PENGUIN BOOKS

I'M NOT THE ONLY ONE

'In an age of boring politicians George Galloway remains anything but dull' Jon Snow

'George Galloway is indomitable. He is one of the very few truly independent voices left in this country' Harold Pinter

'The most eloquent left-winger since Bevan. It is a pleasure to disagree with him' Frank Johnson, *Daily Telegraph*

'A splendid book – at once politically astute, impassioned and hugely entertaining' *Morning Star*

'George Galloway is not only one of the few to whom the word orator applies: he is also an issue politician whose opinions are so succinctly deployed that they are always worth reading' Tam Dalyell

'A controversial and independent thinker . . . one whose passions regularly land him in trouble. He long ago opted out of climbing the traditional political career ladder in favour of speaking out freely, especially in Iraq and Palestine' Ewen MacAskill, Diplomatic Editor, *Guardian*

'An outstanding parliamentarian. He is one of the few great orators in contemporary public life' Sir Peter Tapsell MP

GEORGE GALLOWAY

I'm Not the Only One

PENGUIN BOOKS

PENGUIN BOOKS

Penguin Books Ltd, 80 Strand, London WC2R ORL, England
Penguin Group (USA) Inc., 375 Hudson Street, New York, New York 10014, USA
Penguin Group (Canada), 90 Eglinton Avenue East, Suite 700, Toronto, Ontario, Canada M4P 2Y3
(a division of Pearson Penguin Canada Inc.)
Penguin Ireland, 25 St Stephen's Green, Dublin 2, Ireland
(a division of Penguin Books Ltd)
Penguin Group (Australia), 250 Camberwell Road, Camberwell, Victoria 3124, Australia
(a division of Pearson Australia Group Pty Ltd)
Penguin Books India Pvt Ltd, 11 Community Centre, Panchsheel Park, New Delhi – 110 017, India
Penguin Group (NZ), cnr Airborne and Rosedale Roads, Albany, Auckland 1310, New Zealand
(a division of Pearson New Zealand Ltd)
Penguin Books (South Africa) (Pty) Ltd, 24 Sturdee Avenue, Rosebank, Johannesburg 2196, South Africa

Penguin Books Ltd, Registered Offices: 80 Strand, London WC2R ORL, England

www.penguin.com

First published by Allen Lane 2004
Published in Penguin Books with additional material 2005, 2006
6

Copyright © George Galloway, 2004, 2005, 2006

Set by Rowland Phototypesetting Ltd, Bury St Edmunds, Suffolk
Printed in England by Clays Ltd, St Ives plc

ISBN-13: 978-0-141-01939-0
ISBN-10: 0-141-01939-5

To each and every underdog soldier in the night

Contents

Acknowledgements

It is impossible properly to acknowledge all the hundreds of people with whom I've worked on the issues dealt with in this book and all my other campaigns which will have to be described another day. So any fellow foot-soldiers of the revolution unlisted here should know they have my respect in any case.

But I must thank the staff of the House of Commons Library – the country's finest and, along with the tearoom, the best part of the palace of varieties in which I've spent perhaps too long.

Mr Speaker Weatherill, whose eye I often caught, always cast a kind glance in my direction. As did his successor Betty Boothroyd and hers, Michael Martin. I thank them for recognizing me from the crowd.

The police and security staff in parliament have always protected me from those who offered violence and hate; and most of them never let my views stand in the way of their duty. Who knows: perhaps they're only 'workers in uniform' right enough.

The many friends who sat with me here on the green benches; some departed to the big chamber in the sky, others to retirement and all too few still holding the pass like a mere handful of Spartans. The departed: John Smith, Andrew Faulds, Jimmy Boyce, Bob McTaggart, Ron Leighton, Eddie Loyden, Bob Parry, Ray Powell, Jimmy Dunnachie, Bernie Grant. The retired: my mentor Willie McKelvey, Tony Benn, Michael Foot, Bob Litherland, David Lambie, James Lamont, Don Dixon, John McAllion, Denis Canavan. The still serving, and, some of them with the occasional political wobble, still standing in the Labour cause: Nick Brown, Tam Dalyell, Kelvin Hopkins, George Mudie, Dennis Skinner, Brian Sedgemore, Jeremy Corbyn, Bob Marshall-Andrews QC, John McDonnell, Diane Abbott, Neil

Gerrard, Alice Mahon, Glenda Jackson, Mike Wood, Alan Simpson, John McFall, Tommy McAvoy, Michael Connarty. And those who abandoned me when I ran into really troubled waters, but with whom I had shared many days of parliamentary good fellowship nonetheless: Jimmy Wray, Jimmy Hood, Alan Meale, Tony Banks, Irene Adams, Tom Clark, Kerry Pollard, Brian Donohoe, Gerald Kaufman.

And the Tories and Liberals: the late Alan Clark, the towering Olympian Sir Peter Tapsell, currently Parliamentarian of the Year, Sir Menzies Campbell, who actually was an Olympian and the best leader the Lib-Dems never had, my former 'pair' Theresa Gorman, Crispin Blunt, John Randall, Michael Brown, who were friends across the lines; sometimes proving the great William Gallagher's old adage that 'that's the opposition over there; the enemy are sitting all around us'.

I owe a great debt to my agent Ivan Mulcahey and my lawyers the late Oscar Beuselinck, Kevin Bays and all at Davenport Lyons, Richard Rampton QC, Heather Rodgers, Nicholas de Marco and Ian Smart.

My editor at Penguin, Margaret Bluman, and all at the world's most famous publishing house with whom I am genuinely proud to be working.

My friends, some of them for decades: Seumas Milne, Brian Dempsey, Ron McKay, Bob Wylie, John Boothman, John Craig, John Rees, Lindsey German, Andrew Murray, Colin Rennie, Tom McLaughlin, Jack Stewart, Mickey Duff, the late Tom McDonald, Sa'ad Jabaji, Aida Mishlawi, Dr Azam Tamimi, the late Dr Aida Dabbas, Fawaz Zureikat, Harold Pinter, Ma'an Bashour, Mark Seddon, the late Ahmad Kabbara, Nicholas and Elias Firzli, Ra'if Kasem, Teresa Pearce, David Moxham, Ismail Patel, Ibrahim Hewitt, Dr Sa'ad al Fagih, Zeid Wehbi, the late Dr Yusef Allan, Abu George, Mahmoud Issa, Christopher Silvester, Peter Clark, Victoria Brittain, Ghada Razouki, Linda Smith, the late Hugh Wyper and Alex Kitson, Lynn Henderson, Carmel Brown, Alex Mosson, David Stark, Christine Hamilton, Anas Al-Takriti, Bill Speirs, Pat Stewart, Betty Brown, John Bevan, Andy de la Tour, Wajid Shamsul Hasan, Khawaja Shafique, Salma Yaqoob, Amir Al Hilli, Sabah al Mukhtar, Steve Morgan, Heather Cannon, the late Jim Coulter, Father Noel Barry, Uzi Dekel, Annie Ohayon, Roni Pisker and Yael Demirel. My heartfelt thanks to all of them for picking me up when I fell down, and putting my feet back on higher ground.

My thanks to Eddie and Hesham and all at the Web Café Beirut; to my favourite teacher Miss Helen Littlejohn, my English teacher Richard Bennett, my late headmaster James Hamilton, my friends who opened books to me, Bill Duncan and Alan Alexander. A real debt of gratitude to all at Associated Newspapers, especially Murdoch MacLennan and my *Mail on Sunday* editors Jonathan Holborow and Peter Wright; to Alan Crow, the now departed Jamie Macaskill, Chris Anderson and all the paper's 'backbenchers' who make me look like a better writer than I am. I am grateful to David Morrison for shrewd observations and tireless forensic intellect.

I thank my family: my wife Dr Amineh Abu-Zayyad, former wife Elaine Fyffe, mother Sheila and late father George, brother Graham and sister Colette; and my daughter Lucy and grandson Sean to whom the first edition of this book was in part dedicated.

I could not function at all never mind write a book without the help of my staff. For this book Rima Husseini was indispensable and for everything else Asad Rehman, Yasmin Ataullah, Lara Khalidi and numerous volunteers all helped me make it through many a storm.

And to all the heroes and martyrs, men and women who faced dungeons dark and gallows grim yet kept the banner of freedom flying. Your inspiration is a flame that will never die.

Foreword to the 2005 Edition

Britain today is caught in a systemic political crisis. Victims of a lethal combination: no written constitution or proper mechanisms for dealing with abuses of political power, and a media which is browbeaten or bribed into submission or is in full collusion with the abusers.

Just a year ago the BBC was defenestrated. Its Director General and Chairman were forced out by a ferocious government assault. Its star reporter Andrew Gilligan was crushed to the edge of suicide for reporting and standing by a story which said that Tony Blair and Alastair Campbell had 'sexed up' the intelligence case for war on Iraq.

Is there a sentient being in the land who now believes this charge to be untrue? The Butler Report, though written in that peculiarly understated Whitehall language, Mandarin, concluded exactly that. Every question mark inserted by the intelligence services in their reports on Iraq to the prime minister had been excised. And replaced by an exclamation mark. Documents were sent back and forward between Blair's henchmen and Sir John Scarlett until the latter got it right. Scarlett, without a trace of a blush, was rewarded for his service with promotion as the new head of MI6.

In the Foreign Office – whose principal legal officer resigned on the eve of the war because she could not be a party to the act of brigandry which was about to be launched – leaked papers subsequently showed (apart from the trenchant opposition to the invasion from those we pay to know the Middle East best) that Tony Blair had backed the Bush-whackers' Iraqi 'regime change' as a policy from early in 2002 at a time he was telling us such a policy was illegal. Thus practically every statement Blair made thereafter, to parliament, the country and not least the armed forces, was a calculated deception. Or, in plain terms, a lie.

The bottom line is that Britain has a prime minister who entered into a secret agreement with a foreign power to commit British forces to a military attack on a member state of the United Nations in defiance of domestic and international law. And he is still lying about it.

Moreover, it has turned out to be a catastrophic failure, achieving the very reverse of the benefits claimed for it.

There were no fearsome weapons of mass destruction to disarm. The Iraqis continue to fight the illegal occupation with a bitterness and bloodiness which seems to have taken the great 'war leaders' quite by surprise. Far from paving the way to a road map for a settlement between Israel and the Palestinians the Oslo peace process has been washed away in the bloodshed. Terrorism and Al-Qaeda, which didn't exist in Iraq before the war, have alighted like spores of anthrax upon the gaping wounds of a country shattered by Crusader invasion. Instead of becoming safer, the whole world is now an incomparably more dangerous place.

And still the losses, and the costs, in blood and treasure, ineluctably rise and rise.

At the time of writing, the US air-force is still bombing the Sadr City slums of a capital city it claims to have 'liberated' almost two years ago. And killing the very Shiites they said they came to save.

Success has a thousand parents; failure, alas, is an orphan. This orphan, without any need for a paternity test, belongs to Tony Blair and the rest of the bastards in New Labour.

The British system holds that there is no need for a constitution because it will all be all right on the night the House of Commons performs its function of holding the executive to account. But that depends upon the country having a parliament worthy of the name. We don't.

When the redoubtable Welsh nationalist MP Adam Price introduced a motion to impeach the Prime Minister it was doomed to fail, depending as it did upon the assent of the very sheep who had followed Blair into the lobbies to vote for the slaughter of others.

In 1628 Sir Edward Coke MP, risking torture and execution, moved such a motion against the Duke of Buckingham – henchman of the tyrant Charles I. Accusing Buckingham of 'an act of transparent presumption and dangerous consequences', Coke said this: 'When there is such a downfall of the state, shall we hold our tongues?', adding, 'Not knowing if I shall ever speak in this House again, I shall now speak freely.'

Sir Edward Coke was the real thing: a parliamentarian with some self-respect.

This parliament, in which shivers run vainly along the green benches looking for spines to run up, is a parliament of poodles and pagers and follow-the-leader politicians. They are still barking the same old tunes – a recent survey suggested just one solitary Labour MP now regrets following the leader into the war lobby – and they are still on message, even if the message has had to be rewritten to take account of the unmasking of the weapons of mass destruction hoax – the fundamental falsehood which provided the Attorney-General with his (still unreleased) reason for declaring the invasion legal.

This despite the dawning realization that Blair's action, and perhaps even more the revealed duplicity which lay behind it, will cost Labour perhaps three million of its voters and many of its seats.

When Labour's first prime minister, Ramsay MacDonald, betrayed the party, forming a coalition government with the 'vermin' of Baldwin's Conservatives during the slump of the 1930s, it was said that all over the country Labour people turned his picture to face the wall. This has now happened to Tony Blair. But it will not be enough for New Labour to turn its back on Blair, still waving to the rapturous crowd at party conference but drowning in a sea of contempt and derision in public opinion.

Gordon Brown paid for the war-crime without demur. Alan Milburn, Jack Straw, David Blunkett, Charles Clarke, John Reid – all the pretenders to the Blairite throne sang for their Downing Street cabinet supper from the same hymn sheet as the Vicar of Bray himself.

Britain, like any modern developed country, needs a labour party; a party which speaks for those with nothing to sell except their work, for those who have become too old to work and for their grandchildren; a party which not only speaks for, but legislates for, equality between the races, religions and genders, and for the most vulnerable, the marginalized and the despised.

*

A few hope that the scurvy crew running New Labour can be thrown overboard and the party reclaimed. I wish them luck in this endeavour. They'll need it. But my road is a different one. In 2003 I was expelled from the Labour Party on the orders of Tony Blair after thirty-six years of membership. The same year, New Labour expelled the very trade union – the rail union RMT – which formed the party more than a century before. The Fire Brigades Union, its faith incinerated by the searing experience of its pay dispute, left the Labour Party in disgust.

There are no signs that Britain is going to get its original Labour Party back any time soon.

But a political vacuum will always be filled and I am one of those determined that it shall be. I am now trying to put some Respect back into British politics.

Because I continue to believe the things that drew me into the socialist movement so many years ago, I believe that another Britain is possible. I believe we can build a world without war or exploitation, one by another. I believe in justice and equality and that the earth and all who live upon it deserve respect. You may say I'm a dreamer. But I'm not the only one.

George Galloway MP
House of Commons
London, December 2004

I

The Boys in the Bubble

Britain's political class, its politicians, think tankers and 'official' journalists – those who suck at the fount of power spraying forth the prevailing orthodoxies – are all living in a bubble that is soon to be burst.

For the boys – and girls – in the bubble it is business as usual.

In parliament they yah and boo and bellow and bray as if nothing has changed. Fake tribalism, skin deep, is belied by the sly smiles after each weekly bout between the two team captains, Blair and Howard, at Prime Minister's Question Time, the most pointless half hour in British politics.

It is all just a sport, backbenchers merely the fans cheering from the terraces. The team's tactics and goals are set by the captain; and it doesn't much matter to the terraces if the goals are different from yesterday's. Most don't appear to have noticed that their team has changed ends.

When the Whips, parliament's referees, whistle, into the voting pen they go. Like lambs, silent and uncomplaining to the slaughter.

I have often watched a shiver run along parliament's green benches, looking for a spine to run up. It finds precious few.

Managerialism is the order of the day. The political managers tell us (at great length) there is only an inch or two of political space available, and within this small space we must all live. For them the key things – the worship of the faceless, heartless, free market and Britain's new role in the world as the 'Gurkha' to the new American Empire – are not negotiable.

History has ended on those issues. All we can do, they say, is apply this or that shade of lipstick to the ugly face of today's reality. They don't know that another world is possible.

*

There is no grimmer dictatorship than that of the prevailing orthodoxy.

Grim indeed is the state of the country's fourth estate. Fifty-six channels and nothing on, as the old song said. Now it's more like three hundred channels and still there's nothing on. Certainly nothing that will tell us the truth about the emperors and their clothes.

The BBC – the Bush and Blair Chorus – paid for by a licence-fee poll tax of a people whose wishes take second place to the agenda of the powerful. Rupert Murdoch in all his guises: Australian outbacker, 'Little Englander', American Buccaneer; tomorrow perhaps – as the Far East beckons – Chairman Murdoch Ru Pert.

Foreign owners, craven reporters with no historical memory, columnists largely recruited for their fidelity to the given. Never was Humbert Wolfe's old rhyme more apt:

> You cannot hope
> to bribe or twist,
> thank God! the
> British journalist.
> But, seeing what
> the man will do
> unbribed, there's
> no occasion to.
> ('Over the Fire', 1930)

Great British institutions – the House of Commons, *The Times*, the *Daily Telegraph*, the BBC – either collude or, worse, collaborate in the sale of our country's independence to a foreign power.

They watch the hypocrites, faces waxed with fake grief, poppies ever larger and worn for ever longer, lay wreaths and pay their respects at the Cenotaph.

No one asks why, if war is so terrible, we have become so cavalier at waging it. In the first six years of his government Tony Blair took us in to five wars – Iraq, Yugoslavia, Sierra Leone, Afghanistan, Iraq again. More wars in fewer years than any British ruler, royal or common, before him.

Blair told me privately one day in parliament that, if he could, he'd 'deal with Burma and Zimbabwe' too. The effete public schoolboy, always ready to fight to the last drop of other people's blood. And don't bet against the Bush–Blair axis making more widows in 'dealing with' Iran, Syria, Cuba or North Korea, 'if they can'.

Nor do they ask at the Cenotaph why the generation that defended the country, fought for freedom, for a time standing alone in the world against barbarism, is doomed to shiver on the edge of penury picking up one of the lowest pensions in the European Union. Why, as a matter of New Labour policy, in the fourth richest economy in the world, can't we restore the link between pensions and earnings, without which the incomes of the poorest and most deserving must rise more slowly than those of the rest of us?

The boys in the bubble see children leaving university weighed down with debt. But they never ask how come – when the country was poorer than now – they themselves could be afforded the life-changing opportunities of free study but their children or grandchildren cannot. In the bubble they never ask how it came to pass that a Labour government with the biggest majority in history could have ended up scuttling around in taxis between television studios, denouncing Britain's firefighters, loyal affiliates of the Labour Party for eighty-five years, who hadn't been on strike for a quarter of a century, who'd voted (under the Thatcher anti-trade union laws which Blair not only won't repeal but boasts about) by more than nine to one to strike for pay of £8.50 an hour for plunging into burning buildings for a living.

New Labour spinners – who wouldn't plunge into a darkened room for that kind of money – slandered some of the bravest people in Britain as 'malingerers', 'moonlighters', 'the enemy within' and worse.

One New Labour minister in the Scottish Executive, Richard Simpson, even described them as 'fascist bastards'. He was, admittedly, in spite of desperate attempts by the leadership to save him, eventually forced to resign. But he was never charged with 'bringing the party into disrepute'. Unlike me!

Gordon Brown – who within the tight diameter of the bubble is presented as the only alternative to the dissembler Blair – said the British economy would be 'wrecked' if we paid 40,000 firefighters £8.50 an hour.

That same week Brown wrote a blank cheque – 'whatever it takes', he said – for the war on Iraq. No money to pay those who rescue our own lives and property, unquestioningly and in response to a simple 999 call; but 'whatever it takes' to fly around the world setting fire to other people's countries, incinerating other people's lives.

Politicians, picking up wages and expenses for sitting on their (usually) fat arses equivalent to what four firefighters earn between them, chuntered throughout that long-running dispute into their Tiramisu.

Thanks to corporate invitations, MPs can lunch, dine and drink free, almost every day; many do. The more important guzzle at the troughs of the newspapers, where they're usually briefing against their friends. The less important pretend to be riveted by the latest schemes of Camelot the lottery operator, or the latest news from the ambassador of Kazakhstan. Wherever they were, the political class burped on and on about the 'greed' of the strikers. After a belch into their nosebag of convenience, and another gulp of Burgundy, they might have then tapped their noses, winked and moved on to the issue of 'weapons of mass destruction'.

'If only you knew what I know,' they'd imply.

The truth is that most of them knew nothing.

The bloated British parliament, three times the size it should be – India with a population twenty times that of Britain has a parliament considerably smaller than ours – is one of this country's most ignorant bodies of men (and despite the feminist hopes, most of the women are no better).

And those at the top are liars.

The prime minister, three times in one dodgy dossier day, said Iraq was bristling with chemical and biological weapons. At forty-five minutes' notice, he said, they could threaten British bases on Cyprus. He never explained, by the way, why we have bases on Cyprus. Certainly not to defend Cyprus, as the three decades of Turkish occupation of the island proves.

These were not, in the Churchillian parliamentary euphemism, merely 'terminological inexactitudes'. Blair was not being, as the late Alan Clark might have put it, 'economical with the actualité'.[1] These were not the proceeds of 'Intelligence' of the James Bond or even the Austin Powers variety. These were the sweepings off the Internet floor; this was the paid-for, boomeranging, self-fulfilling war propaganda of hireling exiles, hungry for power, most notably the now discredited Chalabi group – the Iraqi National Congress.

But above all these were lies.

A perfected deception upon the House of Commons, the British people and not least the armed forces; on the basis of this lie the prime minister would soon send other mothers' sons, other women's lovers, to kill and be killed.

When Tony Blair told the press corps aboard what increasingly resembled a presidential jet in the hours after the suicide of Dr David Kelly on Harrowdown Hill in Oxfordshire, that he had 'absolutely nothing to do' with the naming of the weapons expert as the source of Andrew Gilligan's Iraq story on BBC radio, this too proved to be false. When this falsehood was unmasked by Sir Kevin Tebbitt, the chief official at the Ministry of Defence, in his testimony before the Hutton Inquiry, it was all but ignored by the very journalists who had reported Blair's words.

On the day the Hutton Inquiry reported I was with the demonstrators opposite the Houses of Parliament. Just a few yards away, at great public expense, a public inquiry into the shooting dead of unarmed Roman Catholic demonstrators on Bloody Sunday in Derry in 1972 was taking place. It is the second such inquiry. The first, conducted by the Lord Widgery just three months after the event, was such a whitewash, such an establishment cover-up, that its conclusions were eventually utterly discredited. Lord Hutton, as it happens, was counsel for the British Army in the Widgery Inquiry, and his argument, that the men from the Parachute Regiment had opened fire only after they themselves were fired upon, was accepted by Widgery in the face of a mass of contradictory evidence. When the Ulster Unionist Law Lord Hutton – a pillar of the British establishment – with very tightly drawn terms of reference, was placed in charge of the investigation into the death of Dr Kelly, I predicted it would be another 'Widgery'. And so it was. Hutton – once a judge in the Diplock Courts, the no-jury tribunals established by the British to try Northern Ireland terror cases – heard a mass of evidence to the contrary before promptly painting Mr Blair in what they no doubt hoped would be a weatherproof coat of whitewash lasting at least long enough to see Mr Blair limp on to the general election. But like Victor Meldrew, 'I don't believe it.'

Hutton effectively sentenced the BBC to perdition for daring to question the moral probity of the likes of Alastair Campbell. The Chairman and Director-General of the corporation promptly resigned and Andrew Gilligan has packed his bags for an extended stay at Radio Solent or some other freelance broadcasting equivalent of a Siberian power station. The idea that the BBC, the world's best known broadcaster, is truly independent of the British government has taken an almighty blow and surely explains the spontaneous protests of BBC staff at the attack on their journalism by Hutton, Campbell and crew. Less than twenty-four hours after the Hutton Report half of the people polled by the London *Evening Standard* thought it had been a cover-up, a third said it would make them less likely to vote Labour and 70 per cent agreed with the demand for a full public inquiry – this time not into the death of one man but into the deaths of thousands in the fraudulent and disastrous war on Iraq.

If that were to happen, Tony Blair, already with one foot in the political grave, would be dead and buried.

When Blair was caught doing an about-turn over Formula One tobacco advertising just as, coincidentally, Bernie Ecclestone was oiling Labour's wheels to the tune of a million pounds, he described himself as a 'pretty straight sort of guy',[2] a claim now so laughable even Blair wouldn't dare take it out of the pits.

Our prime minister insisted that another dubious Labour donation, this time from the Indian steel magnate Lakshmi Mittal, had come from a 'British business'. This was another lie.

He expected us to believe that Lord Sainsbury's peerage and apparently permanent place in the government had nothing to do with the millions he'd given Blair's funds.

He said Lord Levy – the man who brought the world Alvin Stardust and raised millions for New Labour (he was rewarded with a seat in the Lords and the job of plenipotentiary to the Middle East) – was keeping the Blair family's 'blind trusts' a secret from him as required by law.

Yet Cherie Blair, with the help of Carole Caplin's crystal balls and the Aussie con-man Peter Foster, bought flats in Bristol worth more than half a million pounds out of the trusts' proceeds. They ask us to believe that even under the torture of Caplin's primal screaming and volcanic mud rebirthing rituals, Cherie never breathed a word to Tony that he was now the owner of a fine pair of flats in Bristol.

The Blairites became a byword for twisted spin-doctoring, constantly relaunching the same initiatives as if they were new, double counting up or down on police numbers, crime figures, waiting lists and a hundred other disinformation operations.

The Tories said that Blair's nose grew, like Pinocchio's, with every lie. This was not true. I should know – I sit just ten yards away from him in the House with a perfect view of his increasingly made-up face. (Somewhere in the attic in Downing Street I'm sure there is a portrait like Dorian Gray's, and eventually all the foundation and rouge in the world will not stop him looking just like it.) In fact, no matter how big the whopper, the lawyerish dissembling, the half-truth, the anything-but-the-truth, Blair's nose never grows, and his brass neck never blushes. You only know he's lying because his lips are moving.

Some may think that this persistent mendacity represents a change of personality, perhaps the inevitable consequence of the demands of high office. Not so.

He claimed before becoming prime minister that as a schoolboy he had attempted to stow away at Newcastle Airport on board a plane to the Caribbean, at a time when no such flights existed.

He said he used to 'sit at the Gallowgate End at St James' Park behind the goal' watching 'wor Jackie', Newcastle United's legendary footballer Jackie Milburn. Sorry Tony, seating didn't exist behind the goal there until Milburn was long dead.

Worse, he claimed to the electorate in his first by-election contest, in Beaconsfield in 1982, that he believed in unilateral nuclear disarmament. He even wore a CND badge when it was de rigueur in the Foot and Benn Labour Party of the 1980s. He affected to believe in withdrawal from the Common Market, in state ownership and trade union freedom. He even, though I know you'll think I'm making this bit up, claimed to believe in something called 'Socialism'.

Once when he was the shadow employment minister, I came upon a posse of print union leaders fuming into their bitter on the House of Commons Terrace. Tony Blair had failed to show up for their long-scheduled meeting because he had 'childcare problems'.

The unreconstructed men from the stones of Fleet Street thought this simple onanism. 'Real Men' didn't fail to turn up for their work for such reasons. I often wondered what they would have thought if they'd known that when I went upstairs I found Blair sitting grinning in the Members' tearoom, far from the prying eyes of 'working-class brutes' like Tony Dubbins, the printers' leader.

Blair rejoices in the thuggery of his Home Secretary, the former gauleiter of the 'People's Republic of South Yorkshire', the erstwhile champion of the Sandinistas and 'Nuclear Free Zones', David Blunkett. He encourages him to plumb depths even Mrs Thatcher would have recoiled from. Identity cards, attacks on the right to trial by jury, crushing of the legal aid system through which the poor can access an approximation of justice, the smearing of judges, raft after raft of so-called 'anti-terrorism' legislation, building our very own Guantanamo Bays.

He cheers while Blunkett lays in to the country's immigrants. They should speak only English, even at home, lest they become 'schizophrenic', says the Home Secretary. Just as well they don't follow that policy amongst British expats down in the Costa del Sol.

Blunkett denounces those campaigning against the savage seven-year sentences handed out to the (Muslim) Bradford rioters as 'whining maniacs'[3] – quite a head-doctor is David Blunkett. He sets out to starve asylum seekers into the sea, or anywhere but here. And is forced to deny being 'King Herod' when he proposes to kidnap the children of 'failed' asylum seekers – i.e., those virtually unrepresented applicants he's fast-tracked – and hold them hostage against their parents' return whence they'd fled. Even Saddam Hussein didn't think of that one.

Blunkett told me that such language and such measures were necessary to stop the rise of the BNP and other extreme-right groups. But throwing bones to the beasts of racism in the hope of satisfying them is the road which led to Treblinka and Buchenwald. Feeding the loud and foul mouths of the BNP merely makes them hungry for more. If a self-defined 'social-democrat' cannot see that, cannot stand up, straight, even for anti-racist multiculturalism, then it is worth asking what conceivable purpose in life he serves.

Blunkett's Britain is a land of detention centres – Ann Widdecombe's fantasy – with razor wire, private security firms, German shepherd dogs; the incarceration of people, even children, against whom the only accusation is that they were foolish enough to think they were fleeing for asylum in the free country which sheltered Mazzini, Marx, Mandela, before New Labour had even been invented.

On a trip to India in February 2004 Blunkett announced that he was to introduce measures unprecedented anywhere in the world. We are moving, he said, to an era of 'pre-emptive' justice in terrorism cases: charging people with offences before they have committed them; hearing evidence in secret; imposing state-vetted lawyers on accused people; hearing evidence that will not be shown to the accused; allowing the 'intelligence services' – the same ones who told us Iraq was bristling with weapons of mass destruction – to submit secret testimony to the judge that is not challengeable by the accused, or even seen by him.

Corporate interests queue up for tables at Park Lane fundraising dinners for the Labour Party. They sponsor what are laughably called 'fringe meetings' at the annual party conference.

Consider Nestlé, for instance, whose promotion of infant formula over breastfeeding, in countries where the poor have no access to clean water, has brought it notoriety among healthcare professionals and development organizations. The grotesque spectacle of such a company providing cocktails and canapés for Labour delegates discussing Third World poverty would have had delegates kicking over the tables just a few years ago. The crucifixion of principles is now the first commandment in New Labour.

Nestlé are not alone. Arms companies like British Aerospace, purveyors of harmful chemical fertilizers, the roads lobby, big oil and tobacco companies – even McDonald's, whose hamburgers the smallest child knows are not entirely kosher in an environmental sense – all the cut-throat capitalists have filled New Labour's trough. But not for nothing. There is no such thing as a free canapé.

New Labour has privatized things Maggie Thatcher only dreamed of.

'Our air is not for sale,' the shadow chief secretary to the Treasury Andrew Smith told the last Labour conference before the 'New Dawn' of 1 May 1997. Then he sold it; the darkest hours in Blair's Britain come after the dawn.

Britain became the only country in the world to privatize its air traffic control. Not since Milo Minderbinder rented out his own air force planes to the Germans so they could bomb his base in Joseph Heller's *Catch-22* has such a reckless sell-off been attempted.

Aren't they worried about the potential pitfalls of a Railtrack in the skies? What, New Labour?

They are flogging off the London Underground too, so no doubt we can have a subterranean Railtrack. Potters Bar, Clapham, Hatfield . . . 'We're private. Crash with us,' might be the motto.

The foundation hospitals legislation, the thin end of the wedge of creating a two-tier, creeping privatization of the National Health Service, was rammed through the Commons by the ex-communist apparatchik Dr John Reid, despite the opposition of the Labour Party conference – even that same 2003 conference which gave Tony Blair such a long tear-stained standing ovation that if he hadn't told them to sit down they'd be clapping yet.

Private Finance Initiatives, so-called partnerships between the private sector and public services, have mortgaged our children's, in fact our grandchildren's, future. All their lives they will be paying extortionate sums to private financiers for schools and hospitals being built now under PFI, yet in many cases will never own them.

At least on the back street 'never-never' – after the bloodsucker has had his fill – you get to own the goods in the end. Not with New Labour you don't.

For them, nothing should belong to the public unless it is on the point of collapse, having sucked so many subsidies from the public purse while pretending to be private that the whole joke just becomes unsustainable. The British taxpayer is now shelling out three times the public subsidy to the private owners of the railways that they did when we owned the railways ourselves. Thus we're taking back the track of Britain's railways, but not, of course, sorting out the pickle of the Branson trains. Sir Richard – as Blair ensured we must now know him – will continue to allow his 'fleet' to take longer to get from London to Birmingham than it does to go from Big Ben to the Eiffel Tower.

*

All this betrayal and the deliberate collapsing of expectations have sunk many into political disillusionment and despondency.

Election turn-outs have reached lows not seen since the end of the First World War. Yet at the same time as fewer and fewer people are voting in Britain more and more are demonstrating.

There is hardly a 'conventional' politician in the land who can draw a crowd that couldn't be fitted into a cappuccino bar. Yet I am speaking most nights of the week to audiences of hundreds. And as for Tony Benn – for him they're even selling tickets.

Between September the Eleventh 2001 and the farcical visit of George W. Bush to London in late 2003, there were six national demonstrations in Britain.

There was Britain's biggest ever protest march – perhaps two million people in Hyde Park – just before the invasion of Iraq. This was five times the size of the second biggest – that of the Countryside Alliance – which had a budget of hundreds of thousands of pounds and the full support of the right-wing press, as well as a fair number of landowners exercising 'feudal rights' over their tenants.

It was twenty times the size of Britain's most famous modern demonstration, at the US embassy in Grosvenor Square at the height of the Vietnam War. There was also the largest demonstration ever to take place during wartime and the largest ever working-day protest to boot – when a vast crowd cheered the toppling of the floodlit statue of Bush in Trafalgar Square.

One of the characteristics of all these events was the number of young people marching and the number of young women coming to the fore, as stewards, organizers and speakers. School students staged strikes, walking out of classes often in front of fulminating and foolish head teachers who couldn't see that, for these students, such engagement with the world outside was the best lesson they could learn.

People have not turned off from politics, only from the politicians.

This is not apathy – this is apoplexy.

This is fury at the unresponsive, unrepresentative, blind, deaf heartlessness of the political class that rules them.

During these days that shook the world and through which we are still passing, I was both outside in the streets with the people and inside parliament; inside the bubble with the boys.

At first I couldn't understand it. I'd be overhearing snatches of the same old same old parliamentary badinage in the corridors, in the library, in the tearooms, in the chamber. I couldn't understand what they were all laughing at, while outside the bubble there was all this rage.

It seemed to me like the last days of Pompeii. Or, to roam around the classics, like a House full of Nero's fiddling while Rome burned.

And then I got it.

This parliament, this system, is no longer connected to the people to whom it is supposed to belong, still less the world outside.

No party any longer speaks for those who hate war and the new imperialism. No one is listening to the pensioners, the students, the trade unionists, the immigrants, the ethnic minorities, the asylum seekers – let alone speaking for them.

British politics has become hollowed out, a vacuum. Tens of millions of our citizens are thus locked out of the democratic structures of their country. Even when they take to the streets in unprecedented, overwhelming numbers they are ignored.

This is dangerous. This cannot go on. This cannot be allowed to stand.

It is a national duty to bring about the political end of this warmongering, principle-shredding, mendacious malodorous rancid crew. Blair must go.

This bubble must be burst.

And there are millions massing outside, getting ready to prick it.

2

New World Odour

The singer-songwriter Elvis Costello called it the 'new world odour', saying it 'smelt just as bad as the old one'. That's because there is nothing new about it. The 'world is ill-divided and those who work the hardest are the least provided'.[1] This simple truth is age old and the primary cause of misery and injustice in the world. The rich world is rich because the poor world is poor, just as within the rich world the minority are rich, because the majority are poor.

If humankind was a village of 100 people, with the existing balance in the world maintained, the village would look like this: there would be 57 Asians and only 21 Europeans; just 14 would have come from the western hemisphere, both north and south, and 8 from Africa. Of the 100, 70 would be non-white and 30 white; 70 would be non-Christian and 30 would be Christian. Only 5 people in the village would possess 59 per cent of all the wealth; and all five of them would be from the United States. Some 80 out of the 100 people in the village would live in sub-standard housing, 70 would be unable to read, 50 would be malnourished and only one would have had a college education. And he would be the only one in the whole village who would own a computer.

The First World War Battle of the Somme in northern France was the worst in the history of British arms, 60,000 casualties falling on the first day of the slaughter in July 1916. Yet more people in the world die of poverty every two days than perished that terrible day. Every two weeks more die of being poor than were slain in the US nuclear attacks upon Hiroshima and Nagasaki. And every two years more people die from the want of food and easily obtainable medicine and from utterly preventable disease than have fallen in all the wars in all the countries in all human history. These are the real killing fields. This is the biggest mass grave. But few news crews crowd around it to publicize the wailing, grieving relatives of those snuffed out by poverty.

Sure, if enough of them gather together in telegenic numbers, and a skilled newsman from a prestigious outfit like the BBC captures the drama on film, as happened in Ethiopia, the world can be momentarily diverted. The Orwellian notion that the ultimate obscenity would be when one half of the world could watch the other half starving to death on television, would come to pass. In 1984, of all years, that happened. But most people soon switched off. Even at the height of the Live Aid phenomenon, for every pound that governments and people were raising for the poor, in the rich countries bankers and arms merchants were pocketing two pounds from the indebtedness of the Third World and from the dictatorships that misgoverned it – most of them clients of the west.

London mayor Ken Livingstone was widely attacked when he said that 'capitalism had killed more people than Hitler'.[2] Uncharacteristically, he understated his case. Capitalism – and the imperialism which is its most advanced form – is the greatest mass murderer in all history, quite dwarfing Hitler's genocide. More people died of famine in British India in the last fifty years of the Raj than died in all of Chairman Mao's 'Great Leaps' but, as Michael Caine might say, 'Not a lot of people know that.'

While there was a competitor system, however flawed, in the shape of the USSR and its camp, a kind of equilibrium became established in international affairs. Limits to the behaviour of capitalism in the world were in place. The US could not, for example, invade and occupy Cuba, use nuclear weapons in Korea or take the Korean War into Red China.

Equally, the existence of a possible alternative way, socialism, to which in any case a substantial section of a powerful domestic labour movement was committed, tempered the rapaciousness of capitalism at home.

Social democracy or Labourism was the price capitalism agreed to pay to avoid communism. Though they quibbled about its price and its boundaries, the Welfare State was the settled model for decades of so-called 'Butskellism' – the concept formed by the merger of the names of the 'One Nation' Tory 'Rab' Butler and the moderate Labour leader Hugh Gaitskell who together personified the consensus. Once communism was seen as a busted flush the attempt to roll back the frontiers began and neo-liberalism or 'Thatcher–Reaganomics' declared itself king. Some of the social democrats or Labourites even began to say, 'We are all Thatcherites now.'

The gap between rich and poor in Britain, during the second term of a Labour government, is wider than it was when Charles Dickens was chronicling the gin parlours, opium dens and dank slums of the Victorian era. Pensioners in Glasgow, it was revealed in a 2004 study by Strathclyde University, are more likely to die of the cold than any in Europe – including Siberia.[3]

This is mirrored in the world as a whole.

So-called 'globalization' – just a cover-name for the exploitation of the many by the few – is itself an act of war against the poor. Two people in five in the world go to bed hungry or without access to clean water while in the rich countries many swim in champagne and western parents sue fast food outlets for making their children obese. A quarter of the world's population lives on a dollar a day. In the age of the information super-highway most people in the world have never even made a telephone call.

Fifteen per cent of the world's population consumes almost 80 per cent of its wealth. The USA alone consumes 25 per cent of the entire world's energy resources. The 'drive-by shootings' of the neo-conservative, neo-imperialist foreign policy are aimed at forcing the world to accept neo-liberal economics – the worship of free and unfettered markets, totally free movement of capital (though not of course of people), privatization, low public spending and the corporate domination of all major aspects of economic and social activity by transnational companies with turnovers bigger than many national economies and owing loyalty to no one but their ever richer shareholders – though loyalty to the fat-cat kleptocracy that actually runs the corporations often takes precedence over even that loyalty.

The new world order is policed by many multilateral organizations. But in the end it is the mailed fist of what has become known as the 'coalition of the killing' that is the ultimate enforcer.

The League of Nations, precursor to the United Nations, was described by Lenin as a 'thieves' kitchen'. Today the UN is a thieves' and beggars' kitchen, where the thieves usually make the decisions and the beggars vote for them in exchange for a few crumbs off the thieves' table.

If, as happened with the attack upon Iraq, there is a failure to agree in the kitchen, the thieves merely step outside the door and announce their intention to act unilaterally or, in the case of Yugoslavia, use a different kitchen – in that case NATO.

In such circumstances the beggars merely fall in after the event behind the fait accompli of the thieves – then start begging for a share of the loot. Thus Boris Yeltsin betrayed Russia's traditional Slav ally in Serbia just as, with their messages of 'God speed', did recalcitrant Security Council members like France and Germany once the shooting started in Iraq.

UN Secretary-General Kofi Annan, the dumb waiter of the thieves' and beggars' kitchen, having stated that the attack upon Iraq was an act of international lawlessness, swiftly saw where the bread was buttered at the UN and started serving faithfully again.

In St Augustine's *City of God* the Christian philosopher tells of an encounter between Alexander the Great and a pirate ship on the high seas. Ordering the brigand to heave to, Alexander demands of the captain: 'How dare you terrorize these waters as a thief?'

The captain, who must have been a brave one, answers: 'How dare you terrorize the whole world? I with my one small ship can be called a thief while you, with your great navy, can call yourself an emperor, and can call other men what you will.'

This, precisely, is the situation today.

Self-appointed emperors, though nowadays they call themselves the 'international community', go where they please, do what they want, and arrogate to themselves the right to call other men what they will: rogue states, dictators, terrorists and tyrants.

They decide who may possess certain weapons and who may not; which UN resolutions and international laws are binding and which are not; which dictatorships must be 'regime-changed' and which armed, buttressed and backed.

It is particularly unfortunate for the emperors of today that they are so lily white, protestant and Anglo-Saxon. It tends to give the game away. Those looking for an axis of weasels would find Bush, Blair and Howard, the Australian neo-conservative, hard to beat for smug, smirking, stupid white men.

Bush with his promise of a 'Crusade' after 9/11, and his wallowing in the rapture of Armageddon-worship among the born-again Bible-belting Christian fundamentalists of the American right.

Blair, the sanctimonious vicar, his voice catching with faux sincerity (the act first performed on the death of Princess Diana), sounding for all the world like a TV evangelist caught sleeping with hookers behind the altar and paying for them by skimming the collection.

Howard, the sinister witch-hunter of asylum seekers, quintessential champion of 'Australia fair' (very fair, the fairer the better).

These emperors see the world as a kind of white man's burden which somebody (God?) has asked them to shoulder. The other white men, the 'Johnnie Foreigners' of the old Europe, don't quite have the moral fibre to take up their share of the load, so, what the heck, Uncle Sam, John Bull and their kith and kin Down Under will just have to do it themselves.

These 'Crusaders', these empire builders, have no compunction about calling other men what they will. But any rational enquiry shows that the biggest rogue states, the world's worst leaders, deploying the world's most dangerous weapons, are themselves.

The Security Council of the United Nations has no democratic basis in any case. Huge and important countries like Brazil, Indonesia, India, Pakistan, Japan or Germany have no automatic seat within it. Britain and France on the other hand are permanent members and have veto powers, for no other reason than that they were on the winning side in the Second World War, and have nuclear weapons.

Not only are nuclear-armed states like India and Pakistan outside its power circle, but there are no Muslim, Arab or African seats at the top table. There are no elections to the veto-wielding seats on the Security Council, and the only open forum, the General Assembly of the United Nations, where every member has the same vote, is a little-used and virtually powerless illusion of world government.

But even this cartel of emperors is under no illusion about who is 'boss of bosses'. For many years the US refused even to pay its dues to the UN. It stayed outside UNESCO because it didn't like that organization's political stripe. It removed Boutros Boutros-Ghali from the post of Secretary-General because he was not compliant enough. It has unlawfully refused visas to speakers, like Yasser Arafat, whom the UN General Assembly had invited to address them.

Of course any successful double act has a good-cop/bad-cop routine at its heart. In the recent crisis which paralysed the UN, British diplomats played straight man to the jokers of the Bush administration.

The personae of the two main players could have come straight out of central casting. Looking like he'd just walked off the set of *The Sopranos* was the US ambassador to the UN, John Negroponte. The former Reagan point-man for the illegally funded Contras, the killers of priests and nuns, teachers and midwives in the mountains of Nicaragua, is as big a thug as he looks – and for him that's no insult.

'I don't even want to be here,' his face screamed silently as he went through the motions of trying to persuade lesser men to agree to his proposed savagery in Iraq. Dripping with contempt for the other players, he could hardly conceal his irritation at the diplomatic perpetual motion of his British counterpart.

Sir Jeremy Greenstock was like a British envoy from another era – of the Ealing comedies perhaps, or a Peter Sellers character. He dripped, not with contempt, but with effete patrician snobbery. A master of the fork-tongued subterfuge, Orwellian Newspeak his lingua franca, he was 'perfidious Albion' personified; an intellectual Greek to Negroponte's brute Roman.

Though they could not have been more different, Greenstock and Negroponte could not have been more dedicated to the same thing. Two apologists for the killers, one in a sharp Savile Row suit, the other in loud Godfather garb; the perfect representation of Blair and Bush, of Blair's Britain and Bush's America, of the Jackal and the Jackass of the new empire. Now, as US ambassador in Baghdad, Negroponte is the day-to-day effective ruler of Iraq – the US embassy there is the biggest in the world, situated in one of Saddam Hussein's former palaces, with three thousand 'diplomatic staff'.

The main organs of the international system – like the World Bank and the International Monetary Fund – are completely outwith the

UN's control, a law unto themselves, or rather a law unto their masters whose corporate agenda they faithfully follow and which they force down the throats of the poor countries that they 'restructure' or 'structurally adjust'.

Other parts of the architecture of the new world order are little better.

The European Union is a behemoth without teeth. Corrupt, undemocratic, a gigantic gravy train heading for the buffers of European public opinion. Europe's enormous economic, historic and cultural weight is utterly unmatched by any political or security cohesion.

This will get only worse now that the former Soviet satrapies of eastern and central Europe – often led by the same communist party apparatchiks who failed their countries in their last guise – have gleefully climbed inside Mr Blair's American Trojan horse in the newly enlarged European Union.

The vast bloated Eurocracy of the Commission, stuffed full of taxpayer-supplied pâté de foie gras, billows and blows but in the end is powerless to lead a great continent against the diktat of the emperors.

On the national level, too, democracy is sidelined in the increasingly presidential countries of the axis.

Silvio Berlusconi, in coalition with former Fascists of Mussolini's generation and the neo-Fascists of the Northern League, despite his prime ministerial office, continues to enrich himself and stays out of jail for those crimes of which he has already been convicted by changing the law. José Maria Aznar, the bonsai bouffant leader of Spain during the Iraq war, in coalition with the supporters of the Falangist General Franco, said the equivalent of fuck you to the Pope, the Spanish left and fully 92 per cent of the Spanish electorate, and followed the Bush and Blair line into the war on Iraq. He is now under investigation for illicit spending of Spanish government funds for his own glorification in lobbying in Washington for the award of the Congressional Medal of Honour.

Blair's contempt for the current British House of Commons may on one level be justified given the craven nature of most of its members. But he has no justification for refusing to set a date for the British people's referendum on the new European constitution, except his certainty that he would lose it. Likewise his cynical scheming over

Britain's membership of the European single currency. His 'will he, won't he, will he, won't he join the dance' tango with Gordon Brown over the Euro referendum is designed to bamboozle the audience. He hopes we will concentrate on the sequins rather than the steps he is already taking to deliver what is left of our national democracy to a group of fat bankers in the European Central Bank, whom we never elected and cannot remove.

Any new world order worthy of the name and able to deliver a modicum of justice and peace must start from the concept of democracy. The emperors believe this is a banner they have appropriated for themselves. We must take its standard and hoist them on it; believe me, as they used to say on *Dad's Army* – 'They don't like it up 'em.' Bush – who actually lost the election for the US presidency – and Blair, who was re-elected in 2001 in the smallest electoral turn-out since the First World War, never tire of invoking the word democracy. But democracy is the last thing they want, not only in the heartlands of their favourite dictatorships but on the international level.

They couldn't even face a vote on Iraq by the rigged jury of today's Security Council; nor will they allow free fair elections in Iraq today for the same reason – they couldn't stomach the result.

They certainly don't fancy electing a properly representative Security Council, or allowing a democratically legitimate UN to control the workings of the likes of the World Bank and the IMF.

So, what would a democratic United Nations look like?

- A reformed General Assembly with all member states being more proportionately represented in recognition of differences in their populations – Vanuatu could not have the same vote as India.
- An elected Security Council with every part of the world guaranteed a seat at the top table. And no one country should be able to exercise a veto.
- The Secretary-General and the secretariat to be employees of a reformed General Assembly and the top jobs to be subject to regular election.
- The United Nations to sell its prime real estate in Manhattan and move out of the United States to Geneva in neutral Switzerland.

- The new UN headquarters to be declared extra-territorial, like the Vatican, with sovereignty over the site exercised by the UN itself.
- UN fees to be boosted, with expulsion the punishment for defaulters.
- Enhanced fees to be used to pay for police and military forces for international troubleshooting. Only legitimate international forces whose deployment has been decided democratically will command respect in the world. The alternative – recolonization like the British take-over of Sierra Leone, the French recapture of the Ivory Coast, the American hijacking of Liberia and Haiti – would involve much heavier burdens in the long run.
- Regional security responsibilities to be mandatory. There are regional organizations which are credible and regarded as legitimate in their own parts of the world – the Arab League and the African Union, for example. Europe requires such a regional pact for peace and security and NATO is not it; America rules NATO without being European and Russia is European but not only is it not in NATO but is threatened by it. The genocide in Rwanda was first and foremost an African responsibility, the civil war in Yugoslavia a European one. Both could have and should have been resolved regionally.

Most examples of civil strife will warrant no foreign intervention. Some will. Sovereign states may request regional intervention and each request would have to be treated on its merits; for example, the case would have to be made that the continuation of the emergency would spread beyond national boundaries, that the intervention was not itself compounding injustice, and was not worse than the alternative of non-intervention.

The reason there was no consensus for the attack on Iraq was that world public opinion could see that it was not justified, was being sold on a false prospectus, was worse than the available alternatives and was likely to make existing security problems in the world even worse than they already were. The more justified the case the greater would be the consensus for intervention. National sovereignty cannot be an absolute in today's interdependent world, but as with any drastic surgery it can never be violated lightly, based on a false diagnosis, with consequently a flawed prognosis leading to the death of not just the patient but many others beside.

In a truly new world order with a democratized United Nations at its heart, all Security Council resolutions would have to be implemented, not just those relating to countries whose face doesn't fit with the powerful. Iraq was beggared and destroyed in the name of UN resolutions while the US client Israel is in breach of more UN resolutions than any country in the world (and has been saved from many more by US vetoes). Iraq was destroyed while Israel is constantly rewarded.

The Security Council voted unanimously nearly sixty years ago to demand a plebiscite for the people of the disputed territory of Jammu and Kashmir. The Indian leader Jawaharlal Nehru pledged to implement the resolution but such a vote has never been held, despite the territory being the cause of several wars, a nuclear arms race and a bloody cycle of violence involving tens of thousands of Kashmiri dead and an occupation force of 600,000 Indian soldiers. And all of this in a region where the most desperate poverty and deprivation remains an affront to the eye.

These double standards and the downright hypocrisy that lies beneath them are what discredit the international system. If the world is to get to grips with the hyper-power of the United States (and its auxiliaries) and stabilize a dangerously unjust world then what the *New York Times* called 'the other super-power' of international public opinion will have to be won over to these kinds of changes and to a sustained campaign to achieve them. Every time the emperors preach 'Democracy' we must answer, 'Practise what you preach!'

It is not impossible. There are severe limitations to American power. Though they control the heavens with their military budget, soon to be bigger than the military spending of all other countries put together, the Iraqi resistance is proving daily that they cannot control a single street in Fallujah. For all their 'hard' power, at the same time their 'soft' power is growing ever more flaccid. The dollar sinks, US indebtedness soars and the boycott of American goods and services is a concept beginning to sweep the world. As I write this, in the Lebanese capital of Beirut the local branches of McDonald's are guarded by detachments of the Lebanese army. To no avail; no one with any sense of dignity would be seen dead in them and they are all but empty.

Anti-Americanism – by which I mean the rejection not of the American people themselves but the role of their government and its military around the world – is sweeping the young generation and will be the prevailing mind-set, the most powerful ideology, of the first half of this century.

Europe must find a role in the world that reflects its burgeoning economic power. It will have to find a security profile to enable it to escape its self-imposed defence dependency upon the US. If it is to command the respect and affection of the peoples of Europe, the European Union will have to popularize itself and its potentially positive role in the world. It will have to show the people of Europe that we favour a different model from the US – one based on democracy fairness and justice – and are prepared to implement it at home and work for it abroad. The single currency – in principle a good idea – will have to be under the management of the elected representatives of Europe rather than the bankers and plutocrats who manipulate it now. The Commission must be brought under the control of the Parliament, which will have to be more democratic and more vital than it is now. The idea of a People's Europe can be a flag to which many, especially the young, can rally. That such a People's Europe can help to restore equilibrium in a dangerously unstable, unjust and unsustainable world must become an article of faith worth fighting for.

And democracy must begin at home too.

My long years in the House of Commons have convinced me that British democracy is seriously deficient and in need of major surgery. In this operation on the state we must start at the head. No grown-up democracy can continue with the Ruritanian fantasy that there is a single family born to rule over us. This would be true even if the Windsors were an Olympian example of grace, intellect, beauty and truth. But they are not. I bear no animus towards Queen Elizabeth, who after all did not choose the mind-numbingly boring life she has had to lead. In fact as a youth, when as a waiter I served her wine, I formed the view confirmed by subsequent meetings that she was basically a good egg – as I did more controversially about the much lampooned Prince Philip. But you can't make an omelette without breaking eggs and you can't make exceptions for good eggs.

The Queen will not be with us for ever and even if she lives as long as her mother we should make plans now for a referendum on her succession as the British head of state. Democrats should begin to make the case for a republican future. Even if the referendum confirms the Prince of Wales as sovereign there will have to be many changes. There is no case for the state continuing to finance buffoons like the golfing, philandering Prince Andrew and the gormless Prince Edward from the public purse, let alone the more obscure, even less attractive hangers-on. The royal family cannot go on retaining, even if it may be only formally, powers to declare the country to be at war, to command the House of Commons to do this or that, to create general elections or deny them to the government of the day.

The House of Lords was a constitutional monstrosity when the grouse moors were dragged to bring in the putrefying corpses of the English aristocracy to vote for Mrs Thatcher's poll tax, by which the duke would pay the same as his dustman for local services. It is no less monstrous now that it is stuffed with the rentiers, commission-men and funding cronies of Tony, the new Lloyd George. A flatmate has no more right than a belted earl to a seat in parliament; indeed, given the propensity of cronies to do their pals' bidding it is arguable that the relative independence of mind of the earl makes him more of an adornment to the Palace of Varieties.

There is no case for an unelected second chamber in a modern European state; indeed, if we had a written constitution, a bill of rights and an independent supreme court we wouldn't need a second chamber at all.

The House of Commons is too big. India with a population of one billion people has a parliament of just 500 members. We need half as many MPs as we have, being paid twice as much and having proper offices and staff (employed by the state not the MP). Parliamentarians should have the right to accept or reject cabinet appointments. (Peter Mandelson would have found it easier to get through the eye of a needle than to pass a scrutiny and confirmation hearing.) There should be no secret votes like the one which finances our unaccountable and, as the Hutton Inquiry showed, easily misused intelligence services. No war should be fought on the say-so of a single person – as we did in Yugoslavia and Afghanistan – the prime minister, acting in the name of the queen. Parliamentary select committees should be beefed up, should be chosen by the members of the House, not by the Whips, who are acting on behalf of the government the committees are supposed to be holding to account! In nearly twenty years as one of the most active parliamentarians working on international issues, and despite having won election fourteen times among MPs as the senior vice-chairman of the Parliamentary Labour Party Foreign Affairs Committee, unaccountably I never once caught the Chief Whip's eye for a place on the Foreign Affairs select committee.

Above all, the parliament should be elected fairly, by proportional representation, in multi-member constituencies by single transferable vote. The current system of electing Westminster members of parliament (though not the Scottish parliament, the Welsh and Northern Ireland assemblies or the European parliament members) is a conspiracy against democracy. The Liberal Democrats can poll many millions of votes and elect just dozens of MPs while for a couple of million more the big parties can elect hundreds of MPs. Neither Mr Blair nor Mrs Thatcher in her pomp was ever the choice of the majority of the British people yet each held, and misused, landslide majorities to ram through policies opposed by the majority in the country. This is compounded by a corrupt system of party funding, where a small handful of rich men and powerful corporations are buying the policies of the governing party (though if the alternative party begins to look credible they will start to see those businessmen who were New Labour remembering that they were Conservatives all along). There should be strict limits upon party funding – which should never be secret. The state could provide a basic grant to all democratic political parties based on the number of voters they represent.

The first-past-the-post system not only ensures an increasingly centralized and rigidly controlled duopoly in which men and women of independent mind are increasingly rooted out, but effectively prevents the expression and representation in the democratic system of whole constituencies locked out by the wind shift in the two big parties. Before the launch of Respect: the Unity Coalition (see Chapter 10) voters had a mainstream choice between a governing party of privatization and war and an opposition party of privatization and war (and the Lib-Dems, a party of privatization and against some wars – but only until they start, at which point they say they must support them).

How does a pro-European Conservative vote today when the rabid xenophobes of the Tory right rule the roost? How does a real Labour person vote when Tony Blair has handpicked an anti-Labourite stooge to stand in a first-past-the-post election in their constituency? This is not hypothetical; in the Newport East constituency Blair parachuted in the Tory defector Alan Haworth, whose main claim to fame was that he'd been the brains behind Mrs Thatcher's poll tax.

The Westminster voting system is rigged – and I've been saying so for thirty years, even though I was myself a beneficiary of it.

But democracy mustn't stop at Westminster or even at election times.

Local councils are also too big, unfairly elected and too often resemble a one-party state with all the sclerotic, potentially corrupt, uninspiring politics that implies. No city needs more than twenty to thirty proportionally elected, properly salaried and resourced councillors and a directly elected mayor or civic leader. And why shouldn't the police chief, the fire chief, the education chief be elected?

In the age of the Internet many things could be decided by direct democracy, by referendums or voting on propositions at normal election times, which should in any case cease to be events held years apart on rainy Thursdays in draughty school halls. We should be able to vote on-line, over a whole weekend, or at church, at the supermarket or even in the High Street. The twenty-first should the first truly democratic century on a local, national and international level.

But democracy of outcomes is just as important as the process itself. At the moment the only thing certain about British elections is who is going to lose them – the working people who create, build and provide everything around us. For them at modern election times, the illusion is that everything may change, but in fact everything fundamentally remains the same. The winners, every time, are the few rich and powerful men and their system that holds us all back, the 10 per cent or so of men who own 80 per cent or so of the wealth and who have used it to own and control the main sources of information, and to purchase the commanding heights of the political system – including parliament itself. We must recapture the spirit of democracy to cleanse this Augean stable; a stiff and bracing broom will be required. Which is why I say, 'Forward – to the British Democratic Revolution!'

Only then will Britain be able fully to hold its head up in the world. We can be a force for good. Many in the world still respect us; many more would like to be able to. They admire our culture and perhaps relate above all to our language. But we will have to start speaking it in peace and justice rather than war and militarism.

3

In the Beginning

You deserve some kind of explanation. How did it come to pass that a working-class boy from the Irish quarter of a small Scottish city, the grandchild of immigrants and the child of factory workers, should become so absorbed in the Orient that I could be better known in the souks and bazaars of Arabia and the teeming shanties of Lahore and Karachi than in my own country?

Three million Iraqis turned out onto the streets of Baghdad in November 1999 to hail the red *Big Ben to Baghdad* bus which I and my fellow adventurers had driven there to try to draw the world's attention to the plight of the people after years of devastating sanctions. We had crossed three continents, eleven countries and fifteen thousand kilometres and no British people in history had ever seen a foreign welcome like it. The *Guardian* called me 'the left's Lawrence of Arabia'. As millions on the streets of Baghdad cheered the bus, chanted and sang songs in my honour, I asked myself the same question. How? I have no clear explanation.

My family background has no connection to the Middle East or the world of Islam. True, my maternal grandfather had, as one of Monty's 'Desert Rats', fought at El Alamein and elsewhere in North Africa with the British Eighth Army; but he never discussed the area or its people with me, until I began to fight on his old battlegrounds.

The best I can offer is the story that follows and the Arabic word *kismet* – destiny – as a way of understanding the road which took me here. It may be that though a man of the West I have, as a Tunisian lawyer said between sobs after hearing me speak about the bleeding children of Iraq, '*un coeur oriental*' – an oriental heart.

*

It was a hot weekday afternoon in the north-east Scottish coastal city of Dundee in 1975. I was twenty-one years old. The sunlight streamed in at the window and I clearly remember dust dancing in the warm air. Picked out in capital letters in the window were the words *Dundee City Labour Party*.

I was on guard, alone in the party office. Technically, I was unemployed. In fact I was a full-time political activist, foregoing salary and prospects for the worldwide socialist victory. This was due sometime very soon. I had a map of the world on the office wall festooned with red flags where 'our countries' were. In my lifetime the world map would again be red. It had once sported the red of the British Empire on which, it was said, 'the sun never set'. But twilight had come rapidly in the post-war decades.

Things were going our way. The previous year decades of fascism were shaken off by the Portuguese revolution. On 1 May that year, the Vietcong and their North Vietnamese allies had burst into the presidential palace in Saigon putting the puppet regime to flight, and renamed the city after my hero Ho Chi Minh.

In those cold war days, I chose sides at an early age.

That day in 1975 in the Rattray Street office I was an eight-year party veteran. My promotion through the ranks of the Dundee Labour Party had been rapid, the press referring to me as Labour's 'whiz kid'.*

Anyway when the doorbell rang I almost didn't answer it. Our office was near the Unemployment Assistance Board, precursor of the Department of Social Security, and we were frequently inundated with hard luck cases looking for parliamentary assistance. I had no powers to act on the MP's behalf and so often let the doorbell ring when in the office alone. On this day, for whatever reason, I did not.

'My name is Sa'ad Jabaji,' said the stranger, who to me, never having met any Arabs, looked like the film star Omar Sharif. 'I am the

---

* I had already, several times, been elected to the Scottish Committee of the Labour Party youth wing (its only non-Trotskyite member). I had also been elected the youngest ever Constituency Labour Party secretary. I was the youngest ever elected member of the party's Scottish Executive Committee. (I would later become the party's youngest ever full-time organizer and the youngest ever Chairman of the Labour Party in Scotland at the age of twenty-six.)

representative of the General Union of Palestinian Students at Dundee University; and I would like to discuss our cause with some of the leaders of the Labour Party, if they have time to hear me.'

'None of the leaders are here,' I replied, 'but you are welcome to come in and discuss it with me.'

I had responsibility in the local party for international affairs, because no one else was much interested. We were fully occupied with running the city and planning the takeover of our own country. Don't think I'm joking.

Jabaji sat on the black plastic sofa while I rocked back and forward in the party organizer Willie McKelvey's big chair for at least the next two hours. At the end of Jabaji's story, I was a signed-up member of the Palestinian resistance.

Mesmerizingly, my visitor talked about the Nakbah, or 'Catastrophe', which his people had suffered. A whole country had disappeared from the map. Its people had been scattered. Now millions of them eked out the desperate life of the refugee. Worst of all, hardly anybody seemed to care. This all somehow chimed for me. Another in the long line of crimes of imperialism of the kind I had been ingesting since my childhood. Jabaji and his people were clearly among life's underdogs. It is something I undoubtedly inherited from my father that I have spent my life on the side of the underdog, whether it's a football game or a political struggle. This can be wrong; the underdog is not always right. Sometimes it can be positively perverse. But it is out of my hands, or rather it is in my genes and I cannot help it.

The meeting with Sa'ad Jabaji turned out to be one of the most important of my life. If it had not happened, probably I would have known very little of the Arab world.

Events thereafter moved quickly. I went to work putting to flight the small pro-Israel pocket within our local labour movement. This group included close comrades of mine. Until 1982 it was quite normal to find people who were solidly anti-imperialist, supporting liberation struggles in Latin America and Africa, and yet lined up with Israel against the Palestinians.

It is worth taking a few moments to consider the two main reasons for this.

Zionism was the creation of largely atheistic Jews in the late nineteenth century. Foremost among them was Theodore Herzel, whose theory was that the Jews were not a religious group but a nation. They argued that anti-Semitism was endemic in European Christian 'civilization' and would never be expunged. Thus they believed that assimilation was a chimera; and the only answer to the historic prejudice, discrimination and periodic waves of murderous pogrom was for the Jews to remove themselves from Europe and found their own nation-state elsewhere. At that stage they weren't too troubled where; and serious consideration was given to founding 'Israel' in Patagonia, Uganda and Madagascar. Only later would they fasten on to the idea of 'reclaiming' Palestine, which they falsely categorized as a 'land without a people for a people without a land'.

Ironically, this made Zionism the other side of the coin to anti-Semitism. Both believed the Jews should get out of town and were thus, episodically, able to collaborate with each other in order to stampede Jewish people to Palestine. The Zionists because they (atheists or not) claimed it had been biblically promised to them (what price Patagonia?), the anti-Semites so they would never have to look at a Jewish face on their streets again. As a result of this paradox it became commonplace for racists who actually hated Jewish people nonetheless to be ardent Zionists. The British statesman Arthur Balfour, whose 1917 Declaration authored the Palestinian tragedy, when he promised on behalf of one people (the British) to a second people (the Zionist Jews) the land of a third people (the Palestinians), was actually a notorious anti-Semite. Anyone who thinks the succession of slavishly pro-Israel US presidents each had affection for the Jewish people obviously never visited their golf clubs.

The structural and societal anti-Semitism that was an inherent part of European history ensured that the Jewish people knew all about the conditions of the oppressed. Until recently, the impoverished Jew suffered a double stigma in the eyes of most in society. Even the more affluent members of their community could rarely win equal status with the citizens of whichever country they inhabited. Before Zionism became hegemonic among them, the Jewish people were consistently a large and vital element within the world's progressive movements. They have perhaps contributed more to progressive thought and action than any people in the world. Jewish thinkers and activists formed part of the vanguard of socialist and communist movements, labour unions and intellectual circles. Of course, Marx and Trotsky were both Jewish. Not for nothing did the 'Black Hundreds' of European reaction and fascism routinely denounce the 'Judaeo-Bolshevik conspiracy'. Nazi and other fascist propaganda attacks would often target communists interchangeably with Jews.

The fascists were in a sense right: the Jewish people were deeply engaged, in the vanguard, in the struggle for humanity. The people of Einstein were most usually the allies of people like me in the pre-Zionist days. Many still are. But some of my colleagues hadn't grasped that the settler-state ideology and practice had little or nothing to do with this radical tradition. Older British leftists had worked with progressive Jewish colleagues in their earlier years and tended to be instinctively sympathetic to Israel.

The second explanation for leftist support of Israel is now harder to fathom, since for the last twenty-five years a steady stream of increasingly right-wing governments has ruled Israel. But in the 1960s and 70s, Israeli propagandists put their left foot forward in European circles. They stressed the 'socialist' nature of the kibbutz and made great efforts to entice adventurous young people to spend time living and working over their summer holidays, marvelling at the communal child care and eating arrangements and (relatively) free love. These impressionable young people were never told that the land on which this 'socialist' experiment was being conducted had been seized from other people who were now likely shivering in the miseries of a refugee camp. The kibbutz was to socialism no more than a group of robbers agreeing to share their spoils equally.

The pro-Israel lobby stressed the 'Labour' nature of successive Israeli governments, taking pride in the party's membership of the Socialist International. They did not say that this 'socialist' government was dependent on the USA, that it was helping the apartheid regime in South Africa arm itself against its black majority (while many of the heroes of the anti-apartheid struggle were Jewish),*

---

* When I was undercover in apartheid South Africa, virtually all of the 'safe houses' in which I stayed and cars in which I travelled were made available by Jewish members of the ANC, notably Max and Audrey Coleman.

and that it was arming and training the death squads of grisly generalissimos from the Philippines to El Salvador. The Zionist leaders
had spun the myth that they had seized an unpopulated land for a
landless people – one of the fattest lies in history. Their doyenne
Golda Meir once actually announced, 'There is no such thing as a
Palestinian.'

My stock was high in the Dundee Labour Party, despite my youth, and
older comrades were happy to follow my guidance on the Palestinian
issue, now that – thanks to meeting Jabaji, my reading of David Hirst's
wonderful book *The Gun and the Olive Branch* and the arrogance of
youth – I had become an expert. So my support for the Palestinian
cause didn't arise from a cautious and considered analysis of every
relevant fact. I saw a righteous cause and espoused it. On this issue,
the accumulated knowledge of the subsequent thirty years has proved
that my initial instinct was right.

In the summer of 1977 I made my first visit to the Middle East with
an eclectic bunch of around twenty-five young people from around the
country. Lebanon in the 1960s had, on the face of it, been a Monte
Carlo-type paradise where the elite, at least, could ski in the mountains
in the morning and waterski in the Mediterranean in the afternoon.
But under the surface festered a myriad of class and confessional
divisions. These had both crystallized and been exacerbated by the
arrival of waves of Palestinian refugees. Originally driven from the
north of Palestine, Haifa, Acre and Galilee, they were supplemented
somewhat by the Israeli takeover of remaining mandate Palestine – the
West Bank and Gaza – in 1967, and filled to the brim by the backwash
from 'Black September' 1970, when King Hussein, aided by America,
Israel and Pakistan, crushed the Palestinian resistance in Jordan. When
I arrived in Beirut in the summer of 1977 the vicious civil war had
taken what turned out to be a brief time-out. In this conflict the
Palestinians sided with the country's disadvantaged Muslims, Druze
and a few progressive Christian forces against the dominant and
predominantly right-wing 'isolationist' Christian parties of which the
fascist Phalangists were the strongest. Beirut was and looked like a
war zone, the first I had ever seen in real life. Every building was
pockmarked by shot and shell and every street swarming with swarthy

militiamen armed to the teeth. For me, at the time, I must admit it all added up to radical chic.

The trip was a marvellous, life-changing episode in my life, with exotic Arabic music in the cafés and the whiff of revolution in the air. For a young man who thought like me this was bliss.

The men and many of the women were armed and fighting for the noblest of causes. The plurality of the Palestinian factions was staggering to behold. Every grouplet seemed to have a building with offices, newspapers and a magazine. They had their cadres who sat around smoking and talking revolutionary politics. They had their martyrs, whose faces were plastered on every available wall. Only when the guns boomed in the darkness from the faction fights between the Fatah group and 'Rafed', the 'rejectionists', who scorned the mainstream PLO's readiness to compromise, did the downside of that plurality begin to manifest itself. This disunity, and the disastrous effect it had on the Palestinian position in poor suffering Lebanon, would grow in years to come, but for now was just more evidence of the different world I had entered.

We visited the front, fraternized with the Fedayeen (which means 'he who is ready to sacrifice'), and toured PLO institutions like *SAMED* (an acronym from 'sons of the martyrs'), which made furniture, produced sweets for the fighters and grew crops in sympathetic countries like Sudan and, embarrassingly, Idi Amin's Uganda.

In a sign of how isolated in the West the Palestinian leadership then was, our crew of powerless youngsters was introduced to virtually everyone in the Palestinian leadership. We met Abu Jihad, the hero of Fatah's military wing later assassinated in Tunisia, and Abu Iyad, who was later killed in the same way. We went to see Dr George Habash, the erudite leader of the Popular Front for the Liberation of Palestine, which in those pre-Hamas and Islamic Jihad days was the most militant of all the factions. And we heard Nayef Hawatmeh outline his then audacious (and for him potentially fatal) theory, that the Israelis living in Palestine had now acquired 'national rights', and that there would have to be a 'two-state solution' to the conflict.

We met the 'foreign minister' Farouk Khadoumi, who told us that this tragedy could be boiled down to Shakespeare's 'to be or not to be'; for the Palestinians that was the question. And he left us in no doubt that for them it had proved 'nobler to take up arms against their sea of troubles and by opposing, end them'. We met, one midnight, the impossibly glamorous Salah Tammari, married to the ex-wife of King Hussein, and still a Palestinian hero. And many others, including, in the back of a shop somewhere, a man they said was the leader of the Munich Olympics operation, a product of 'Black September'.

Those who have never been in a Palestinian refugee camp cannot imagine what it is like. No refugee camp is a land of milk and honey, but one that has stood for decades is in a class of its own. The mixture of permanent and temporary ensures an oppressive, squalid atmosphere. A ramshackle jumble of concrete breeze blocks, corrugated iron, cardboard, plastic and canvas is crossed by a labyrinth of terrifyingly dangerous electricity and telephone wires. The open sewers run with filth in which children play. The presence of three generations of refugees hits you directly after the appalling smell of insanitary poverty.

There is grandfather sitting on a rocking chair smoking his hookah pipe. In his pocket quite often is a pay book from some branch or other of the former British mandate in Palestine for whom he worked; which he will produce in an instant if you proclaim yourself a visitor from the land of Balfour. Most British people have forgotten (or have never known) the role our country played in all this. No Palestinian will ever forget it. Behind the old man, carefully preserved in the chaos of the one- or two-room shack in which the three generations bed down every night (making it one of the wonders of the world how all these children come to be), he will have stored, like the crown jewels, the title deeds to his land, his orange grove, his olive trees; the paradise he left behind more than half a century ago. He knows that foreigners live there now; people who often had houses of their own in Brooklyn, London or wherever, but who came to Palestine and took his. On the door of this rancid rat-infested shack, he will have carefully hung the key to the door which he locked before he fled his country, and which, despite the odds and the decades, he sincerely believes will reopen the door to his life one day.

Standing around in suffocating, enforced idleness and nursing his wrath will be his son. He was probably born in the camp and has known only this. He cannot work because there is none and in any case the host government dare not 'accept' that the refugee is anything but a temporary visitor. This would do Israel's work, accepting their fait accompli and conceding that the fight was over. So he is forbidden work in almost all jobs outside the camp. He can and has married and makes as many children as he can; for the revolution, for security in case he's still stuck here when he's as old as his father, and because – well, what else is there to do? He takes an interest in politics in a usually desultory way, listening to the BBC with his father, endlessly chewing the fat with the other able-bodied men of the camp. Almost certainly he will be battle-scarred. He will have fought Israel, either in an operation over the border or more usually in defence of the camps when Israel visited him. He will have an allegiance, usually to Arafat but sometimes to the other smaller splinter groups. Nowadays he will not hate members of the rival Palestinian groups; by and large there is now none of the factional bitterness that so divides competing revolutionary movements in other parts of the world.

He is dependent on the diminishing services of the United Nations Relief and Works Agency (UNRWA), which provides food, basic medical care and rudimentary schooling in all Palestinian camps. He will be acutely aware of the agency's shrinking budget but maintain his almost mystical belief in the power of education. Despite everything the Palestinians still have the highest percentage of university graduates in the Arab world as well as more PhDs – their only serious rival being Saddam Hussein's Iraq.

Playing in the gutters are his many children. In the sixties and seventies he will have named them after 'Universalist' revolutionary heroes, like the brave female Palestinian Al Jazeera television-reporter Guevara al-Budeiri. Palestinians called Gyap – after the legendary Vietnamese general – were to be found in refugee camps around the Arab world. Later, in despair, it was little Saddam or more recently Usama whom you would hear being called in for his tea. Yet these children had never seen Palestine, indeed were the children of parents who had never seen Palestine. If you asked them where they came from they would answer Haifa, Jaffa, Acre, Jerusalem; anywhere but this wasteland. The children would be members of the Ashbal – the PLO boy and girl scouts – but tying knots and orienteering have a very different purpose in their curriculum.

To spend time in these camps is to understand fully why generations of Palestinians have been willing to sacrifice their lives to strike back at their usurpers. When life is a living hell what's wrong with going to heaven in a ball of fire? The Liberal Democrats' sacking of their front bencher Jenny Tonge MP for the 'crime' of saying she 'understood' why suicide bombers are created rather than born – there was a similar brouhaha when Cherie Blair said much the same – was as ludicrous as it was cowardly. The wonder is that there are not more such acts of self-immolation, not that they occur at all.

I had been appointed the youngest ever full-time Labour organizer – defeating, by 21 votes to 3, the present Chairman of New Labour, Ian McCartney, for the job – and was due to start work soon. Yet I gave serious thought to staying on in Beirut among my new friends; in the end I did for several months. But while the pull of Beirut was strong I seemed to have a bright political future ahead of me which pulled my growing oriental heart back westwards.

I might have become a kind of foreign legion figure with the Palestinians. I might have fought, maybe died, with them in the internecine wars that would soon rage. One thing I believe is that I would have been unlikely to have made as much of an impact on the Palestinian issue as I did by making what remains one of the hardest decisions of my life. I went home.

In the end it was a political decision; the siren of Beirut's majestic Pigeon Rock, where nightly I would sip sweet Arabic coffee, proved fractionally less seductive than my place in the surely inevitable revolutionary days ahead at home.

About a week later, standing in The Tavern bar in Dundee's Hawkhill district with a local comrade and with Elaine Fyffe (who would later become my first wife and mother of my child), I made a statement which I meant and mean still, though it elicited strong disapproval from my listeners.

'Whatever the consequences for my own political future, I intend to devote the rest of my life to the Palestinian and Arab cause.' Which, more or less, I have done.

In 1980 Dundee's Town Hall became the first public building anywhere in the western world to fly the Palestinian flag when we twinned the city with the West Bank town of Nablus and brought their mayor Bassam Al Shaaka as chief guest at our annual festival. He was a striking sight, given that he had no legs, those having been blown off in an Israeli terrorist attack. He marched in our parade on a pair of excruciatingly painful tin legs. But this was not the reason for the hysterical outrage that greeted the twinning.

The Zionist movement had got busy in a way which only they can. Our other, previously twinned, towns – Alexandria in the USA (adjacent to Langley, Virginia, home of the CIA), Würzburg in Germany and Orleans in France – were pressurized into threatening to sever relations with us if we didn't ditch Nablus. The entire Board of Deputies of British Jews came to Dundee and staged a sit-down strike in the city square. An ailing department store, Goldberg's, closed down making sixty staff redundant and blamed the twinning. The local press attacked us mercilessly and for many years.

One night at Hampden Park, on the occasion of a midweek Scottish international football match, a giant pitch-side advertising hoarding bearing the strange logo *No Pub Like Ours in Dundee* puzzled television viewers. Only when it grew dark did the floodlighting pick out the luminous first letters of each word of the slogan, which transformed it into *No PLO in Dundee*.

My involvement in Arab affairs was growing wider and deeper. I was regularly travelling to Beirut and became closer to Yasser Arafat, whose mainstream Fatah group I had always supported over the more radical factions. But I was also visiting Syria, Morocco, Egypt, and most other Arab countries.

About the only Arab country to which I wasn't invited during this period was Iraq. I would have been arrested if I'd turned up in Baghdad because I was a known opponent of the Ba'athist regime. Saddam Hussein, described throughout the British media as the 'Iraqi strongman vice-president', had taken full power and begun a purge of the then powerful Iraqi Communist Party. As their leading cadres flooded abroad in terror they slotted in to my world view as being on 'our side'. Thus I was one of the first to join the Campaign against Repression and for Democratic Rights in Iraq (CARDRI) – essentially a front of the British and Iraqi communist parties – in the late seventies, acting as the contact point within the Dundee Labour movement for the dissemination of anti-Saddam propaganda, giving the no doubt some-times bemused local Labour membership regular and graphic accounts of Ba'athist atrocities.

One evening when I'd put on a film show of a Palestinian documen-tary that was a little too conciliatory for the local Ba'athist students' liking, they staged a noisy walk-out of the event shouting 'Rejectionist' slogans as they went. They had then a reputation for dishing out violence to their opponents. Sa'ad Jabaji's successor as Palestinian student leader in Dundee, Dr Yusef Allan, had to sleep with another activist on the floor of the Dundee Labour Party office where I lived in the back room at the time, for fear of an Iraqi attack upon my person.

In those days, having driven out the communists with whom he had been in coalition in a National Front government, Saddam was a blue-eyed boy of Britain and America, who were doing a roaring trade of all kinds with him, including arms, and yes, 'weapons of mass destruction'. Thus I was pleased to be able to say, while under attack as an apologist for Saddam Hussein, that I used to be outside the Iraqi embassy in London demonstrating for democracy and human rights while British businessmen and ministers were inside selling guns and gas. Later Tariq Aziz would tell me that on one occasion when he was inside Number 10 Downing Street and we were demonstrating outside, the urbane appeaser and later Foreign Secretary Douglas (now Lord) Hurd told him, above our incessant chants: 'Don't worry about them, they're only communist troublemakers.'

When Iraq invaded Iran in 1980 it did so at the behest of countries like Britain and America who armed it and financed it with credits in order that the taxpayer could guarantee the payments for Saddam's weapons supplies. They were on Saddam's side.

In a classic demonstration of the West's blundering approach to the Orient, Britain and the US had orchestrated the 1953 coup to depose the democratic socialist regime of Dr Mossadeq in Iran. His crime had been, like Colonel Nasser over Suez, to nationalize an asset important to Western private interests, in this case oil. The West reinstalled the tyrant Shah of Persia, who went on to build the foulest dictatorship the region has ever seen. His secret police force, SAVAK, became a byword for torture, murder, the disappearance of opponents and the complete crushing of anything called democracy or human rights, let alone a secular opposition.

Britain supported the Shah until virtually the hour he fell at the hands of tens of millions of Iranians who swept his regime from the streets after the arrival home from exile of Ayatollah Khomeini. Indeed one of the last acts of Dr David Owen, the Labour Foreign Secretary in James Callaghan's government, had been to declare undying loyalty to the Shah – on the very day the tyrant fell.

It is worth speculating that if Britain and the US had not overthrown Mossadeq there would have been no Shah and therefore no Khomeini. If no Khomeini there would have been no Iran–Iraq war, no need to arm Saddam to the teeth. Saddam would not have had his million-strong army all dressed up with nowhere to go but Kuwait and there would have been no first Gulf War. If so there would have been no sanctions, more than a million dead Iraqis – most of them children – would still be alive today and there would have been no subsequent invasion and occupation of Iraq. A small pebble was thus thrown into the deep waters of the Gulf fifty years ago; and it created a tidal wave engulfing so many millions of lives.

In the absence of a powerful socialist or secular opposition in Iran, my perspective led me to support the Islamic revolution of Khomeini as a people's movement that promised an end to the oppressive dictatorship. I believed that Khomeini, and the revolutionary crowds, would strike a spark that could burn down the whole corrupt edifice of dictatorship in the region, as the British and American governments feared. So they implored Saddam to try and crush this incipient revolution at birth. I particularly recall the grim photographs of the current US Defense Secretary Donald Rumsfeld handing surveillance information to Saddam, the better for him to target chemical weapons at Iranian troops. Rumsfeld enjoyed Hussein's company so much he went back a second time for afters.

Tariq Aziz tells the story of his final meeting with Rumsfeld. This was in the late 1980s. The old airman Rumsfeld had faded away into a seller of saccharine, in the form of artificial sweeteners. While addressing a reception in New York, Aziz spotted Rumsfeld at the back of the room and acknowledged him. At the end of his speech the owlish Iraqi minister blinked nervously as Rumsfeld approached bearing a huge sack in both arms. But it was only a gift – a sack of sweeteners for Aziz's personal use (though perhaps Rumsfeld knew that *aziz* means *sweet* in the Arabic language). Rumsfeld smiled ingratiatingly and hoped Aziz might find them pleasing and, if so, might then see his way to recommending their purchase for the state-controlled Iraqi economy.

Throughout the long eight-year attrition, in which perhaps a million people died and during which the Iraqi chemical weapons attack upon Halabja took place, it looked likely that Iraq would be over-run by Iran and their Kurdish opportunistic allies. I supported Iran, as did Syria, the Arab country to which I was then closest. The US maintained for many months after the Halabja attack that it had in fact been mounted by Iran and not Iraq. They also said that 400 people had died there. Later they would say that Iraq had been responsible; and that the death toll had been first 4,000 and then 8,000. Britain continued to sell weapons systems to Saddam long after Halabja.

It was only after the Iraqi 'victory' in the war, when Saddam Hussein emerged with a million-man army, equipped with the best that British taxpayers' money could buy him, that his former paymasters, armourers and, well, apologists and mouthpieces, began to get nervous.

After the Iran–Iraq war and long before the events in Kuwait, Saddam Hussein made a fateful and typically grandiose boast, which set alarm bells ringing shrilly and began the long countdown to Iraq's destruction. At the 1989 Arab League summit in Jordan, Saddam Hussein said, 'If Israel attacks any Arab country . . . we have the means to burn half of Israel.' It was then, I believe, and not when he had been deliberately lured into his Kuwait adventure the following year, that a decision was made that Iraq was too strong and a threat to the West's settler-state sentinel, Israel. Saddam Hussein was also a threat – a radical Arab nationalist one – to the potentates in the Middle East every bit as dangerous as the Ayatollahs in Tehran, and sooner or later he would have to be dealt with.

The siren on the rocks, on which Iraq would later be smashed, was called Kuwait.

Many think the recovery of Kuwait to Iraq was an original idea of

Saddam Hussein's or a policy emerging from the pan-Arab nationalism of the Ba'ath party. In fact it had been a national article of faith during all previous Iraqi governments. For Iraqis of all political persuasions, Kuwait had been stolen from the motherland by perfidious Albion – Great Britain, the former colonial power. I recall my colleague Tam Dalyell MP explaining to wide-eyed Iraqi leaders that his father, who had been secretary to Sir Percy Cox, the British Resident in Iraq, had actually been in the tent with Cox when, tiring of the haggling between local chieftains, he took his stick and drew a line in the sand.

'This is Kuwait and that is Iraq and that's the end of it,' Tam reported Cox as saying. At the time the severance of Kuwait (not so much a limb as a big toe) hurt for reasons other than the obvious. First there was pride. In the 400-year Ottoman era that had just passed, Kuwait had been part of the governorate of Basra, a single province in an empire ruled for centuries by the Caliph from behind the Sublime Porte in Istanbul. The area now known as Kuwait was clearly a part of the larger Iraqi whole.

Shorn of the Kuwaiti coastline, the remaining Iraq became virtually landlocked with only one small outlet to the Gulf, and that in difficult shipping waters. Later it was obvious that the few thousand backward Bedouin who called themselves Kuwaitis were sitting on top of an ocean of black gold – oil.

An example of this long-standing Iraqi yearning for the recovery of Kuwait comes from the life and strange death of Iraq's penultimate royal ruler, King Ghazi. Long before Saddam Hussein – in the 1930s – Iraq had in this flamboyant leader a champion of Palestine and of Arab nationalism. Ghazi installed powerful radio transmitters in his royal palaces in Baghdad and Mosul from where he would personally exhort, through the microphone, the Arab revolt in Palestine against British rule and the steadily building Zionist threat to the land. He would call for Arab unity and, virtually daily, demand the return of Kuwait to her motherland. Ghazi was a bisexual playboy and his colourful private life would lead to his downfall. He was first undermined by British-inspired gossip, and then when that failed to stop him he was lured out of the palace for a homosexual assignation. There he was mysteriously killed – officially in an automobile accident when his car hit a telegraph pole. But his head had been pierced by a sharp object, his driver disappeared never to be seen again, and neither the car nor the telegraph pole looked like they'd collided. Widespread rioting broke out in Iraq and the British consul in Mosul was murdered by an angry mob on the roof of the consulate. British diplomatic cables from the time have – unusually for the Rolls-Royce British civil service – gone missing from our historical archives.

So Iraqi royal rulers like King Ghazi, nationalists and leftists like Karim Abdel Qassem, the military officer whose revolution overthrew the monarchy in 1958, and who was in turn executed in the first Ba'athist coup in 1963, and of course the later Ba'ath party governments all harboured – sometimes secretly, sometimes openly – the hope that one day the statelet known as Kuwait would 'regain' its motherland.

When the crisis erupted in the summer of 1990, it had several new elements. With its tiny population, its lazy and despotic 'family business' leadership – 'more Corleone than Sainsbury', as I said in parliament in 1991 – and its poor treatment of foreign (especially Arab) guest workers, Kuwait had felt extremely vulnerable to the sweep of the Khomeini hordes of the Iranian revolution. So they paid Saddam Hussein to protect them, giving him billions of dollars to support his war against Iran. When he had done so, they wanted their money back. They now told the Iraqis that these had all been loans, not grants.

There were also the two tiny uninhabited islands in the Gulf, Warbu and Bubiyan. Iraq wanted to lease them from Kuwait to help with the bottleneck in their only deep-water port facility at Um al Qassr. Kuwait said no.

The Iraqis further alleged that the Kuwaitis were pumping well in excess of agreed production limits and were plundering the Al-Rumaillah oil field (which straddled the Iraq–Kuwait border), depleting stocks and helping to drive down prices as a deliberate policy of over-supply in the delicately balanced international market.

Now it would be a very good question, beyond the scope of this book, why such a Ruritanian monarchy, with lots of expensive, Western weapons rusting in the desert but absolutely no one ready or able to use them, would risk poking such sticks in the face of their much larger neighbour – especially as he was not even caged at that time.

That question would deepen when linked with the mysterious conversations between the US ambassador to Baghdad, April Glaspie – now convented in the State Department and subject apparently to a Carmelite vow of total silence over the affair – and Saddam Hussein. According to the Iraqi transcript of the conversations – not seriously challenged by even the US government – Ambassador Glaspie informed the bellicose Saddam, who was contemplating swallowing his small neighbour, that the US 'had no opinion' on their 'Arab–Arab border dispute with Kuwait'; and that Americans, like Iraq, 'knew all about' the problems created by 'colonialism'. Whether deliberately or not, the United States government thus helped whet the Iraqi appetite for the invasion, which occurred over the night of 2 August 1990.

The world woke up to the patently absurd news out of Baghdad that there had been a Kuwaiti coup and that its perpetrators had quickly transformed the country, a sovereign state of the United Nations and a member of the Arab League, into a province of Iraq. In truth the Iraqi forces had swept unopposed all the way to Kuwait City, putting the ruling potentates to flight with hardly a shot being fired.

The question I discussed with many in Baghdad in the years that followed was why, if Kuwait was such a sitting duck (its regime so unloved that no one would fight to save it), the Iraqi regime chose the most provocative and intolerable way of taking it over? There were hundreds of thousands of foreign workers including Iraqis and Palestinians who could have been the building blocks of a genuine revolution. There were many Ba'athists in Kuwait and many Islamists (though of a milder variety than today's) who could have been the agitators and organizers of unrest. The Kuwaitis would have cracked down hard on such civil unrest; but that too could have worked to Baghdad's advantage. After weeks of demonstrations and repression at least Baghdad might have created a pretext for its aggression, one that might have won them some international understanding and buttressed their Arab support against the unloved Kuwaiti royal house. The royal dictatorship there might even have asked Saddam to come in and save them!

By imitating the Vietnamese in Cambodia, when they invaded, overthrew Pol Pot, and withdrew leaving a pro-Vietnamese government behind, Saddam might conceivably have organized the removal of the Al-Sabah dictatorship in Kuwait successfully. Instead he chose the worst way. The full-scale military invasion of a neighbouring country and an overnight annexation of one of the world's most important oil producers were always doomed to reversal. Like the original catastrophic decision to invade Iran, it was another colossal blunder by the Iraqi leadership. This was explicable in only two ways; either Iraq was a country run by fools – a regional giant with the mind of a child – or someone had twice made a fool of the people who were running Iraq.

In 1990 I was an enemy of the Iraqi regime and had, purposely, never visited the country. The sympathy I had for former colonies undoing the fake boundaries of imperialism could not support the naked aggression committed against Kuwait. That action copied elsewhere in the developing world would be a recipe for endless chaos and bloodshed. Yet as 1990 moved ominously towards a cataclysmic war I made my stand with Iraq.

The differences I had with the Iraqi regime were not as great as those that I had with the bigger villains of imperialism. The US and its loyal auxiliary Great Britain were preparing to invade Kuwait not out of concern for the fate of small nations, nor for the high-flown reasons they advanced. There was much talk of Iraq as a dictatorship. Yet Kuwait was governed from top to bottom, not by one party, but one family!

In January 1991 I tabled the following motion in the House of Commons:

That this House notes that British forces are currently fighting, some perchance to die, for the restoration of the legitimate government of Kuwait: and notes that this legitimate government, vis: the Amir Jaber As-Sabah, the Crown Prince Sa'ad As-Sabah, the Prime Minister Sa'ad As-Sabah, the Deputy Prime Minister Sa'bah As-Sabah, the Foreign Minister Sa'bah As-Sabah, the Minister of Amiri Diwan Affairs Khalid As-Sabah, the Minister of Information Jaber As-Sabah, the Minister of the Interior Salim As-Sabah, the Minister of Defence Nawaf As-Sabah, the Minister of Oil Ali As-Sabah, the Governor of Ahmadi Province Al Sabah As-Sabah, the Governor of Jahra Province Ali Abdullah As-Sabah, the Governor of Kuwait Province Jaber As-Sabah, the Governor of

Faranawiya Province Ahmad As-Sabah, are an unelected government who appear to be related: further notes that the Kuwaiti National Assembly, which had a limited franchise and even more limited powers, was suspended by the Amir's decree in 1986: and wonders if this war aim of restoration can be justified.

Propaganda started to raise the scare about Iraq having 'weapons of mass destruction'. The sale of these by Britain, the USA and West Germany to Baghdad not many years before was not emphasized. Those preparing to attack Iraq were the financiers and armourers of Israel with its mountain of weapons of mass destruction, chemical, biological and nuclear weapons and the means to deliver them. (Israeli nuclear capability had been revealed thanks to the extraordinarily brave Israeli Mordechai Vanunu, who was sentenced to twenty years' solitary confinement for telling us.)

This was a war for oil; the big powers were anxious to stop an Arab nationalist government increasing its share of the world's oil reserves. It was also a war for Israel, to cut down to size a potentially trouble-some Arab government. I believed the result – reversing an invasion – would not justify the means. The inevitably disproportionate response would sow the seeds of further conflict through the defeat, dismember-ment and national humiliation of Iraq. I and the great majority of the British left took up our places in the ranks of the Stop the War movement (part 1, as it turned out).

A cold chill settled on the invertebrates on the opposition Labour front bench. But there were many honourable exceptions. Several luminaries resigned from the Labour team of shadow ministers, most notably Clare Short. Sadly, a million dead Iraqis and a dozen years later, Clare was to act shamefully at the time of the second Iraq war; first apparently intending to resign then staying in the War Cabinet at Blair's right hand and denouncing opponents of the war as 'appeasers' and then, after the war, resigning and laying in to Blair as a liar who fooled us all – no one more than poor Clare herself – into an unneces-sary and disastrous conflict.

It should be stressed that the 1991 war was intellectually quite difficult for many to oppose. There was a pretext: Iraq had been wrong to invade Kuwait and extremely foolish not to withdraw its forces once it saw the certain consequences. There was an international consensus among states. There was a coalition not of two but of more than thirty countries participating in the attack. There were even Arab armies lined up alongside the big Western powers, most notably those of Egypt, Syria, Saudi Arabia and Morocco. Despite this Clare Short and others maintained a principled and spirited opposition within Parliament and on the streets of Britain.

I was a first-term Labour MP and made many House of Commons sorties, one or two of them quite effective. On the afternoon when the news pictures of the massacre perpetrated by the US air force on the Al-Amariya air-raid shelter in Baghdad had just come through on the lunchtime news, I asked a distinctly pale-faced Douglas Hurd (the normally unflappable Foreign Secretary), in front of a baying hostile House:

'As the Foreign Secretary watched the pictures this afternoon, of the ribbons of women and children being swept (Interruption) . . . yes, swept out of the air-raid shelter in Baghdad did he think, even for a moment, that some of the blood of those women and children belonged on his hands?'

Hansard, the official record of parliamentary proceedings, euphemistically describes the reaction as 'Interruption'. In reality the savage faces around me on both sides of the House made an epic study in rage. Mouths open and eyes bulging, the red-faced MPs howled at the gall of this squalid nuisance, on whom till that point they had had a hard time laying a glove given my anti-Saddam record and their profitable and shameless decade of giving succour and comfort to what I had described in the House as the 'bestial dictatorship in Baghdad'.

Sometimes these sorties were flown at night and here I should explain some important facts. In those days, though much less so now, the House of Commons was a very boozy place. There were around nineteen bars in the building, open all hours while the House was sitting, often beyond midnight and sometimes all through the night. Drink was cheap because it was subsidized, unbelievably, by the taxpayers, most of whom earned a lot less than parliamentarians. Given the captive nature of the clientele (most of us 'whipped' by the party managers not to leave the building, to go to the pictures, visit a gallery, meet a friend or – heaven forbid – go home), the atmosphere was often highly charged late at night. I don't drink alcohol. But many who enjoyed the blurring of their ignorance on Middle Eastern politics and the fuelling of their spurious moral indignation made an angry beeline for me as they stumbled out of the bars. One such was Dr John Reid, now a general in the New Blair Army but then a mere Kinnockite subaltern as deputy spokesman on children. One night I accused him of 'going from defending the rights of children to apologizing for their mass murder'. Reid, well fuelled as he then almost always was, lunged violently at me in the voting lobby. I managed to deliver two straight lefts to his florid face before a powerful lunge of woman-power in the formidable shape of Diane Abbott MP intervened to stop the fight. Incredibly, a full twelve years later, the same Diane Abbott threw another punch to save another well-oiled Blairite stooge MP from the same fate after he insulted and then tried to assault me in the library corridor of the House on the night of the parliamentary vote authorizing the latest war on Iraq.

This was the beginning of my long civil war in the Labour Party over Iraq. In it I would sustain many wounding attacks from which I shall always bear ugly scars. It need not have ended in my discharge – I believe honourable discharge – from the ranks if the strategy, indeed the whole doctrine of the party, had not wheeled so far right that effectively the forces of Labour were eventually rented out to our enemies.

4

My War with Uncle Sam

I happened to be watching the smoking tailfin of the first plane to hit the Twin Towers on 11 September 2001, live on television. Thus I saw the second plane smash into the second tower. I immediately turned to my horrified wife, whose face paled as she instantly recognized the consequences. (Interestingly, my sister, who had recently sat in the towers on a New York holiday, texted me shortly after, saying, 'What terrible vengeance will now follow?')

'It's Bin Laden,' I said.

Within thirty minutes I was writing a hastily commissioned piece for the Guardian. 'Remember, remember the eleventh of September,' I wrote. Gunpowder, treason and plot were already apparent in the first hours of that fateful day. I pointed out that though these monstrous mosquitoes seemed to have come out of a clear blue sky, they had in fact been incubated in a deep swamp of bitterness and hatred, fertilized by the West's double standards – towards Israel–Palestine, Iraq and the corrupt kings and puppet presidents who, virtually without exception, ruled the Muslim world. In the course of that week and in parliament when it was recalled, I pointed out that while the attack on 9/11 was a great crime, it was neither the first nor the greatest crime. And that our apparent belief that it was represented, yet again, those double standards.

In a simultaneous broadcast, swimming in the grief of the three thousand who died in New York and Washington, Mrs Blair and Mrs Bush would beseech us 'not to forget' (as if we could) the heartbreaking messages of love and farewell sent from mobile phones on board the planes or in the Twin Towers, left to the answering machines of their loved ones.

'Just because Afghan women don't have mobile phones, their loved ones any answering machines, doesn't make their incineration, delivered from the skies, any less obscene than the deaths of those American women,' I said. I could tell from the faces around me in parliament that what for me was a simple truth was not a belief shared universally. In fact it was to become abundantly clear that the blood of Americans, Israelis, Europeans, Australians was worth far more than the blood of Afghans, Iraqis, Palestinians . . .

I argued in the House that if it were merely a case of a conveniently bearded, helpfully turbaned Mephistophelean 'Dr Evil' in a cave in the Tora Bora, whom we could find and dispatch with a mighty 'Kerpow' to solve the problem, we would be lucky indeed. But that it was not that simple.

But I was also the first to highlight some uncomfortable truths about that Dr Evil.

'I despise Usama Bin Laden, the mediaeval, obscurantist savage,' I told the House. 'The difference is, I have always despised him.' Even when Britain and America were stuffing guns and money down his throat, on the basis that 'my enemy's enemy is my friend', I was against him. I was practically the last man standing in parliament against the so-called 'Mujahidin' – the cut-throats powered into control of Kabul by Reagan and Thatcher. I told Mrs Thatcher: 'You have opened the gates to the barbarians . . . and a long dark night will now descend upon the people of Afghanistan.' I never spoke a truer word.

Usama Bin Laden, the Taliban and their spiritual fathers were created, financed, armed, trained and supported by diplomacy during that first grisly transatlantic love-fest, the Ronnie and Maggie show (Jimmy Carter did his bit too, although it was peanuts compared to their contribution). This process received a lot of help from tame media fans with microphones and typewriters, like the ITN correspondent Sandy Gall, whose breathless panegyrics to the struggle of these 'noble savages' fighting the Soviet Red Army in Afghanistan were such a feature of *News at Ten* at the time.

Later, thanks to the mighty Michael Moore, in his book *Dude, Where's My Country?*[1] we would learn just how labyrinthine was the web of connections, greased with millions of dollars, linking the Bush family and the Bin Ladens. According to Moore, the Bush family – whose grandfather had made much of the family fortune dealing with Hitler – and the Bin Ladens were practically kinsmen. Daddy Bush inveigled Bin Laden bullion into his sons' failed business ventures, the Bin Ladens were multi-million-dollar investors in the Carlyle Group (on whose board Daddy Bush and his buddy John Major sit). The Saudi oligarchy – of whom the Bin Laden family are a part – has one trillion dollars invested in the American stock market and another trillion dollars sitting in American banks, the merest hint of the withdrawal of which would send the US economy through the floor.

In a still unexplained, indeed inexplicable, chain of events in the hours after 9/11, when all American flights were grounded, Bush (himself on the run from underground base to underground base like a frightened rabbit) allowed twenty-four Bin Laden family members – some of whom had attended Usama's son's wedding in the Tora Bora just six months before the Twin Towers attack – to leave the country 'for their protection'. They were all allowed to fly to Europe and out of the reach of any questions (or, more specifically, answers). To hold them for questioning would have been, said Bush, 'to take hostages, and we don't do that'.

I warned the House of Commons on the day of parliament's recall that if we responded in the wrong way to 9/11, and deepened instead of drained the swamp of hatred, we would create 'ten thousand new Bin Ladens'. Which is of course precisely what we've done.

During the war on Yugoslavia, Clare Short – then known by the sobriquet bestowed upon her by the *Guardian*'s peerless diarist, Mathew Norman, 'Bomber Short' – accused Tony Benn and me of being motivated by a 'visceral anti-Americanism'. This was particularly harsh on Benn, who had been blissfully married to an American for half a century. But it was wrong about me too. The love-hate relationship with America I share with half the world really is a paradox and not a defence mechanism. I am the great-great-grandson of what must have been practically the only woman in the nineteenth century to emigrate *from* America *to* Scotland – something I found out only very recently in researching my family tree. The American Maggie Smith had married the illegitimate butcher Andrew Galloway and lived, according to the census of 1901, 'in two rooms with one or more windows' with their two small children and a boarder!

I first became aware of America as a small boy hiding under my bedclothes as an aeroplane from the nearby Leuchars airbase flew overhead. The air at the time was thick with talk about a nuclear war between the US and the Soviet Union over the Cuban missile crisis. In my childish fear I imagined the plane overhead was about to obliterate my world. Although I grew up to be a friend of Fidel Castro – the young revolutionary at the heart of that crisis – at the time I, a small child, had no side in the thirteen-day stand-off, when the world stood on the brink of thermonuclear war. Indeed my party piece, when others were singing 'Ho Ro My Nut Brown Maiden', was reciting sizeable chunks from the speeches of John F. Kennedy, to the delight of my Irish relatives.

It was common for families like ours to display pictures of JFK (under that of the Pope) on the living room wall, such was the pride in the first Catholic president of the United States. I can say I loved JFK, and all the Kennedys. The love affair was definitively over when one of them turned out electioneering for her husband, Arnold Schwarzenegger.

I was playing football in our housing scheme's dark streets when my father, on his way out to a darts match, told me President Kennedy had been assassinated. I burst into tears. I remember, too, where I was when Bobby Kennedy was killed. My reaction was identical. I continue to believe Ted Kennedy is the greatest president the US never had. When he ran against Carter for the Democratic nomination in 1980 I wore his badge and sent him a Scottish pound note for his campaign fund. I used parts of his magnificent concession speech of that year in my funeral oration for my own father in 1997. I cried for every lost Kennedy and I weep for the America that lost them.

In my childhood America was Bonanza; Hoss and Little Joe, Adam and Pa. I had a picture on my wall of the Lone Ranger aboard Trigger signed when they both clattered through the Greens Playhouse in Dundee. (They said it was he, but with the mask on who could tell; and I was shocked when I learnt what Kimo Sabi meant!)

Then America was Davy Crockett (I had a fur-tailed hat just like his), Elvis, Maverick, John Wayne's *She Wore a Yellow Ribbon* (I had a fort and a full toy regiment of the US Cavalry, though I didn't know then about all the hearts they buried at Wounded Knee). I drank sarsaparilla in a café in my home city's Hilltown district and I began a life-long love affair with American cars: Buicks and Cadillacs especially, things of beauty and a joy for ever. I've tried to buy huge American cars, hopelessly impractical, in Havana, Damascus and Johannesburg.

Later in the sixties I found Bob Dylan and I have never let him go, still believing him to be the greatest writer since Shakespeare. Joseph Heller's *Catch-22* is my all-time favourite novel. I am a film fanatic and I especially like Hollywood films, of which I have an amateur's encyclopedic knowledge. I've read virtually everything I could find on the American Civil War and have a point of view about the military skills of every general (the Confederate Stonewall Jackson was the greatest).

Who could have thought that the small Dundee boy who pulled the covers over his head to avoid the consequences of the Cuban missile crisis would end up firm friends with Fidel?

In one late-night conversation with Castro (they are all late-night conversations – once we talked so long we went swimming in the Caribbean together at dawn) we discussed the extraordinary sight that day of an American president – Clinton – jogging in a Malcolm X baseball cap.

'What did you think of Malcolm?' I asked.

'He was a great man, Malcolm,' said Fidel, the forty-year American whipping boy, 'but he was a little . . . dangerous!'

Such paradoxes are routine when discussing America. The country today is no more synonymous with George W. Bush than it was when the leaders of the victorious Cuban revolution visited New York for the UN General Assembly back in 1960. Fidel, Che Guevara and the other young bearded guerrillas first stayed in a fashionable Manhattan hotel until a posse of gold-toothed Cuban émigrés, rattling their ill-gotten jewellery, turned up to protest. The manager asked Fidel for an indemnity against any damage they might do. Standing on the revolution's dignity Castro refused and the manager ordered them to leave. Malcolm X came to the rescue, offering lodgings in the famous

St Theresa's Hotel in Harlem – with Black Muslim protection for the duration.

From there Fidel began receiving all the greats of the era, who would not normally have been found in Harlem. Khrushchev came, as did Nehru (with the young Mrs Gandhi in tow), the Chinese foreign minister Chou en Lai plus Tito and numerous others.

The Muslim guard (with their incongruously named pork pie hats) couldn't keep the girls away from Che, however, and every time Fidel needed him the first place he'd look was the fire escape, where Guevara was usually found tossing flowers down to his admiring fans.

'What was your main memory of the visit?' I asked Fidel.

'The day Malcolm arranged a picnic for all of us in Central Park, with army-surplus chairs and tables. The Cuban leadership and Malcolm's Muslim brothers all stretched out in the heart of New York City. I was terrified the water bottles would get mixed up and our Cuban rum would find its way down the throats of Malcolm's non-drinking brethren,' he laughed.

In my teens I did develop a visceral hatred of American imperialism that used to be shared by the likes of Robin Cook and Clare Short. Later they chose to share its bed along with ex-communists like Health Secretary Dr John Reid and many others in the Blair clique today.

In my first year at secondary school I began wearing the badge of the Vietnam Solidarity Campaign, and at the age of fourteen I attended my first major demonstration: the legendary rumble in London's Grosvenor Square, where police horses lost their footing on ball-bearings, police truncheons flew and where we followed the leadership of a handsome young Oxford student by the name of Tariq Ali – with whom I march at the head of anti-war demonstrations today.

'Ho! Ho! Ho Chi Minh!' we'd chant and 'LBJ [the US president Lyndon Baines Johnson]; how many kids did you kill today?'

I kicked every ball with the Vietcong, cheered their victories and mourned their every defeat. I was no different from the hundreds of thousands of American demonstrators and the millions there who opposed the war. This war was not just a disaster for the people of Vietnam – who lost two million dead in that era and whose country was drowned in an ocean of American chemical weapons, the consequences of which can still be found in the maternity wards of Vietnam today – but was a catastrophe for the US itself. America sent half a million of its young men to the quagmire of Vietnam; 58,000 came back in body bags. Mostly they were the poor, both black and white. The American elite took overseas university courses to avoid the draft – like Bill Clinton – or just dodged it like George W. Bush and his Vice-President Dick Cheney. The draft tore American society apart; the descent into a drug-fuelled inferno in 'Nam drove many of the soldiers crazy. Thousands committed suicide when they came back; many were never the same people again. Films like Oliver Stone's *Platoon* and *Born on the Fourth of July*, based on the life of my friend Ron Kovic, were no exaggeration. This really was *Apocalypse Now*.

The day the American ambassador clattered off the roof escaping the US embassy in Saigon – swiftly renamed Ho Chi Minh City – his files scattering in the tail draught as he scrambled desperately to clamber aboard, was one of the greatest of my life. The wrath of the Vietnamese people chased him for his life. The US had been given a bloody good hiding. It was a vindication of everything I was openly proselytizing.

Vietnam was not the only soundtrack of my seventies. In the other September the Eleventh, the one nobody ever talks about any more, a democratic parliament came under assault from the air, and a presidential palace was in flames. Inside the burning building a president lay dead. Thousands were rounded up in a football stadium to be tortured or murdered. Tens of thousands were scattered to the four winds where they remained for decades in bitter exile. The long dark night of military dictatorship began. It was, of course, Chile on 11 September 1973, and the terrorists organizing the attack on democracy were not bearded fanatics but sharp-suited killers in the operations room of the White House. Their names were President Richard Milhous Nixon and his Secretary of State 'Dr' Henry Kissinger.

The fate of the Nixon presidency encompasses all the reasons to both love and hate America. That such a low and venal character could serve twice as vice-president and twice as president tells you much about the system. A creature of the corrupt corporate coitus between the big parties and big business, Nixon was as shifty as he looked. His close links to the Cuban émigrés and their Mafia associates are only now being properly exposed. He may even have been involved in the conspiracy against JFK – whose narrow victory over him in 1960 he never forgave. Nixon bugged and burgled his way through political life right from his student days. Tricky Dicky as he was called practically invented the concept of dirty tricks – cancelling opponents' bookings of venues for their rallies, distributing bogus and damaging forged leaflets and documents, employing goons to strong-arm his political enemies, smearing rival candidates.

Nixon knew the difference between a smear and a boomerang, however. During his battle with the Democratic Party's presidential candidate Hubert H. Humphrey in 1968, Nixon's bloodhounds came up with information that the venerable goody-two-shoes Humphrey had been 'seeing to' a young woman in her twenties.

'Shall we leak it?' asked his aides.

'Don't be silly,' said Nixon, 'if this gets out he'll sweep the country!'

And yet for all that Watergate exposed the seedy underbelly of America, it also showed many of the ways in which the US – which rose to the occasion – has much to teach the rest of us.

For a start it is very unlikely that any of the British newspapers would have had the dogged persistence or editorial freedom to pursue the story to the death in the way that *Washington Post* editor Ben Bradlee and reporters Bob Woodward and Carl Bernstein did. Or that under our own 'unwritten constitution' such a scandal could have defenestrated a powerful elected government in the way the American constitution destroyed Nixon. In Britain the whole matter would have been swept under the carpet like the Hutton Inquiry whitewash; an underling would have taken the rap – or not, if the judge was particularly brazen – the establishment would have hung together for fear of hanging separately and the whole thing would have blown over. The truth is the United States is the least secretive of societies with the best constitution, and Watergate was both the best of times and the worst of times all rolled into one. Another American paradox.

But they are suckers when it comes to politicians and especially presidents. A nation whose best known political contemporaries are George W. Bush and Arnold Schwarzenegger and which, overwhelmingly, believes that the old hack B-movie star Ronald Reagan should have his face carved alongside Washington and Lincoln in the rock of Mount Rushmore needs a good civics class.

What more can be said about Bush, the man who said we are all 'mis-underestimating' him? The man who thought the people who live in Greece are called Grecians, in Kosovo, Kosovarians; who said the problem with American imports was that most of them come from overseas. The man who weeks before he became the most powerful man on the planet, when asked on TV who the leader of Pakistan was replied, 'The General.' Pressed by the interviewer for, say, a name, he smirked, 'We just call him the General.'

In America politicians routinely don the mantle of religious men; it plays in Peoria as they say. But few manage to look and sound as much like an Elmer Gantry snake-oil salesman as George W. Bush. The president is down on his knees as often as possible in the White House – a change from his predecessor Bill Clinton in so many ways. Every meeting habitually begins with a prayer, and, appropriately, we learn from a newspaper in the holy land, *Haaretz*, that the president even speaks to God before the big decisions. The Israeli newspaper quoted Bush as telling the then Palestinian prime minister Mahmoud Abbas, 'God told me to strike at Al-Qaeda and I struck them, and then He instructed me to strike at Saddam, which I did, and now I am determined to solve the problem in the Middle East.'

We must, I suppose, be grateful that someone is talking to this world-class ignoramus, with his shrunken bar-room view of the world, living proof that 'a little knowledge is a dangerous thing'.

In his ignorance about the world Bush is of course merely speaking for his people. In a poll of US adults between the ages of 18 and 25, 65 per cent could not place Great Britain on the map (so much for the special relationship). 92 per cent of Americans have no passport and they certainly don't travel the world via their news broadcasts, most of which carry very little foreign news. On the main American networks ABC, CBS and NBC, wrote Sheldon Rampton and John Stauber, time devoted to foreign coverage fell from a scant 4,032 minutes in 1989 to 1,382 minutes in the year 2000. Once wars – which account for most of this shrivelled coverage – are over, the countries quickly fade away. Afghanistan received 306 minutes of coverage while the war raged there in November 2001 but three months later it fell to 28 minutes. In March 2003 it was just one minute.[2]

*

Bush himself before his election thought 'abroad' was the bordellos and casinos of Acapulco.

But though Bush may appear to be inches from imbecility, those around him are not. I don't believe for a minute that this alcoholic former cocaine sniffer, a thrice-arrested, draft-dodging former playboy who has 'issues' with the chewing of pretzels, has really found God and been born again. Bush didn't find God as much as find the party of God, America's own Hezbollah, the militant, Bible-belting fundamentalists of the Christian Right. He knew this was a force that should be with him, and he went out and lassoed it. Fundamentalist right-wingers like Karl Rove, Bush's main pollster and muse, know how to arouse the seventy million or so American voters who view the Bible literally and vote accordingly. After eight years of the fornicating 'slick Willie' Clinton, this group found a kind of rapture in George W. And he seems to see things their way. They believe in the concept of Armageddon, the inevitable world-wide conflagration between Good and Evil or, to put it another way, the Clash of Civilizations. Bush seems to want to get there as fast as possible. Though historically hostile to Jews, they believe that Israel is their ally in this, at least until the consequential return of the Messiah, when all the rest can go to hell and in their view certainly shall.

Thus the Bush administration roams the world like a giant with the mind of a child. The 'Toxic Texan' who left his state governorship literally under a cloud of corporate pollution resulting from his deregulation of environmental constraints on profits, has wrecked the Kyoto protocol designed to bring global warming under control by reducing the emission of climate-changing greenhouse gases. Not only did he declare as an article of faith that he would not ratify the treaty, he has bribed and bullied enough others to ensure its inoperability.

The man who wants to rampage around the world regime-changing and putting 'rogue state' leaders on trial is the same man who has destroyed the International Criminal Court. Why this should be so can be illustrated best by a brief look at the life and times of Henry Kissinger.

By his wilful sabotage of the 1968 Paris peace negotiations, being conducted by the Lyndon Johnson presidency to end the war in Vietnam, Kissinger played a key role in prolonging America's involvement in the war. Between 1968 and 1972 more than half of America's

58,000 dead soldiers perished. During these negotiations Kissinger was secretly working for the Republican challenger in the 1968 presidential election, Richard M. Nixon.

Between Nixon's election and the end of the war Kissinger served as Nixon's National Security Advisor and Secretary of State. In effect, such was his power in the Nixon White House that he was in truth Nixon's deputy. In that period he presided over the intensification of a war that could have been over – to the electoral advantage of Nixon's opponent Hubert Humphrey – four years earlier. In those four years perhaps one and a half million Vietnamese needlessly died and the country was comprehensively ruined, before Kissinger negotiated virtually the identical peace deal with the Vietnamese to the one he had sabotaged in 1968. For which, on the day that satire died, he was awarded the Nobel Peace prize. (Satire would be murdered all over again in 2004 with the nomination of Bush and Blair for the prize.)

During this period Kissinger recommended – in defence of the 'credibility' of American power – the opening of a second front, a 'sideshow' over the Vietnamese border in Cambodia. The neutral neighbour, under the rule of Prince Sihanouk, was illegally bombed in a terrifying firestorm that claimed over half a million Cambodian lives. No congressional approval had been obtained for this secret war – indeed approval would have been refused if it had been sought because Nixon had pledged to end the war, not expand it. When news leaked out of the subterfuge (US pilots were ordered to lie when filling in their work-sheets about where they had flown, inventing Vietnamese villages they had been 'bombing'), Kissinger ordered the illegal wire-tapping of journalists, state department officials, the CIA and even his own staff and friends. Thus the 'plumbers' unit, the people who went on to burgle the Democratic Party headquarters at the Watergate building in Washington, was born.

In the United States news of the spreading of the war sent 500 university campuses up in smoke as the anti-war movement went wild. Four young American students were shot dead by the National Guard at the Kent State University in what became an emblematic moment for a generation.

Kissinger then coordinated the overthrow of Sihanouk and his replacement with the US stooge dictator Lon Nol. This in turn created the triumph of the Khmer Rouge, the victory in Cambodia of Pol Pot, the genocide of the 'Killing Fields' and the deaths of countless more Cambodians.

The overthrow of the democratically elected socialist government of Salvador Allende and the subsequent murder, torture and enforced exile of tens of thousands of Chileans was another Henry Kissinger masterpiece. Kissinger first tried to sabotage Allende's victory, and when that failed he carefully coordinated the military coup of his favourite Generalissimo, Augusto Pinochet. It was the other 9/11, 11 September 1973.

By 1975 Kissinger was working for President Gerald Ford who, despite famously not being able to 'chew gum and walk in a straight line at the same time' (sound familiar?), had been appointed president in the stead of Nixon, whom he'd pardoned for his illegal acts (they had to go to Ford because Vice-President Spiro Agnew had been sent to prison, along with Attorney General John Mitchell and a clutch of other White House officials). Kissinger's appetite for blood was apparently unsated.

Kissinger actually sat in the operations room with the Indonesian General Staff while they planned the illegal invasion and occupation of the Portuguese colony of East Timor. He connived at ways of avoiding the ban on the use, by the blood-spattered Indonesian president General Suharto, of American weapons, supplied strictly for 'self-defence'. And he congratulated the beasts after their operation, which in the end cost the lives of nearly one quarter of the colony's Christian population.

All this and more is to be found in the now apostate Christopher Hitchens' coruscating indictment entitled *The Trial of Henry Kissinger*.[3] Unlike Nixon and the rest of his gang, 'Dr' Henry Kissinger remains alive; the greatest living war criminal and mass murderer in the world today. In days when General Pinochet, the now 'senile' retired dictator of Chile can be apprehended, like the common criminal he is, by the Metropolitan Police on the orders of a Spanish magistrate, and held as – officially – a 'prisoner' in the UK, there is plenty of reason to believe that a similar fate could one day befall Pinochet's puppet-master, the murderous Dr Strangelove, Henry K.

*

Precisely to avoid such an indignity befalling him or any other politician, officer or soldier wearing the stars and stripes, Bush was determined from the start to wreck the International Criminal Court. Just like with the Kyoto protocol, he not only refused to ratify the setting up of the court himself, he made it a loyalty test among the countries in the 'coalition of the killing' that they should refuse to join it either. Sadly it is likely to be long after Kissinger has descended to the bowels of the seventh circle of hell that any American leader does face justice in the new world order.

Bush has similarly wrecked the treaty banning the use of anti-personnel landmines (I wonder if they discussed that during Bush's B&B at Buckingham Palace; everyone present could have 'dissed' the life and works of Princess Diana); the treaty to check the proliferation of small arms (Bush too goes bowling in Columbine and is happy to be held at pistol-point by the gun-nuts of the National Rifle Association, despite the fact that more than one million Americans have been killed by gunshot by other Americans since JFK's assassination), and – I'm not making this up – the treaty to stop the proliferation of chemical weapons (on the grounds that allowing inspectors into US chemical warfare plants would be a breach of the commercial confidentiality of the president's indecently close corporate friends).

The US is a behemoth and would, even if ably and sensitively led, always excite a mixture of fear, envy and admiration. But Bush, Cheney, Wolfowitz, Perle et al. and the terrifying outer circles of the neo-con, brazenly imperialist 'Project for a New American Century', the right-wing fundamentalist fanatics who have power on the Potomac today, have succeeded in uniting whole continents against them. America for many is not Hoss Cartwright, Lassie or Calamity Jane whip-crackin' lovably away. Rather it is George Bush's simian swagger and smirking face, speaking in air-force hangars to hordes of uniformed personnel roaring 'USA!–USA!–USA!' and hollering for the order to kick ass, any ass, anywhere. It is a deeply troubling face, which will terrify our children for many years to come.

5

Last Refuge of the Scoundrel

Almost thirty years ago I heard the 'Red Clydeside' leader Jimmy Reid say: 'Nationalism is like electricity; it can kill a man in the electric chair or it can keep a baby alive in an incubator.' The question, he implied, was: nationalism for what? Against what? The nationalism of whom?

In the decades since then I have watched this pulsating powerful current course through the international circuit. I have watched it putting lights out in Yugoslavia and am now watching it, by internal combustion, firing a liberation struggle in Iraq against British and American occupation.

In its so-called 'tribal' form it has butchered hundreds of thousands. In its more 'advanced' western guise it has murdered millions.

First we should define our terms. 'Breathes there the man,' asked Sir Walter Scott in *The Lay of the Last Minstrel*, 'with soul so dead, / Who never to himself hath said, / This is my own, my native land!'

A love of what is good about one's native land and its people is natural, even admirable. It can be the well-spring of cohesion, cooperation and a healthy spirit of competition. But 'countries' are more problematic. Which is my country, for example? Scotland, where I was born? Great Britain, the state from which I draw my citizenship? Ireland, from where half of my family came? Or Palestine, Iraq, Cuba, Vietnam, Nicaragua or any of the other places and causes for which I've fought?

If Scotland had had its way in the eighteenth century she would now be joined with France. If Napoleon had won at Waterloo we might now be citizens (or subjects?) of a 'country' called Europe.

To which 'country' does the Muslim youth of Pakistani parents (or grandparents) in Bradford truly belong? If measured by where he wants to live and bring up his own children he is British. If by which cricket team he supports or how he wants to live he is something else. My maternal grandparents wanted to be Irish living in Ireland, but poverty drove them across the seas. Which country do you imagine I cheer for when the rugby teams line up at Lansdowne Road?

Countries, or nation states, are a modern invention. For longer than we have lived like this we lived in different units, some smaller than 'countries', others larger.

The Arabs, for example, lived for four hundred years – until comparatively recently – not as Syrians or Lebanese, Iraqis or Saudis, but as Arab subjects of the huge, Muslim, Ottoman empire run from Constantinople, the fundamental characteristic of which was its faith, not its ethnicity.

Britain is an older nation state; but someone my age could have met someone who lived before Germany existed. My grandfather could have met those who created the state of Italy.

I grew up with the apparent permanence of the USSR. Those of my grandson's generation will have to read the history books to know that such a state ever existed, even though the allegiance of many peoples to that state was once a mighty political force.

Great Britain is not the state it was even thirty years ago. Then, it was unitary, centralized and 'offshore' from the European heartland in every way. Now Scotland and Wales have their own devolved parliaments and the north of Ireland may be evolving into something quite different still.

If Britain is not, as Mr Blair promised it would be, 'at the heart of Europe', it is at least in all presently conceivable circumstances a part of an ever deepening and larger European whole.

In such a historical state of flux, it is patently absurd to adopt the watchword 'My country, right or wrong'. And yet that mind-set has been surging through the politics of Britain and the United States in the current era. It has led to the branding of dissidents – myself included – as traitors facing the threat of prosecution under ancient Treason Acts. It has sent yet another generation of my countrymen off to war, to 'civilize' Johnny Foreigner. It is my belief that we each have many and different sets of allegiances in this complex world. Of these the most important is to our own conscience.

My opposition to the war on Iraq was shared by at least half of the British people – a majority before it began. But if only five hundred of us had felt that way, it would have changed nothing for me. I was against it because I was against it; not because of a head count.

It follows that if against it, I must act against it, using all my powers of persuasion and any platform at my disposal. I believed my country was doing something wrong, and that therefore I had a special responsibility to try to stop it.

Britain is a relatively relaxed state, and we British are admirably reluctant to flag-wave compared with many others – after 9/11, when Jack Straw and some other ministers started mimicking their American counterparts by wearing badges on their expensive suits bearing the British and American flags conjoined, their natural sense of embarrassment soon saw them removed. With that, and with a tradition of parliamentary democracy (of sorts) going back centuries, you might have thought that this free-thinking sense of tolerance would by now be a given.

Especially perhaps in the case of a politician, elected to parliament precisely because of his opinions and expected, once elected, to make up his own mind and express his views for others to judge.

Not so. If you like, I'll show you my scars.

I have a file in my office marked 'Poison'. It contains not the most virulent threats and attacks, insults and obscene abuse; those are always sent to the police.

In fact it is not a file, but a filing cabinet. In over a decade, peculiarly anally obsessed correspondents have told me to go back, bend over, suck this, eat that, and otherwise prepare to meet my doom, for speaking out against the policies of successive governments towards Iraq.

Sometimes I recognize where the correspondents are coming from; for example, in the case of Scottish hate mail, it is often religiously sectarian.

But often I am left stunned and my staff shaken by the kind of vitriol that someone has taken the trouble to write or type, put in an envelope and post – remarkably often giving their name and address and clearly expecting a response!

When the government minister Adam Ingram planted on the *Sun* newspaper the story about my 'wolves' interview on Abu Dhabi TV, when I described Bush and Blair as having fallen on the almost defence-less people of Iraq like wolves, the balloon really went up. He had earlier tried to run it in the Scottish *Daily Record* whose editor Peter Cox, having refused to publish it, wrote to me saying:

Well that was a fine stooshie! I decided not to partake of the Galloway blood because I: a) couldn't see the point b) couldn't bring myself to attack you for being one of the few Westminster souls with principle.

Maybe I'm a sucker but you made your points with passion at our recent lunch and I agreed with much of what you said. It's just your timing that's awful!

So why write? Just to say – don't let the buggers get you down, George!

For declining the minister's scoop Peter Cox got the sack after the *Sun* splashed it. That's what happens to ethical editors nowadays.

I knew Adam Ingram – who was overheard planting the story by *Tribune* editor Mark Seddon in the Old Labour eaterie Soho's Gay Hussar – when he was a member of a sectarian, anti-Catholic, Protestant-supremacist Orange Order lodge. Yes, that's right: the man whom Mr Blair made Armed Forces Minister in his government has a long history of marching to martial music.

I also knew him when he had changed his orange stripe for one of the deepest red and become a Trotskyist. But I'll say one thing for him, he has always been consistent. Consistently a fanatic of one kind or another.

But the subsequent *Sun* front page – a full-colour, full-frontal assault headlined 'Traitor' – changed my life.[1]

Written by the paper's slightly sinister-looking chief political correspondent, a suede-shoed, right-wing journalistic 'assassin' called Trevor Kavanagh – who was to become Tony Blair's favourite muse – the article invited their six million-plus readers, including Britain's infamous 'White Van' men and their 'footballer's wives' spouses, to let me have it. Being the *Sun*, they gave out the wrong telephone number – leading to a plague of threatening calls on someone else's phone – and even the wrong e-mail address. But waves of morons did get through, and for many days made the lives of my young female staff a misery.

Every filthy suggestion was made to them, and not just from the *Sun*'s own staff. An executive from the newspaper offered one secretary a good price to display her 'Page Three assets' for Mr Murdoch, that gallant Papal Knight. John Reid, the former IRA songster, ex-mouthpiece of the Bosnian Serbs, then sergeant-major of Tony Blair's war and the unelected chairman of the Labour Party, promised that I would be 'dealt with' after the war.[2] Which of course I was.

So, whom had I betrayed in my interview by speaking out?

Clearly I had betrayed neither my conscience nor my duty as a parliamentarian to speak out against what I saw as a crime being committed by my government. The people who elected me would in due course have the right to turn me out if they disapproved of my stand. And in the end, though in defiance of their own rules, my party could, and did, terminate my thirty-six years of membership.

Nor had I betrayed the armed forces personnel, whom I described on Abu Dhabi TV as 'lions'. Those who had done that were the political leaders – the 'donkeys' who had sent them in to harm's way on the basis of a pack of lies.

Who were the real traitors?

By tying us so closely to the increasingly discredited Bush administration, by becoming, not 'the heart of Europe', but a cancer at its heart, by being seen as an agent for American interests in Europe, by putting us in the first ranks of the hated amongst the one and a half billion Muslims in the world – in this way it was Mr Blair who was undermining the very state he claimed to lead.

But thanks to the patriotic fervour of the *Sun* and the government manipulators, millions of British people didn't see it that way. How prescient and chilling were the words of George Orwell in *1984*: 'All that was required of them was a primitive patriotism which could be appealed to whenever necessary.'

Once the drum-beats of war propaganda began, once the shrill false notes of the tinny bugle of 'patriotism' started blowing, many fell in again behind the colours. Including many who should have known better, not least because for them history was repeating itself as tragedy and farce rolled into one.

Just at the outbreak of the First World War, Europe's 'Labour' or 'social-democratic' parties gathered in Brussels at an augmented meeting of the Socialist International bureaux from 28–30 July 1914, and expertly analysed the imperialist character of the coming storm in which the scramble for colonies and the exploitation of resources – too important to be left in the hands of 'savages' – threatened to destroy a generation.

They pledged themselves to put their loyalty to their ideals of solidarity, equality and peace before their loyalty to their own imperialist states. Then promptly went home to their parliaments and voted for the war credits to fund the carnage.

I sat in a British parliament three generations later, with the biggest social-democratic majority in the country's history. Its benches were stuffed with former peaceniks, veterans of the anti-Vietnam War demonstrations, and 'feminists' who had told us throughout the eighties that politics would change, become less aggressive, if we only made room for those who would later bathe in the spotlight as 'Blair's babes'. And I watched them vote, in their hundreds, for another imperialist war.

Saddam Hussein could have been the Kaiser. The war propaganda was of the 'Huns rape Belgian Nuns' variety: 'Boy prisoners', 'severed prostitutes' heads', 'ships of death' sailing concentrically laden with WMD ready to scuttle and poison the seas for ever, deadly toxins ready to splash all over us, duty-free bottles of vodka which were really cocktails of agony and death being smuggled by Saddam through Customs at the Channel ports, underground nuclear facilities, massive purchases of uranium from Niger, links to Al-Qaeda, terrorists training on mock hijacked aircraft to slit stewardesses' throats, 'forty-five minutes to doom!'

Grown men and women, elected politicians, educated journalists, worked themselves into a frenzy of war hysteria. One day I sat in front of a little-known provincial MP by the name of Phil Holt. For fully ten minutes, while an anti-war speech was being made (from the Tory benches) he repeatedly shouted the words 'Saddam Ussain [sic]' after virtually every sentence of the speaker's remarks.

Air-headed blow-dried telly-dollies (and some women broadcasters), chosen for their dentistry and ability to read an autocue, would question me on television about 'weapons of mass destruction' for all the world as if they knew what they were talking about. And in a tone of voice which clearly conveyed that they couldn't understand how anyone could doubt the truth of what the political leaders were telling us. Only the venal, they seemed to drip, could be standing up for 'the enemy' like I was.

The language of 'us' and 'them' even infected the flagship crews of Channel 4 news – the thinking person's broadcasters. One presenter asked me how I could go on 'foreign television stations' and speak against my own country; and looked genuinely puzzled when I told him I just didn't see the world that way.

Jon Snow, the progressive heart-throb newsman, talking of an incident in Basra, spoke of 'us, losing the south' as if he were a member of the 'coalition' rather than a journalist.

The Liberal Democrats' attitude to the war in Iraq was typical of this bogus patriotism, the kind described by Dr Johnson as the 'last refuge of the scoundrel'.

In the long run-up to the war the Lib-Dems provided the only significant parliamentary opposition. They openly questioned the 'intelligence' brouhaha; made central the issue of Security Council authority to the legality of any war; spoke against the contemptuous way in which European opposition to the war was being treated by the US. They spoke for almost all progressive opinion in Britain – and were reaping political dividends for it. Charles Kennedy stood on the platform with me and other leaders of the anti-war movement in Hyde Park on 15 February 2003 and pledged his troth to peace.

But at the first whiff of grape-shot he and the other sad sacks of the Lib-Dems fell in with the rest.

We didn't want this war, they said, it is wrong and illegal, but if it has begun we must support 'our boys'.

But why, if something was wrong and illegal before it was done, should it be any different once it has started?

Only if, in the end, the watchword is, 'my country, right or wrong'.

This kind of nationalism – used to disinherit, invade, occupy and exploit others – is the destructive, execution-chamber kind of electricity that Jimmy Reid was talking about. It became commonplace in the nineteenth century, in what Tariq Ali calls the 'colonial moment'.[3]

It was an inevitable corollary to colonialism. After all, how else could conquest be justified, but by the concept of superiority? The language of 'civilization' as the nemesis of backwardness and bar-barism is as much a part of the discourse of the new imperialism as it was of the old – from the Hottentot election in Germany through Mussolini invading the dark continent of Abyssinia to the 'they're not yet ready for independence' verbiage of the British over half the world.

When the rivals 'scrambled for Africa' in the nineteenth century they did not tell their public opinion that they were embarked on an act of brigandry, of piracy. They dressed it up in the language of humanitarianism or religion. As I heard Archbishop Desmond Tutu say in South Africa: 'The colonialists came with the Bible in one hand and the rifle in the other. They taught us to pray with our eyes closed. And when we opened them again they had stolen our country.' 'We' were not going 'there' to rob and pillage, perish the thought, but rather to hold the hands of 'the savages' and to lead them to the sunny uplands of 'civilization'. Meanwhile we would take only what was our due.

Thus the Indian independence leader Mahatma Gandhi, when asked by an American journalist what he thought of western civilization could reply, 'Yes, I think that would be a good idea.'

But another kind of nationalism is boiling up, sometimes foolishly being fomented within developed countries and even in the imperialist heartland itself. This sometimes has a superficial attraction to progressive people, although its consequences can be far from progressive.

This regressive 'electric chair' kind of neo-nationalism, which seeks to turn the clock back and break up long-established multinational states, is one of the great perils of the twenty-first century and may prove a dangerous diversion.

The Western countries, Britain, Germany, France and latterly the USA, invested decades and billions to subvert and destroy the Federal Republic of Yugoslavia. The best way to do this was obviously to stimulate and assist the nationalist serpents who had been crushed but not killed by the rocks of pan-nationalism.

Yugoslavia was a sufficiently strong national entity by the Second World War that the Partisans, led by the communist leader Tito, were able to tie down a large portion of the Wehrmacht and, eventually, cause Yugoslavia to become one of the only Nazi-occupied countries to liberate itself without the direct intervention of either the Red Army or the Western Allies.

In the Cold War the BBC World Service, broadcasting in Serbo-Croat, became a nest of sedition against socialist Yugoslavia – even though Tito eventually took the country out of the Soviet bloc and into non-alignment.

Western governments – who cared nothing for the national, cultural or civil rights of the Slovenian, Montenegrin, Bosnian, Croatian, Albanian, Macedonian, Serbian, Hungarian and other minorities who made up the patchwork quilt of the modern Yugoslav (pan-Slav) state – began to harbour secessionist, even terrorist, forces working to destroy Yugoslavia.

Tito, a Croat and a titanic figure of great wartime stature, was able to see off all destabilization efforts and build a state in which its citizens wanted to live. After his death in 1980 Yugoslavia began to fall apart. Lesser men failed to fill his shoes on the federal level. Austerity policies imposed by the IMF and the World Bank began to bite into the faltering economy. And in the constituent parts of the whole, divisive forces began to re-emerge.

The Communists, like Croatia's Trudjman, tried to reinvent themselves in increasingly nationalist colours, encouraged by the West. With the then near collapse of the Soviet Union and the temporary weakness of the resultant Russian state, the imperialist countries saw the chance of breaking up Yugoslavia once and for all, to destroy a society that while not fully socialist was at least not fully open for business to international capitalism. At the same time, such an intervention crucially encroached on ailing Russia's natural hinterland.

Croatia was encouraged to break away principally by a resurgent Germany. Inevitably the Serbs – themselves now led by revanchist nationalists – came to the defence of their compatriots who were a significant minority within Croatia. A series of murderous civil wars followed in the heart of Europe which ended with the transformation of Bosnia into a NATO protectorate in 1995 and the foreign invasion of what remained of Yugoslavia in defence of the Kosovo Liberation Army in 1999.

Apart from the destruction of a long-standing European state, the slaughter of tens of thousands of people and the beggaring of most of its citizens, what had been achieved by helping to conjure forth these serpentine ancient enmities in our own continent?

The planting of the seeds of new conflicts had been one dubious achievement. Albanian chauvinism had been greatly encouraged, and the threat posed by the Albanian minority to the stability of the former Yugoslav republic of Macedonia, which quickly emerged after the Kosovo War, has only gone quieter, not gone away. 'Greater Albania' is an idea whose time is coming in the region, a dagger at the heart of the surrounding mini-states. The reverse ethnic cleansing, this time of Serbs by Albanians in Kosovo, has engendered bitter hatred among the dispossessed Serbs, whose many ancient Orthodox Christian sites have been destroyed in the new vacuum.

Nationalism among the Serbs in Serbia proper has begun to rise dangerously. The 2003 parliamentary elections saw not only Slobodan Milosevic elected to parliament from the dock in the Hague but the much more rabid Radical Party, led by another war crimes prisoner, Vojislav Seselj, win the elections and emerge as the largest party and the fastest growing political force in the region.

This situation is pregnant with many unresolved problems.

The Serbs, when they can, will seek to settle scores with all their neighbours.

Bosnia-Herzegovina is a failed state that will depend upon foreign forces and international largesse long into the future.

Kosovo, though requiring the same force and finances from the international community, has become at the same time one of Europe's biggest problems. Drugs, prostitution, people-trafficking, crime and the logistics of fundamentalist terrorism have become Kosovo's main exports and their only foreseeable earner in the future. The beggars on our streets, the vice barons in the red-light districts, the junk in the veins of our young people, the terror trail into the European heartland – these are all the unexpected gifts to the future from the humanitarian warriors Blair, Clinton and their ilk.

And, of course, encouraging nationalist feelings where it suits the West – in Yugoslavia or Chechnya – but calling it terrorism where it doesn't like it – in Kashmir or Palestine – not only exposes yet again the double standards for which the West is famous but undermines the case against the break-up of our own countries.

In Scotland, in Catalonia and in the Basque country of Spain, among the northern regions of Italy, between the Flemish and the Walloons in Belgium, separatist forces are at work. Sometimes they are violent or openly racist and sometimes not; sometimes hovering between the two. But if Yugoslavia should be broken up into its constituent parts, why not Great Britain or Spain?

Clearly, every nation has the right of self-determination. But a nation also has the right not to exercise that right. It has the right to decide instead to be a part of a larger multinational state, and indeed in the modern world it seems sensible that it should do so. After all, there are many factors in favour of fewer, larger entities rather than the Balkanizing of existing modern states: economies of scale (how much shall we pay to create new Scottish armed forces, a chain of Scottish embassies around the world?); weight in multilateral negotiations; ease of life for citizens moving around; diminishing of tensions among neighbours; and increased mobility leading to ever larger minorities within states. There are not too few states in the world but too many.

Britain is a successful, relatively modern, democratic, wealthy country, largely free of national strife. Many English people live in Scotland; far more Scottish people live in England, where they have been remarkably successful – look at the three great offices of state recently being in the hands of Scots at the same time, namely Tony Blair (who was born and educated in Scotland), Gordon Brown and Robin Cook. And even Sir Alex Ferguson had to come south of the border to bring undreamt of success to Manchester United.

The Scottish economy and civil society has grafted together with the English like bone. Why break it?

Yet between 20 and 25 per cent of Scottish voters do want to fracture the country and partition this small island. And I can tell you as a parliamentary candidate on numerous occasions that the younger the voter encountered on the way to the polls the more likely he or she is to be voting for divorce with England.

At the height of the bombing in Yugoslavia the first Scottish parliament was being elected. I encountered a group of shipyard workers heading in to vote. They have been among my most loyal supporters and I asked them to vote Labour this time as they had always done for me at Westminster elections.

'No, for this election we are voting SNP,' they replied.

I went into my routine about not breaking up Britain to try to talk them round.

'Britain?' they said, though in industrial language. 'What's Britain? . . . Going around the world bombing people?' And of course the irony was that we *were* engaged in bombing people, in our self-appointed role as air force to the separatist Kosovo Liberation Army!

Although separatism in Scotland has been largely, though not exclusively, peaceful nationalism, in Ireland of course it has not. The armed campaign of the Irish republicans was in large measure supported by people in the USA, with the American political class at least ambivalent about the 'armed struggle'.

The British state ruthlessly suppressed this attempt to break up what it insisted was its territory – at least as ruthlessly, over nearly a hundred years, as did Milosevic in Kosovo. People in Britain deeply resented American fanning of the flames in the north of Ireland, yet both countries happily joined in doing so in Yugoslavia.

Now that Spain has elected a left-wing government, were it to take a consistent stand against the neo-liberal economics and the neo-con new imperialist policies of the Bush–Blair axis, it would not take long I believe for 'concerns' about Spain's role in Catalonia or the Basque land to rise up the western media and political agenda. The 'rights' of the Basques to their 'Euskadi' homeland would be miraculously discovered. And before we knew it we might be bombing Madrid, in the beginning at least with propaganda and economic subversion.

Playing with nationalism in this hypocritical double-standard way is playing with fire. Just like playing with Islamist fundamentalism was against Nasser in Egypt, against Najibullah in Afghanistan, and against Iraq with the Mullahs of the Supreme Council of the Islamic Revolution in Iraq (now the coalition's most important ally in the occupied country).

Where a country is illegally and violently occupied by another or where the national religious, cultural or linguistic rights of minorities are trampled on by the majority in multinational states, a nationalist response is inevitable.

The role of others in those circumstances is to encourage, by political means, the resolution of those differences, the ending of the cause of the problem. And that role must be consistent and be seen to be sincere. Such sensitive and complex situations cannot be helped by armed attacks from outside, which are far more likely to make matters worse. Electricity, in the wrong hands, can be very dangerous indeed.

For myself, I must enter a guilty plea. Although of all the places I spend time I am fondest of this sceptred isle although I love its language, literature, manners and style and above all its people, I have no nationalist feelings of any kind. Not for Scotland, Ireland, Britain or even Europe, though I cherish them all. I never could see the Beatles as foreigners to me. When I cross the Severn Bridge into Wales I don't feel I have traversed a river of blood to somewhere mysteriously 'other'. When I have addressed gatherings of people who see the world like me in Paris, Madrid, Amsterdam, Athens, even Managua, Hiroshima, Beijing, I have never felt I stood on foreign land.

As I told my daughter Lucy many years ago, when she asked me if I was Scottish or British, 'My flag is red, my country is the future.'

6

A Line in the Sand

In the great slave revolt against Rome and after the brave slave army had been defeated and only a few hundred of them remained alive, the victorious Roman commander came among them on the field.

'You may all go free; all I require of you is one thing. Point out from among you which one is the slave Spartacus,' he said.

As Spartacus was about to stand up and sacrifice himself that his friends might go free, one after the other after the other his comrades rose and roared, 'I am Spartacus. I am Spartacus.'

In that spirit we say tonight, 'I am a Palestinian, I am an Iraqi.' (George Galloway MP, Algiers 1999)

Over time I came to love Iraq the way a man loves a woman. For nearly ten years whenever I heard the word Iraq, in the conversation of passers-by or on radio or television, I would turn around as if someone had called my name. In a few short years, after a previous lifetime of estrangement through political disagreement with the regime, Iraq entered my bloodstream and it will never leave it.

First there was the beauty of the land between the two rivers, the Tigris and the Euphrates. The sense of history in the place where Abraham, the father of all the prophets, once walked, where the alphabet was first written down, where the number 0 was invented, where agriculture was first developed, which had the world's greatest library when my ancestors were painting their faces blue and living in the forests. Almost a millennium ago Baghdad was sacked by the Mongol hordes. The Tigris turned colour twice in the same day; first red with the blood of the defenders and second black with the ink from the books thrown into the river by the illiterate invaders. Iraq, the land where laws were first codified, the land of the hanging gardens of Babylon, of the Ziggurat at Ur. The captivating loveliness of the Tigris, as the sun was going down and the faithful were being called from the minarets atop the tortoiseshell or cobalt blue mosques for the 'Isha prayer, makes me ache with longing now that I am separated from it by war and occupation. But most of all, more than the beauty and the history, I fell in love with the people of Iraq.

'Good friends and bad enemies' is what other Arabs say about the Iraqis. For me, they were always good friends.

They are rough people by Arab standards; not as decorous as others in the Gulf, but more sincere. When they ask how you or your family are, they listen, intently, to your answer, questioning you further if you merely answer by rote. If they invite you to come to their home, they mean it; it is not part of an elaborate show of courtesy.

I am used to things not being quite what they seem and well aware of the tactics of reduction and demonization routinely used to destroy enemies. I knew for example that Anthony Eden, the British prime minister at the time of the Anglo-French-Israeli invasion of Egypt over Suez, routinely described President Gamal Abdel Nasser, one of the greatest men of the twentieth century, as 'the Mad Dog of Cairo'. I knew that any Arab ruler who was not a lapdog had, by definition, to be a mad dog. Sometimes they would be rehabilitated as a teddy bear, and sometimes, as in the case of Yasser Arafat, they would become mad dogs all over again. In the case of Iraq, 23 million people had been reduced to one man, Saddam Hussein, and he had been so demonized that thereafter any and all crimes against the 23 million could be, and were, justified. Thus – in the manner of the American commander in Vietnam who infamously declared 'this village will have to be destroyed in order to save it' – maybe more than a million Iraqis, most of them children, were killed in pursuit of a leader they did not elect and could not remove. Saddam Hussein committed real and serious crimes against the people of Iraq, most of them during the period he was a key friend and customer of the West. But his crimes do not compare with those committed against Iraq by us, in the name of human rights and democracy.

Unlike the vast majority of those who took the decisions that led to what Pope John Paul II called 'the slaughter of the innocents' in Iraq, what the then Chief Whip of the Democrats in the US Congress David Bonior described as 'infanticide masquerading as politics', I walked in the killing fields of Iraq between the wars. I saw the suffering, smelt the death, heard the cries of the people. And I brought others to bear witness. A few brave Members of the House of Commons, Kerry Pollard MP and Bob Wareing MP, and Lords Ahmad and Rea. The Canadian shadow foreign secretary, personalities like the radio presenter Andy Kershaw and above all journalists hitched a ride with me across the ten hours of flat featureless desert in a taxi to Baghdad and around the country.

Virtually all of them saw things differently after they'd experienced the excruciating suffering of the Iraqis under the embargo. To venture forth in the sea of coughing, spluttering misery in Iraq was a life-changing experience for those few foreigners who dared. When I first toured the country's hospitals I thought them little more than cesspits in which, if the patients weren't very sick when they went in, they soon would be. Mostly they were dark through constant power cuts. They were filthy because at the time detergents were banned under sanctions – being potentially of 'dual use' – and because cleaners, on the equivalent of US$5 per month, often didn't show up for work, having to hustle in various ways down on the street to make enough to live. They were full of flies; all the windows were open because air conditioning had long since broken down (parts being banned under sanctions). Pharmacy shelves were usually all but bare, both because so many medical supplies were blocked by sanctions and because for medicine, just like for everything else, Iraq had no money.

Until the oil for food programme began in 1995 – that is, five agonizing years under total embargo – Iraq was not allowed to sell a drop of oil, its only means of earning the money for the multitude of things she had to import.

IV fluid bags hung limp and empty by hospital bedsides, because this fluid too was banned under sanctions; X-ray equipment, scanners of all kinds, computers, medical diagnostic equipment, even vitamins and insulin – being, officially, neither food nor medicine – were all on the forbidden list. Baghdad had two functioning ambulances for a capital city of millions of people, because ambulances – dual-use potential again – were banned by the sanctions. Pencils were banned under sanctions; not in case Saddam would sharpen them for use as arrows but because the lead in them might have a military purpose. Ping-pong balls were blocked by the US/UK representatives on the sanctions committee at the UN in New York as, laughably, on one occasion was bull's semen.

Far from funny though was the occasion when the Americans blocked an application by Bulgaria to ship baby food to Iraq on the grounds that 'it might be eaten by adults'. At that time Iraqi children were dying at the rate of one every six minutes of every day and night as a result of the embargo.[1] This suffering was testified to by UNICEF, by Harvard medical school academics, and by the *Lancet* (a magazine that itself was banned, like all trade, educational and scientific journals, under the embargo). At one stage an Iraqi member of the British Library, amazingly through all this still studying for his PhD in the works of James Joyce, was told in writing by the Library that they could not send him a photocopied chapter of *Ulysses* because it would breach the embargo. It was attested to by the former president of Finland, Dr Martti Ahtisaari, and later by two successive assistant general secretaries of the UN itself – who both resigned their posts in protest – the Irish Quaker Denis Halliday and the German diplomat Hans Von Sponeck.

Ahtisaari described a 'near apocalyptic' situation in his 1991 report to the United Nations. The UN's Food and Agriculture Organization said of Iraq in July 1993:

it is a country whose economy has been devastated . . . above all by the continued sanctions . . . which have virtually paralysed the whole economy and generated persistent deprivation, chronic hunger, endemic under-nutrition, massive unemployment and widespread human suffering . . . a vast majority of the Iraqi population is living under most deplorable conditions and is simply engaged in a struggle for survival . . . a grave humanitarian tragedy is unfolding . . . the nutritional status of the population continues to deteriorate at an alarming rate . . . large numbers of Iraqis now have food intakes lower than those of the populations in the disaster stricken African countries.

This report, I remind you, was produced by the United Nations, the author of the sanctions.

In September 1995 the UN's World Food Programme updated us. 'Alarming food shortages are causing irreparable damage to an entire generation of Iraqi children . . . after 24 years in the field, mostly in Africa starting with Biafra, I didn't think anything could shock me,' said Dieter Hannusch, WFP's chief emergency support officer, 'but this was comparable to the worst scenarios I have ever seen.'

Mona Hamman, WFP's Regional Manager, said:

There actually are more than four million people, a fifth of Iraq's population, at severe nutritional risk. That number includes 2.4 million children under five, about 600,000 pregnant/nursing women and destitute women heads of households as well as hundreds of thousands of elderly without anyone to help them . . . seventy per cent of the population has little or no access to food . . . Nearly everyone seems to be emaciated. We are at the point of no return in Iraq . . . The social fabric of the nation is disintegrating. People have exhausted their ability to cope.

Writing in the *Lancet* on 2 December 1995 researchers said, 'findings illustrate a strong association between economic sanctions and increase in child mortality and malnutrition rates . . . The moral, financial and political standing of an international community intent on maintaining sanctions is challenged by the estimate that since August 1990, 567,000 children in Iraq have died as a consequence.'

Two days later writing in the *Guardian* the peerless foreign correspondent Victoria Brittain said, 'The Red Cross has strongly criticized the "dire effects" of sanctions on civilians . . . There is chronic hunger . . . with 20,000 new cases of child malnutrition every month.'

In March 1996 the UN's World Health Organization said, 'Health conditions . . . are deteriorating at an alarming rate under the sanctions regime . . . the vast majority of Iraqis continue to survive on a semi-starvation diet . . . The damaging effects of poor nutrition are being compounded by epidemics . . . and by a precipitous decline in health care . . . the most visible impact of these problems is seen in the dramatic rise of mortality rates among infants and children.'

This all constituted a war crime to me. This was mass murder of children, by politicians who called themselves the 'international community'. This was the biggest of the 'mass graves' in Iraq, and it was being dug in our name.

Practically the only English-language author to concentrate his formidable research powers on this slaughter was the writer Geoff Simons, steadily building an international audience for his indictment of the sanctions genocide on Iraq. In the preface to his masterpiece *The Scourging of Iraq*, published in 1996 by Palgrave Macmillan, Simons wrote of the feelings he experienced trying, like a man heading a brick wall, to move policy makers, journalists and the ranks of the complacent in our midst about the suffering in Iraq:

Tell them about the innocent thousands, hundreds of thousands, forced to drink sewage; about the silent shrivelled women holding their dying babies; about the thousands of children trapped in unrelieved trauma; about the stick-infants, the ballooning 'sugar-bellies'; about the children now going blind for want of insulin; about the millions today being denied adequate food and medicine – and what is the response? Incomprehension, blocking out, a refusal to believe or feel – what psychologists have called *psychic numbing*. And *guilt transference*: if people are suffering, it cannot be *our* fault, *my* fault ... There must be someone else to blame. Let us rely on the propaganda to tell us who it is.

The London-based charity Medical Aid to Iraq noted that 'even under the pressure of the Iran–Iraq war, between 1980 and 1990, Iraq's infant death rate had halved ... while under sanctions child mortality had quadrupled'.

The report described Iraq as comparable to a refugee camp of more than 18 million people. Two-thirds of all people in seven out of Iraq's nine governorates had lost their access to tap water. The US blocked a Danish proposal to supply a Baghdad children's hospital with heaters, saying they 'might be used elsewhere'.

Other items for Iraq vetoed at this time by Britain or America or both included baby food, rice, agricultural pesticides, shirts, boots, children's clothes, shoelaces, school books, glue for text books, badminton racquets, notebooks, paper, pencils, pencil sharpeners, erasers, children's bicycles, blankets, nail polish, lipstick, soap, sanitary towels, deodorants, tissues, toothpaste, toothbrushes, toilet paper, shampoo, disinfectant, PVC sheets, water purification materials, medical swabs, medical gauze, medical syringes, medical journals, cancer drugs, a heart stabilizer, X-ray film and equipment, catheters for babies, umbilical catheters, nasal gastric tubes, medication for epilepsy, surgical gloves, bandages, oxygen tents, surgical instruments, stethoscopes, ECG monitors, dialysis equipment, angina drugs, all electrical equipment, all concrete additives, granite shipments and all building materials. Oh – and tennis balls.

British and American leaders repeated the meaningless mantra that they 'had no quarrel with the Iraqi people' while making their lives an endless misery, and killing them in large numbers. Even after death they were not beyond the reach of their tormentors. An application to export shroud materials – without which no Muslim could be decently buried – was vetoed by the US. The would-be exporter protested to Britain's DTI: 'This material can be used for nothing except dressing the dead.' Iraqis, he said, 'do not bury people in smart suits or shiny shoes. We have no funeral homes. We wash them, tend them, buy six or seven metres of shroud cloth and put them in the ground wrapped in a shroud.'

Mr Peter Mayne, a British civil servant, had the unenviable duty of replying to this heartfelt plea. 'I refer to your application to export shroud cloth to Iraq. The application has been considered . . . I have to inform you that a licence has not been granted under the current climate. The US representative on the UN Sanctions Committee are [*sic*] currently blocking the export of cloth to Iraq.' So much for dressing the dead.

The UK Customs and Excise department intercepted a pair of hand-knitted baby leggings, sent by a proud grandmother in Baghdad to her first grandchild in England. The baby's mother was contacted by Customs and informed that before being allowed to receive the leggings she had to apply to the Sanction Committee in New York for an import licence.

By 1993 UNICEF were reporting that one in five schoolchildren had stopped attending Iraqi schools, which were increasingly leaking (dirty) water, had fewer and fewer text books or exercise books or even paper or pencils, and were presided over by teachers who themselves were beginning to suffer malnutrition. By 1994 a quarter of all Iraqi babies had low birth weights. In 1995 the French MP Yves Bonnet described his visit to the Saddam Children's Hospital, where three years later I would discover Mariam Hamza. Speaking after he had seen a dying baby and been unable to look her mother in the eye, he said:

Yet again the UN Sanctions Committee has endorsed its implacable mission: the death of 100 innocent under-fives each day through respiratory infections, diarrhoea, gastroenteritis and malnutrition, and the death of 200 over-fives a day of heart problems, hypertension, diabetes, renal and liver disease and leukaemia. I am filled with shame and anger at myself, at my cowardliness, my silence, my complicity with those who, despite their claims to the contrary, have killed hundreds of thousands of civilians without incurring the wrath of the war crimes tribunal of the Hague, implacably going about their dirty, evil work.

Yet the standard response of British ministers was to deny this truth and to denounce those telling it as 'mouthpieces' for the Iraqi dictator.

American leaders were much more candid. Asked on the prestigious *Sixty Minutes* show on CBS television by Leslie Stahl, who had just seen the situation in Iraq for herself, 'Half a million Iraqi children have died . . . how can we justify that?', the US Secretary of State Madeleine Albright replied in words that will follow her to hell: 'It's hard . . . but we think . . . we think the price is worth it.'[2]

Giving the lie to their own denials the British government then supported the establishment of the oil for food programme through which the Iraqi government would be allowed to sell a tightly restricted amount of oil, under close UN supervision, with the proceeds going into an escrow account in New York. Iraq could then buy a savagely limited range of goods for their civilian population through, and only through, that escrow account. But every contract had to go through the filter of the sanctions committee, to be considered by killers in smart suits appointed by the US and British governments (99 per cent of all blocked contracts were stopped by either the British or American representatives, or both).

Even before the oil for food agreement, the Anglo-American axis repeatedly asserted that the embargo did not cover food or medicine. This lie ignored the fact that Iraq had no income with which to buy food or medicine and that all its assets overseas had been frozen. Moreover, it ignored the cruel and deliberately pedantic definition of food and medicine. And above all it ignored the sheer murderousness of the systematic subterfuge fashioned by our men at the UN. Take cancer drugs for example. Everyone knows that cancer is treated by a protocol of different drugs which if not taken at the same time, or taken and then interrupted, are rendered expensively useless. The smooth savages working for Britain and the US in the sanctions committee were particularly skilful at that. They would release one batch of medicine or medical equipment but place a query on another, indispensable, part of the order.

Virtually every cancer patient I came across – and there was a virtual epidemic of cancer, a tenfold increase in the number of childhood cancers after the first Gulf War – had suffered from the shortage or interruption of their drugs supply. Doctors would explain to me, sometimes close to tears, that they refused to play God and decide which cancer-stricken child would have the few drugs available and which would go without. The result was an equality of misery, with all children receiving some medicine, but few receiving sufficient for it to do them much good.

International pressure in response to the humanitarian catastrophe forced the axis of London and Washington into the introduction of the oil for food scheme, but it affected the situation only marginally. Iraq struggled to pump their permitted volumes of oil; the attrition of oil extraction and distribution systems by bombing and the embargo on spare parts had taken their toll. The new arrangements banned virtually all spare parts as having potentially military use. The sanctions committee continued to be the eye of a needle through which little got through without difficulty. The cumulative effect of years of war and sanctions had in any case caused the health situation to go into a freefall which no palliatives could greatly alter. Most children got sick with water-borne disease. The sewage and water systems were in a state of collapse and could not be repaired. Sometimes sewage would come out of domestic water taps – I have seen this with my own eyes. Children went down like flies with diarrhoea, which soon became something worse. Dysentery, kwashiorkor, typhoid, yellow fever, even cholera; curses long ago banished, returned with a vengeance. A child would become sick in her stomach and two weeks later would be dead – I personally witnessed many such cases. Again, when we shouted this from the rooftops, we were traduced as Saddam apologists. The oil for food programme had solved the problems of suffering, they said – problems they had earlier denied even existed.

Later, they were again forced to give the lie to their own propaganda, when they doubled the amount of oil the Iraqis were allowed to sell, which implied, if they were now correct, that until then they had been allowing Iraq only half of what it needed. But they were still lying. They would talk about the total value of Iraq's exports as being sufficient if only Saddam wasn't spending it on 'palaces' or 'weapons of mass destruction'. But Iraq wasn't getting what they were claiming. They knew, but never said so, that fully thirty per cent of the value of oil sales was being immediately confiscated by the Compensation regime and handed out to cash-rich Kuwait and other US-friendly claimants for losses incurred in the 1990 invasion. A US-dominated panel operating under nominal UN control met in Geneva – with Iraq having no representation or rights – and decided which country, organization or individual *might* have made such and such a profit, if only the invasion of Kuwait hadn't happened, and promptly wrote them a cheque. This at a time when Iraqis were suffering and dying for the want of this cash.

Saddam couldn't have been spending the oil revenue on weapons. First of all, he never saw the cash; it was paid straight from the UN to the suppliers of carefully vetted goods. Secondly, Iraq was completely besieged by land, sea and air. How could Iraq be bringing in weapons? If it could, what was the use of the sanctions that were working the killing fields? Neither could the palaces – grotesque and grandiose as they were, designed to show the world that Iraq had not been cut down to size – be the 'opportunity cost' of feeding and looking after Iraq's needs. Virtually all of the materials and labour used in these monstrosities was local; and none of it came through the oil for food programme. How could it? Wouldn't Britain and America's diplomats in New York have blocked it along with the ping-pong balls and bull's semen? These palaces were, in effect, 'work for food' programmes, utilizing idle labour, and paid for in the 'Monopoly' money, Iraqi dinar. Before the 1991 war this could be exchanged at $3.50 for one

Iraqi dinar, but by the 2003 war the rate had sunk to 2,500 dinars to one dollar.

I never understood why the Iraqi regime didn't set this idle labour and these local materials to work on something more worthwhile than palaces for the head of state, in which he scarcely set foot and never slept. Although I asked this question many times of the Iraqi leadership, I never received a satisfactory reply. It seems heads of state love palaces; and the more insecure they feel the more they have to have.

These canards were simply disinformation; and those who spun these lies – including Robin Cook whose new-found candour about matters Iraqi is as welcome as it is overdue – knew exactly what they were doing. Cook bitterly defended the line that Iraqi children had to be starved because their leader was 'building palaces' and 'buying weapons of mass destruction'. Cook said this to me over and over again in the chamber of the House of Commons, at party meetings, in private discussions at the Foreign Office and elsewhere, and over the airwaves. He defended the murderous bombardment of Iraq during Operation Desert Fox at Ramadan and Christmas 1998 on exactly the same bogus grounds for which he now criticizes Tony Blair. Then there was Cook's tour of the basest of black propaganda, crude disinformation pranks like the Iraqi Boy Prisoner story, made famous by its lampooning by Mathew Norman in the *Guardian* Diary.

Cook told a Parliamentary Labour Party meeting (as he had earlier told the party's National Executive Committee) about a boy who had been imprisoned at the age of five for throwing a stone at a mural of Saddam Hussein and years later was still in a dungeon for this 'crime'. This story was supposed to justify our sanctions killing hundreds of thousands of Iraqi children. I immediately challenged Cook.

'Give me the name and any details you have about that boy,' I said, 'and I will travel to Baghdad immediately and sit down in a public square and refuse to move until he is released.' Cook could not or would not provide further and better particulars. Tam Dalyell put down a parliamentary question – which Cook could not ignore but could transfer. Now claiming that the information he had so boldly trumpeted had come from the Ministry of Defence, Cookie tossed the buck to the Defence Secretary George Robertson. Tam's question to Robertson was then itself transferred to the House of Lords and the

Defence Minister there, Lord Gilbert. Gilbert stalled and stalled again. Finally he announced that he would not answer the question on the grounds of national security!

Years later Mathew Norman would return to this issue again. His co-diarist Marina Hyde had spoken to Lord Gilbert about the mysterious Iraqi boy prisoner. At first the now ex-Defence Minister seemed to have quite forgotten him. And then he remembered that the information – which had been the subject of a major propaganda offensive by Blair's ministers – had come from 'a reliable source who had been in Baghdad at the time' who had given it to him at a drinks party!

So, said Marina, there was but a 'single source', at a drinks party, for a story used to justify a bombing wave and which had been trumpeted by both the British Defence Secretary and the Foreign Secretary?

'Oh yes,' said Gilbert, 'but it comes down to trust. If you believe the person and deem them to be of good character.'

Cook was fond of black war propaganda, which is why it is a little difficult to take him seriously now. Perhaps we really should try harder. During the Yugoslav war, in the same portentous voice in which he evoked the boy prisoner, he told us that the Serbs had killed twenty-one Kosovan schoolteachers and stuffed them down a local village well. Later, an expert wrote to the *Guardian* pointing out that in the village in question there could not have been more than thirty children of all ages. If the village really had that number of schoolteachers then socialism in Yugoslavia had achieved pupil–teacher ratios hitherto undreamed of.

On one occasion I wrote to the House of Commons authorities asking for the use of the committee-room corridor gallery space to display drawings and paintings by Iraqi schoolchildren. This is a normal thing; most weeks there is an exhibition there of one kind or another. The authorities agreed but said it was usual, though a formality, to obtain the agreement of the government department most relevant to the subject of the exhibition. To my amazement Robin Cook banned the pencil drawings of Iraqi schoolchildren being displayed in parliament. He said the drawings – though he had never seen them – would imply that the suffering in Iraq was a result of sanctions and this he could not tolerate. Soon afterwards a display of schoolchildren's drawings from the refugee families from Kosovo was posted in the same exhibition space. This time there was no difficulty in obtaining the Foreign Office's permission. The exhibition was Robin Cook's.

George Robertson and I go back a long way. During all these wars, it was strictly personal between us. I first met Robertson in 1973, when we both appeared on Peter Jay's *Weekend World* programme. Robertson drove me from Aberdeen to Dundee after the show. It was the only good turn he ever did me. At the outset I should say that though I bitterly dislike him, I respect George Robertson, now Lord Robertson of Cable and Wireless and sundry arms companies. During that drive thirty years ago, Robertson laid out his right-wing Atlantacist politics. He clearly sincerely believed in them. And in all the years since he has never wavered from them, even in the albeit brief period when it was highly fashionable in Labour politics to pretend to believe otherwise. Unlike Tony Blair, Robertson never wore a CND badge in order to curry favour – indeed, he campaigned against unilateral nuclear disarmament when Blair was a member of CND. When Robin Cook, in his brown corduroy suit and red tie, was roaming the country making incendiary speeches against Reagan, the Republicans, Cruise missiles, the Contras, and American imperialism in general, George Robertson was plodding on in his life-long quest for 'transatlantic understanding'. This was his world view and he was always faithful to it, as Defence Secretary, as head of NATO and no doubt in the boardrooms of the merchants of death in which he sits today.

Robertson loved the 'presidential palaces' routine. Once he said that Saddam had a palace and grounds 'bigger than Paris'. When it turned out on examination by the UN inspectors to be smaller than Paddington he was entirely unembarrassed. France always was a useful yardstick for the war party. In the run-up to the 2003 war, when saying how inspections were useless, they would routinely describe Iraq as 'bigger than France', sometimes even 'twice as big as France'. In fact Iraq is smaller than Texas, which just showed the ignorance of those who would shatter it into a new Balkans in the Middle East.

Once Robertson superimposed a map of what he said was a 'presidential palace' onto a map of my Glasgow constituency, which he held up in the chamber of the House, quite dwarfing Glasgow's city centre.

He and royalists like him didn't like it when I pointed out that our own head of state, with Buckingham Palace, Windsor Castle, Balmoral, Sandringham, Highgrove, St James's Palace, Kensington Palace, etc., had a fair bit of real estate herself.

Robertson was always fonder of the theatrical gesture than his dour Presbyterian demeanour would suggest. He used to hold up a small glass of water at the Despatch Box saying: 'This small glass, if it were full of Saddam's WMD, would contain enough toxins to kill everyone in Britain/Europe/the world,' depending on how pessimistic he was feeling that day. Leaving aside the failure to find even this single glassful once they had conquered Iraq, ignoring the fact that virtually every country in the world had an abundance of such weapons, including Britain and especially Israel and the United States, ignoring the fact that in Robertson's and my youth the USAF was dropping an ocean of such WMD on the people of Vietnam – leaving all that aside, Robertson never quite explained how besieged Iraq was going to find a way of splashing that small glassful of toxins on all the people of Britain or Europe or the world.

By 1998 the oil for food programme was providing each Iraqi with the equivalent of thirty cents per day for everything. For food, for medicine, for schools, police, water supplies, sewage works, power generation and distribution; all the multitude of services on which a highly urbanized society, which had stood on the verge of first-world-equivalent status just a few years before, had come to depend. People were still dying like flies, with mass funerals of little coffins tied to the roofs of taxis tearing at the heartstrings of informed public opinion everywhere. Britain and America, which had first said the suffering was synthetic, had then introduced a permissible level of Iraqi oil exports that they said was adequate to address the suffering before having to double it; now they doubled it again.

But by now Iraq could not produce enough oil to take up its allowable quota. The degradation of plant, machinery and systems was such that, once the 'compensation' and 'UN costs' had been deducted, once the blockages in the sanctions committee in the UN were taken into account, and once the emaciated capacity for Iraqi oil production was acknowledged, the material benefits to the Iraqi people were pitifully meagre.

The lies still came thick and fast. Saddam was hoarding and creating shortages, was maldistributing the available goods; Iraqi incompetence was partly responsible for shortages, and so on. In the real world the United Nations repeatedly praised the Iraqi rationing system, which they always said was scrupulously fair and highly efficient – indeed 'the most efficient food distribution system of its type in the world'. Later Paul Bremer, the Bush plenipotentiary in Baghdad, would insist the ration system must be scrapped because it was 'pure socialism'.

There was no hoarding or incompetence. On the contrary, any comparison between the system of feeding the population run by the besieged Ba'athists and that of the 'liberators' of the coalition reflects increasingly well on the Iraqis. Again Cook, because he was the best at propaganda, was exploited by Blair to the full.

When I claimed that the UNSCOM arms inspectors were spies, Cook denounced me, saying the source of these allegations was Saddam himself. This denunciation took place just before the inspectors started writing books about how they were spying. I said some of the UNSCOM inspectors were working for Israel. Cook rubbished this too – just in time for the inspectors to admit it was true. One of Cook's most repulsive lies at this time was that the Iraqi regime was importing (through the UN) liposuction equipment 'for the cosmetic uses of the wives of the Iraqi elite'. This he repeated on every opportunity he could, clearly thinking he had scored a bull's-eye. But it was bollocks; a vulgar lie. The liposuction apparatus was not destined for the 'wives of the elite'; in any case I have met most of the wives of the elite and none of them would get a spot on *Sex and the City*. The liposuction was required for restorative surgery for mastectomy patients and those suffering from horrific disfiguring burns. I visited some of those patients, desperately in need of this equipment, which Robin Cook gloried in having halted. If he had seen what I saw he might not have been so smug.

While on the heartlessness of attitudes to women I should make some observations about issues somehow missed by most of those now crying crocodile tears about the position of women in Muslim countries.

Iraqi women suffered the highest rates of miscarriage in the world.

They suffered the highest levels of mental illness. They recorded the highest levels of infertility. They gave birth to record numbers of children with cancer. Unmarried Iraqi girls began producing milk in their breasts. Young Iraqi mothers frequently couldn't produce any milk. Many Iraqi women, once among the least 'conservative' Arab women, wore the cover-all black chador because their hair was falling out, because they couldn't get hair dye, or because it had been some years since they had seen a hairdresser. One night in the Al-Rashid hotel I was approached by a tearful young woman, just three months married. She told me a story Mr Cook might have thought trivial, might even have used in the House against 'the wives of the Iraqi elite'. She had a problem of facial hair she said, which her new husband didn't know about. She had controlled it for years with facial hair remover. None was now available and she was excruciatingly embarrassed to the point of distraction about what she saw as the inevitable loss of her husband's love. Could I help her get some supplies of Immac? She cried at this point. And so did I.

In early 1998 I walked into the children's ward of a Baghdad hospital and made the acquaintance of someone who became a very important part of my life and to whom this book is partly dedicated. In the first bed in the first ward with a name as holy as she looked angelic was a four-year-old cancer patient named Mariam Hamza. By her bedside was her black-clad grandmother, swatting the flies away from the child and occasionally firing off what I would come to recognize as her trademark line in complaints. The girl stopped me in my tracks. I listened carefully while the doctor explained her condition and her prognosis – bad.

I knew instinctively that this child personified the suffering of the Iraqi children under the embargo. I never had one second of doubt about that. I knew too that if she stayed in this filthy squalor without the right medicine in the right combination she would surely die. I knew that both the Bible and the Koran declare that to save the life of one child is as if to save all humanity. I knew I must try and take her to Britain to save her life. I had no idea at that point if her family would allow this, if the Iraqi regime would allow it, if Robin Cook, who banned the exhibition of Iraqi children's drawings, would allow it. I hadn't thought about how the money would be raised, or whether I would be attacked for doing so. I just knew that I had to do it.

Of course I hoped that her presence in Britain would have a beneficial effect on British policy. I have never denied that. I said from the beginning that we were saving one Mariam but that there were millions of Mariams left behind who could only be saved if the embargo was lifted. I said she was a small candle who hopefully would illuminate a dark and terrible tragedy – a crime – which had been visited on a whole nation by some of the most respectable politicians representing the 'international community'. I didn't know then that Mariam would end up famous all around the world – and be described in the gutter press as 'Saddam's secret weapon'. I didn't know where this road would take me. I just knew I had to take it. I thought of my favourite Spanish poem by Antonio Machado, part of which I'd seen written on a wall in Havana: 'Walker: there IS no path; the path is made by walking.'

7

Ave Mariam

Perhaps embarrassed by the initially positive press generated by the idea of bringing Mariam Hamza to Britain for life-saving leukaemia treatment, Robin Cook cooperated fully with visas, permission to fly her out (breaking the air embargo) and even embassy assistance in neighbouring Jordan. This was his opportunity to show that he had 'no quarrel with the Iraqi people', but only their leadership. This could have been better shown by allowing the medical care to come to Mariam rather than vice versa. No matter. But the government's sensitivity to her case was not shared by others.

I had wanted Mariam to be cared for by the world-famous Royal Marsden Hospital near London. They refused to accept her on the grounds that her case was the centre of 'political controversy'. Even as I write these words, years after the event, I find it hard to believe that a hospital, a place of healing, could turn a small child away because of a political storm swirling way above her head. But they did.

The Queen is the patron of the hospital and I wrote to her asking her to intervene. It went nowhere. The matter was urgent and so I took her home to the city of Glasgow. After a night in a Greenwich hospital, where she was visibly revived from death's door, we took her to Heathrow to fly her up to Glasgow, and into a hurricane of hatred. As if by agreement somewhere, the initially sympathetic coverage had grown almost universally hostile, summed up in a *Daily Telegraph* leader column attack upon me that day as 'Saddam's Useful Idiot'.[1]

We could have arranged to be picked up on the tarmac and whisked out of the airport without a word or a picture for the waiting pack of press wolves in the terminal. But we could not resist their frantic pleading for 'just a couple of minutes', 'just a couple of pictures', 'just a couple of words'. For forty-eight hours before our arrival they begged my staff for a photo opportunity on our arrival with the child. Then they accused me of publicity-seeking!

BBC Scotland in particular, in the form of reporter Alan McKay, who thus earned my undying enmity, badgered me practically hourly to appear live on their evening television show *Reporting Scotland*. I didn't want to do it just for practical reasons – we had only just arrived at the hospital – but McKay's desperation persuaded me. I appeared on the show only to be attacked by a presenter called Jackie Bird for 'grandstanding' – on a programme they had made perhaps twenty calls to get me on.

'Saddam's Secret Weapon' was how this sick little girl was described on the front page of a Scottish national newspaper.[2] Reviewing the press coverage is enough to make you sick so I recommend it only for those with strong stomachs. But the biscuit was taken by the 'psychologist' quoted prominently in a national paper saying that I was guilty of 'child cruelty' by bringing Mariam to Britain to save her life because of the 'trauma' she must have experienced at Glasgow airport on 'seeing women wearing short skirts'!

Such was the trauma experienced by the hospital administrators at Glasgow's Royal Hospital for Sick Children at Yorkhill in my constituency, however, that this was the last biscuit taken free of charge in this story.

Children from other wars and conflicts have regularly been 'mercy-treated' by British hospitals, and many have since from Iraq – including another Iraqi child called Mariam after the invasion – either for government propaganda reasons or out of Christian charity. But there was to be no mercy on Mariam's bill. With the foul breath of sections of the Scottish press down their necks, the hospital was forced to tally up every last chocolate biscuit consumed by Mariam and her still black-clad, still complaining grandmother.

The hospital performed a miracle. This may be the most impressive sick children's hospital in the whole country, and those who work there truly deserve the appellation 'angels'. Nothing can be more heartbreaking than dealing with small children with cancer, and having to cope with their distraught families. But they do, and with skill and dedication that would humble a saint.

Despite the press storm, from the very first days members of the public were arriving at the hospital with nightclothes, teddy bears, money for the grandmother to stuff inside her tunic for the huge number of hungry Hamza children left behind.

Slowly but surely even the Scottish press began to come round to Mariam's side. By the end even the papers that had been rabidly attacking her presence in the country were eating out of her hand.

I never made any bones about my purpose in bringing Mariam Hamza to Britain. It was not only to save her life; it was also to highlight and to campaign against the devastating effects of sanctions on the Iraqi population, largely imposed by Britain and the United States. This I stated in a hundred interviews and hundreds of public speeches. This was why I founded the Mariam Appeal. This was why the Mariam Appeal was never intended to be a charity; indeed, we had legal advice that it could not be – charities are not allowed to be set up for a single child and they must not have a political objective. If I had asked the Charity Commission for England and Wales to register the Mariam Appeal as a charity they would have refused on both these grounds.

And yet, in the days following the collapse of Baghdad and the axis 'victory', Tony Blair's Attorney General Lord Goldsmith (apparently the only senior lawman in the country who considered the attack on Iraq to be legal) ordered the Charity Commission for England and Wales to investigate the Mariam Appeal, to ascertain whether it was de facto a charity and therefore whether the funds it had expended on political campaigning were improperly spent (and thus repayable – to the Charity Commission!).

Not a single person who had donated a penny to the Mariam Appeal had made a complaint about any of its expenditure. The appeal was launched not in England and Wales but in Scotland, where the Commission has no authority. In 2001 the appeal left Britain altogether when it closed its London offices and moved with its new chairman Fawaz Zureikat, a Jordanian businessman, to his offices in Baghdad. At the end of 2002 the organization ceased to exist. Yet despite all this the Charity Commission's politically inspired witch-hunt continued. In the worst case, they could have found that all the expenditure of close to one million pounds – on Mariam's hospital and other medical and family care, on meetings, rallies, conferences, staff salaries, leaflets, booklets, buses to Baghdad, air-embargo-breaking flights to Baghdad and campaigning of all kinds – was improper and the money would have had to be sequestered from me and my friends, leaving us bankrupt and in my case out of public office. That's justice New Labour-style; the war was legal, my anti-war, anti-sanctions work effectively illicit and subject to crippling sanctions. After almost a year of thorough investigation and vast expenditure of scarce public funds the Charity Commission was forced to conclude in its report closing the investigation that it had found no evidence of any impropriety of any kind in the running of the Mariam Appeal. This confounded the hopes of many of my enemies, not least Robert Murdoch's *Sunday Times*, which was forced to pay me substantial damages after claiming just a few days before the Charity Commission reported that it would conclude exactly the opposite.

I remain very proud of the work I did to try to end the man-made suffering in Iraq. Together with a small group of my friends we played a decisive role in changing public perceptions about the sanctions in Iraq – in Britain, but elsewhere too. There were a few others on this battlefield, like the authors Geoff Simons and Felicity Arbuthnot, the Cambridge-based Campaign against Sanctions on Iraq, Voices in the Wilderness, Sabah Al-Mukhtar's Arab Lawyers Network, Riad al Taher's Friendship without Frontiers and the journalists Mark Thomas and the incomparable John Pilger. But it was a thin red line. I did not give my all in this battle for any conceivable political advantage – indeed it has led me into the political wilderness from which I may never find my way back.

The Mariam Appeal played a key role in highlighting the role of depleted-uranium (DU) weapons in the cancer epidemic in Iraq, long before the issue became as widely understood as it is today. In the Gulf War of 1991 Britain and (mainly) America fired 30,000 DU-tipped shells, and over 900,000 DU-tipped bullets. The more than thirty tons of radioactive residue this left had entered the air, the water, the food, the bodies and ultimately the children of Iraq. It was our belief that this was also linked to the so-called Gulf War Syndrome afflicting thousands of coalition war veterans. But if DU made you sick handling it before it exploded, it was fatal for those on the receiving end. The World Health Organization was prevented by the US from carrying out the necessary epidemiological study to get to the bottom of this link, but the Mariam Appeal helped put the whole issue firmly on the political map. My wife, Dr Amineh Abu-Zayyad, devoted most of her time over several years to studying this issue; her work presumably went up in smoke in the sacking of Baghdad or lies still under the piles of debris. Debris which will include still more DU; this weapon has continued to be used, in Yugoslavia, Afghanistan and, once more with feeling, in Iraq.

In 1999 the Mariam Appeal reached tens of millions of television viewers with our epic journey in a 1963 London Routemaster bus through Britain, France and Spain and then across to Morocco, Algeria, Tunisia, Libya, Egypt and Jordan, finally reaching Baghdad, where three million Iraqis turned out to receive us; the greatest welcome in history for British people in the Middle East.*

This mission, financed by the ruler of the UAE, Sheikh Zayed, as we said on the front of the bus, brought together an eclectic bunch of labour activists, ex-student radicals, musicians, bus drivers, vegetarians – and a professional pall-bearer! For sixty days we all held together famously, though it may be significant that we've never been together since. Sleeping (sort of), washing (well ...), cooking and eating on the bus, we were the best of British. I had stipulated (I know, I'm old-fashioned) that the crew should be all-male not only because, travelling across mainly Muslim countries, we didn't want our enemies characterizing us as an orgy on wheels, but also because I feared trouble indoors for the married men when they informed their wives that we were all going on a summer holiday; oh ... and there would be single women on the upper deck! But I was fooled by the bus driver called Alex; when she turned up in the flesh she was all woman. Ten men driven by one woman; not mad, but all the way from Big Ben to Baghdad. I had my doubts.

Alex proved me wrong and was the second most interviewed crew member after me; though I fear ten pairs of sweaty feet may have put her off men for life. When asked in the Arab world why we didn't

* A one-hour video film of the expedition – narrated by Julie Christie – is available for £10.00 plus post and packaging from rob@respectcoalition.org.

continue the journey all the way to Saudi Arabia, I was able to answer that we couldn't as women aren't allowed to drive there. We might have made as big an impact there as we had in Egypt, where thousands of people mobbed around the bus every time we went out in it. We were even asked to leave the pyramids because we were proving too popular a rival attraction. One Egyptian minister told me as we were leaving that it was just as well we were going: 'Another week and you might have started a revolution!'

Incidentally, when our bus pulled in to the Jordanian capital, Amman, we were mobbed by a large crowd. In the crush of well-wishers a man hugged me close and whispered in my ear, 'I am Sa'ad Jabaji from Dundee University.' Then he started to cry. In the twenty years and more since I had seen or heard from him, I, the young man he had converted to the Palestinian cause, had made it practically my life's work. He had gone into business and become a prosperous architect and builder. But he can never have built anything as strong as the bridge he created between me and Palestine.

In public meetings every night and in uncountable media interviews across three continents we laid into the policy of sanctions and war on Iraq, as a policy of mass murder. This is how history, I believe, will view the Iraq story. It is how much of the world sees it already.

'Labour MP punches hole in air embargo over Iraq,' said the headline in *The Times*[3] after I flew in the first aeroplane from London to Baghdad in 2000.

With a Roman Catholic priest, two journalists, and activists close to me I pretended to be flying on a religious pilgrimage to Bulgaria then changed the flight path for Baghdad. We left in a minibus from the Palace of Westminster and bumped into the deputy prime minister John Prescott, who seemed instinctively to know we were up to something; or perhaps our 'very active' intelligence services had already told him. We flew from a small airfield in Kent, and as we crossed into Iraqi airspace I took control of the communications – in case the Iraqis tried to shoot us down.

When I announced to the control tower in Baghdad that the plane was carrying me and my friends from London, the ecstasy from the less-than-busy air traffic controllers was unforgettable. However, our arrival took the Iraqi authorities and media entirely by surprise and we had to circle the airport while officials were turned out of their beds and the media drummed up for the event. At a press conference in the deserted airport my first words were: 'Peter Hain – it's Good Morning from Baghdad.' (Incidentally, it is this airport that the US has turned into a Guantanamo Bay, holding thousands of Iraqi prisoners without charge or status, including the former deputy prime minister Tariq Aziz.)

Some projects never came to fruition although they were good ones. Plans for the recruitment of International Work Brigades – young people from around the world coming to a camp on the outskirts of Baghdad for two weeks at a time to build a children's recuperation and leisure facility and be educated about the injustices of imperialism in their spare time – had to be abandoned at an advanced stage, though a beautiful piece of derelict parkland had been identified and prepared.

An idea for a 'Big Ben to Basra' boat, sailing from the Thames to the Gulf flying the flag of the anti-sanctions campaign and stopping at the Mediterranean ports, going through the Suez Canal, and around the Horn of Africa, was sunk by the unavailability of an affordable vessel. We had even designed a special radical-chic matelot's uniform for the crew and had decided that we would learn to tango and salsa on deck during the long sea-miles. This time there would be no ban on females.

For conferences, rallies, receptions, a daily Internet briefing for thousands – the Iraq Sanctions Monitor – I travelled tens of thousands of miles in this campaign. Not only did I obtain no personal benefit from all this, I and my associates drove ourselves to the point of exhaustion and sorely tested the patience of some of our closest friends and family. I would never have asked the Iraqi regime for financial recompense for this work. Millions of pounds would have been too small a price for such a workload which had been so effective, an effectiveness concealed by my old enemy Con Coughlan in the *Sunday Telegraph* (10 October 2004). But I was not interested in money; it was a labour of love for the people of Iraq. Nor did any Iraqi official ever make any improper suggestion of financial support. I was meeting top Iraqi officials all the time. I knew the rumours that this politician from this or that country was receiving financial support to help their work on Iraq, but I never raised such a subject and nor did they with me. I knew that any support from the Iraqi regime for my work would have been the death of my campaign, into which I had already invested much of my political credibility. And I put a priceless tag on that.

Apart from Tariq Aziz, with whose family I remain in touch, the only Iraqi leader to whom I became personally close was Mohammed Saed Al-Sahaf. I first met him when he was Foreign Minister, though he was poorly suited to this post, being a mercurial, passionate and angry man. But in his next post he became famous throughout the world as 'Comical Ali' – the Information Minister who could 'see no ships', turning a 'Nelson's eye' at the progress of the invading armies.

Yet I believe his war-time role was his finest hour. Showing great courage he faced the barrage of hundreds of Western pressmen every day while his country was being overwhelmed, yet somehow kept his good humour and dignity throughout. In the later stages of the war he even faced a real barrage, with Coalition bombs several times whistling Dixie past his ears during and immediately after press briefings and site visits. But in the early stages of the war he was telling the truth while Coalition briefers were lying through their teeth.

On the first day of the invasion, the tiny port of Um al Qassr on the Kuwaiti border was reported – by the spinners to the 'embedded' Western journalists – to have been captured and pacified. Sahaf reported that it was still resisting. It was, as it still was when its 'capture' was announced over and over again. Then a story about an 'uprising' was spun out of Basra by American and British briefers; Sahaf said it was a figment of their imaginations. It was. WMD finds were regularly splashed across the news as the coalition fought its way through the country. Sahaf said the reports were lies. They were.

Sahaf is a Shiite Muslim – like many of the leading members of the supposedly Sunni regime. Tariq Aziz of course is a Christian. I was regularly at late-night dinners with both men. They would speak openly, drink copiously, and laugh at their troubles. Both had decades of service for the Ba'athists, and had lived through days when they were the closest friends of those now trying to kill them.

My last night spent with them was Tariq Aziz's wedding anniversary, which also happened to be the birthday of his younger son Saddam.

The boy blew out the candles on his birthday cake. I don't know what he wished for – perhaps that his father had given him a different name – but his mother made a loud wish on behalf of all of us: that Bush would not invade Iraq. It was a wish that would come untrue soon enough.

Aziz had been sure that war would come ever since 9/11.

Soon after the attack upon the Twin Towers I was with him in his office in Baghdad. He had just taken a call from Moscow and he believed that a huge attack of 200 Cruise missiles was imminent, that night, upon Baghdad. His story was interrupted by a summons to the president, and he rushed out warning me to sleep in the shelter of the hotel. I sat out in a suburban garden instead, looking at the moon, waiting for the explosive blizzard. When it didn't come I was surprised that Aziz had got it so wrong. Later we learned – from among others Bush's own cabinet colleague Paul O'Neill, the former Treasury Secretary – that there had indeed been such a threat and that Bush had begun planning an invasion of Iraq the previous January; immediately he took office and nine months before 9/11.

Sahaf, on the other hand, believed that the Coalition was bluffing.

The same kind of optimism he was later to display in his role as 'Comical Ali' led him to believe there would be no war. Sahaf was a journalist, with a much greater understanding of the power of information in the Western world than some others, and he and I would regularly discuss the need for an English-language Arab television station; a sort of Al-Jazeera aimed at the West. He knew that such a station would have to be independent of any state but nonetheless possessed of a 'point of view'; just like all the Western stations have, only opposite to theirs. I had pushed this idea to several Arab governments who already had satellite stations broadcasting to their own people, and who had the wherewithal to make an English-language station viable.

Too late to make any difference, just such a station, ATV – involving friends of mine – would finally get on air, broadcasting from London but only to the United States. Its finest hour was getting the exclusive of Tony Benn's interview with Saddam Hussein just before the attack began, which was seen all over the world.

It is still the single biggest thing the Arabs could do to redress the hopeless imbalance of media power in the world. They suffer from lack of confidence in their ability to change things, and from a paralysing 'conspiracy theory' mentality among the Arab elite. I once put it to a Gulf prince who had just donated a Boeing 747 to Iraq – which the Iraqis couldn't use – that the Express group of newspapers was on the market for less than the cost of this aeroplane. Two daily newspapers and a Sunday paper – historic parts of Britain's journalistic architecture – could be bought by Arab interests, thereby obtaining the first foothold in the Western media.

'They' would never allow 'us' to own British newspapers, he said.

What do you mean, I said, and who are 'they'? And it's not a question of 'allowing'; the papers are for sale and the first person to write the cheque will get the papers. The Express suitors at the time were the Hinduja brothers, on trial in India in an arms scandal, and the pro-Israeli pornographer and false friend of Tony Blair, Richard Desmond. Desmond got the prize; and the guttersnipe *Sunday Express* columns of Robert Kilroy-Silk with his now notorious views about the Arabs is one of the results.

Though Mariam Hamza is now free of leukaemia, for reasons which are not clear but are probably linked to deficient treatment on her return to Baghdad she is now blind and slightly mentally impaired. The last time I saw her, the waif who had left for London at death's door had become an otherwise healthy, happy and loving child, now quite grown-up. She has several new brothers and sisters. Although the Mariam Appeal is long wound-up, its funder and chairman Fawaz Zureikat has undertaken to continue with the family's subvention of $100 a month as long as the child lives. A large number of Hamzas, including a huge extended family in their home village near Najaf, have been living on that money, and their immediate future is grim. Mariam urgently needed medicines during the height of the attack upon her country, when all communications between Baghdad and the outside world were cut. Her father made a televised appeal to me through an Arab television station during the fighting and somehow Zureikat got the tablets through; something, again, he has promised to supply for as long as she needs them. At the height of the press attacks against me, many journalists tried to persuade Mariam's father to attack me, for somehow 'exploiting' the girl for the benefit of Saddam and the regime. But the father would have none of it, saying, quite simply, that I had saved his daughter's life, and that nothing would ever change that.

When we took Mariam back to Baghdad, clear of her cancer, I told her that one day I would return to see her graduate. And then on another day, to attend her wedding. Alas, now neither event is ever likely to happen. Like so many others in Iraq, Mariam Hamza's life has been broken, shattered perhaps beyond repair. I believe that what the West did to Iraq is one of the greatest crimes of the twentieth century. That this crime was committed by men in soft shoes rather than jack-boots, smart suits rather than the garb of fascism, for me just makes the whole thing more despicable. In the end I could not remain in the same party as these men; indeed it had become intellectually and morally untenable long before my expulsion. I should have resigned when the majority of my parliamentary colleagues voted for the invasion of Iraq.

I consider Tony Blair to be a blood-soaked criminal, who at the bar of history will be utterly condemned. Few people know what political achievements Anthony Eden, prime minister at the time of the invasion of Suez, had to his name. That's the point. The only thing Eden is remembered for is the criminal blunder of invading Egypt. The only thing Anthony Blair will be remembered for is the blundering crime of Iraq. Strange, for a man we are told is increasingly obsessed about his 'legacy' and his place in history. The bonfire of Blair's vanities has been lit and will soon engulf him, and the whole Blair 'project' will turn to ashes.

8

Saddam and Me

Frankly it was the last call in the world I wanted to take. Not because it was a famous and glamorous Arab film star who called me up out of the blue as I sat in the Lebanese capital Beirut finishing this book. But, although I would have been pleased to see her, it was definitely not a 'come up and see me sometime' call.

She was calling, she said, on behalf of a cousin of Saddam Hussein. Saddam needed my help to find a lawyer to save him from the hangman's noose. My heart sank.

I knew that her calls were almost certainly monitored – she is a well-known dissident in her country. I figured any cousin of prisoner No. 1 in Cell-Block Iraq was likely to be monitored also. And I have always proceeded on the basis that 'Big Brother' was watching me.

I wanted to say 'Why me?' but she was already into an explanation. He wants an English Queen's Counsel. He respects the British legal system and he thought I would know the right person to approach. I could have said no but I did not for several reasons.

Saddam Hussein could have had no legitimate complaint if having lived by the sword – ruthlessly cutting down any and all opposition – he had died by the sword (or the rope) at the hands of Iraqis.

But that was not the situation. No trial arranged by illegal occupiers could have any validity in law. Nothing legal could come from the invasion of Iraq carried out in flagrant defiance of the United Nations. The people who deserved to be on trial for crimes against the Iraqi people were first and foremost George Bush and Tony Blair. Saddam had committed many awful crimes against his people, most of them when I was demonstrating against him at a time when he was a highly profitable client of the same Anglo-American axis now holding him.

The so-called 'governing council' – the fiction of a government in Baghdad – was not entitled to take any action in the country. This was not the government of Iraq. It had been imposed upon Iraq by the tanks, guns and planes of foreign invaders. Most of its members were little more than 'foreigners'. Some had left Iraq forty years or more before and could walk down any street in Baghdad without being recognized. And some of them were criminals themselves, like the chief American stooge Ahmad Chalabi. In 1992 the US government paid for the creation of the so-called Iraqi National Congress (INC) – even inventing its name. It was given $12 million over the next four years to organize itself under Chalabi's leadership.

Scion of a hugely wealthy Shiite landowning family, in league with the British-invented monarchy Chalabi had established the Petra Bank – the second biggest in Jordan – in 1977. In 1989 King Hussein's government was forced to seize the bank and inject $164 million to avert its collapse and a resulting financial meltdown of the entire Jordanian banking system. Chalabi – for a time paraded as a future US-imposed 'president' of Iraq, one of the world's most oil-rich countries – escaped the kingdom in the boot of a car, was tried in absentia and sentenced to twenty-two years' hard labour in prison for embezzlement, fraud and currency trading irregularities. The Jordanian government, which is still seeking to arrest Chalabi and bring him back to serve his sentence, says he escaped with over $70 million. Though distrusted by the State Department and the CIA, Chalabi repaid the investment of the $12 million, at least in the eyes of the Pentagon and the neo-cons Donald Rumsfeld, Paul Wolfowitz and Richard Perle who control it, by playing a key role in persuading the fools on the hill in Washington that the Iraqis would welcome the invasion.

That George Bush, the man who had done so much to wreck the international criminal court, should not only try and convict someone in a country he'd invaded but, in a TV interview the night before my telephone call from the actress, actually pass sentence (death; his favourite verdict executed well over a hundred times during his governorship of Texas, the execution capital of the western world) – the very idea made me sick to the stomach.

All accused persons have the right to the best defence possible; in the view of just people at least. It is one of the things which should distinguish us from prison-states like Saddam's Iraq. Surprised by the dictator's apparent belief that Britain had the best lawyers, I made a call to Michael Mansfield QC.

He was in Belfast – he has been a major player in the Bloody Sunday inquiry into the events more than thirty years ago in Derry – and didn't get back to me until the next day. He suspected – as I knew he would – that I would pass on to him an offer to take up the highest profile legal case in the world. Not that he was short of them at that moment: that very day the long-awaited inquest into the death of Princess Diana and Dodi Fayed had been announced. Mansfield was, he said, acting for Mohammed Fayed, Dodi's father and Arab 'conspiracy theorist' par excellence (he believes the Duke of Edinburgh had Diana murdered because she was carrying a Muslim child).

Mansfield is a man of the left with a long record of representing unpopular clients. In the best traditions of the Bar, he gives his (considerable) all for whomsoever he's representing. He was clearly interested in some level of involvement in the case, despite his enormous workload. He mentioned that the other 'silks' (QCs) in his 'set' (chambers) were outstanding figures whom he was sure would be interested in a front-line role in the case. I inferred from this that he would have a semi-detached part to play, which cooled my interest a little. I saw him, sword of justice in hand, as the best representative in such a case. He mentioned – because he thought the potential client might want to know – that the colleagues he had in mind were Jewish. I was sure that this would constitute no barrier. Whatever his other sins Saddam Hussein is a secular man who ruthlessly suppressed Islamic fundamentalism in his country. His Ba'ath party is a mixture of Arab nationalism and Stalinist authoritarianism. He hates Israel, no doubt, but in my experience, none of the Ba'ath leaders have displayed any hostility to Jews.

In any case I was sure that having a Jewish legal team representing him was in his best interests. My own limited experience was that some of the most highly skilled lawyers were Jewish, and that they employed the highest ethical tenets in their approach to the job. I had led the campaign against the deportation of the Saudi opposition leader Mohammed Al-Massari. Michael Howard, then home secretary, had bowed to the demands of those British arms companies making hay with the Saudi regime and sought to expel the Muslim cleric to Dominica, where there were no other Muslims and the staple diet was pork. I sat through every day of the tribunal and was deeply impressed by the quality of the justice meted out. The verdict was not only a victory for our campaign but was accompanied by what I described as a public judicial flaying of Howard. Both Al-Massari's lawyer and the judge were Jews.

That phone call from the film actress had made my heart sink for another reason. It confirmed something I would rather have forgotten. Saddam Hussein and George Galloway were, it seemed, doomed to be an item. Saddam and me – we go way back.

Yet there has been no Arab ruler whom I have more mercilessly attacked, about whom I've made more scathing comments, against whom I have campaigned more energetically.

When hardly anyone knew Saddam's name, I was disseminating literature, drawing (or rather failing in my attempt to draw) attention to his crimes. I had met him only twice – the same number of times as Donald Rumsfeld had – and one of those occasions was as part of a large group meeting. The difference between Rumsfeld and me was that he was visiting to sell Saddam weapons of mass destruction and give him surveillance photographs the better to target them, whereas I was meeting him to try to avert more war, more killing and more suffering.

In parliament – therefore in the public record – on television, in the press and at public meetings I have carpet-bombed the record of Saddam Hussein, both before and since I met him for the first time in 1994. But it was what I said on that occasion that made it much easier for my enemies to grotesquely caricature my views:

'Sir, I salute your courage, your strength, your indefatigability.'

How many times have I had those comments rammed down my throat by people with not a scintilla of my record on human rights and democracy in Iraq? How much do I regret the potential for damage in those words? How long have you got?

Just a couple of months before this speech I had described, in parliament, the regime in Baghdad as a 'bestial dictatorship'. And here I was, apparently praising the very same regime, in the beast's own Takriti lair.

The 'your' in question in those remarks is not a singular possessive pronoun but a plural. Those being praised for their courage, strength and indefatigability (one of the strange archaic English words my brain persists in throwing up and which I am sure no Iraqi translator had ever interpreted before) are the 23 million Iraqis, not their president. As a correspondent to the letters columns of the *Guardian* pointed out at the time, the comments burst like a bombshell in the British media; if I'd used the good old Scottish word 'youse' instead of 'your' the ruthlessly exploited misinterpretation of my comments would have been disabled. But I should have known better. I entirely misjudged the way in which those comments could be taken out of context. I have given literally thousands of speeches and interviews in my time and not always of the same quality.

I am an emotional person and the couple of weeks before my interview with Saddam had been a roller-coaster. I had come to Iraq from Palestine, always an emotionally charged tour in the prison camp that is the Occupied Territories. The bitter and brutal reality of the life of the captive Palestinian people there was weighing heavily on me. And Iraq itself, especially in 1994, fully two years before the first oil for food programme, was simply a sea of misery. It is hard now to convey the shock and awe inspired by a tour of the Iraqi killing fields when the country was under total siege. The mass grave of those slaughtered by sanctions is yet to be uncovered by most of the Western media and politicians. But it will be when journalism – history's first draft – gives way to the real thing. Iraqi children were dying at the rate of one every six minutes then – a rate of attrition which dwarfs any of the crimes of Saddam. Most of these children were too young even to know that they were Iraqis. Yet they died for no other reason than that they were Iraqis – and small and vulnerable ones, about whom few outside the Muslim world cared a fig. The day before the ill-fated meeting in Takrit – to which we had been conducted in circumstances of great secrecy – I had listened at the door of a labour ward while a woman gave birth by Caesarean section, without anaesthetic. At the meeting with Saddam I allowed my emotions to run away with me. I said things in a way I shouldn't have. Only a fool has no regrets. And I will regret the gift I inadvertently gave my enemies, always.

Amazingly I set off the night of the meeting, across the long desert road from Baghdad to Jordan and a flight home, completely oblivious to any damage. I arrived in the early morning at the airport in Amman, weary and bedraggled. On arrival at Heathrow I was met by an official of the airline at the door of the plane who passed me a note from a BBC journalist friend in Scotland, warning me that the media had gone bananas and were waiting for me. I still did not know what for. As I was reading the note I was aware of a flash then another then another. Photographers had, presumably improperly, managed to get airside and were now swarming all around me. I kept my head up and walked as tall as I could, my mind spinning, trying to work out what had happened. It was not until I made my way out into the arrivals hall and a huge scrum of cameras, journalists and film crews and was asked the first question that I knew the offence of which I was accused.

At the same time my flat in Glasgow, where my wife was studying for her PhD, was under siege. Journalists were offering the usual financial inducements for the woman to 'tell her side of the story', promising a sympathetic hearing of course. Showing the casual racism commonplace in the media, because she was an Arab they inferred she must be an Iraqi. Was it true, they asked, that she was the niece of Saddam Hussein?

Hilariously, my office that day had asked our TV rental shop to send an engineer to fix the erratic picture on our set. When the man arrived my wife shouted through the door.

'Who is it?'

'It's the TV man,' he replied.

'I have no comment to make,' she said – probably the strangest ever response from a customer wanting their television fixed.

The whole affair felt, I imagine, like picking up a live electricity cable. I was burned very badly.

Foolishly I asked some Iraqi kids in Britain to write to my daughter Lucy, knowing she was taking some stick at school, to encourage her and set out the defence of what I had done. She was furious with me, implying as it did the possibility of disloyalty on her part. She was twelve years old. My friends in my constituency remained absolutely solid and the electorate in Glasgow would later double my parliamentary majority (a fact strangely missed by the legion of commentators who had predicted my certain defeat in the wake of the row). However, the atmosphere elsewhere can be judged by the fact that my account of the meeting, written under total media siege and for which I was paid thousands of pounds by a newspaper, was never published.

David Hill, now the chief spin doctor of New Labour but at that time the chief aide to the born-again left-winger Roy Hattersley, and Murray (now Lord) Elder, the then right-hand man to the party leader John Smith, sat with me in a Commons antechamber while we composed – me at metaphorical gun-point – an 'apology' for any offence caused to families of servicemen by the misreporting of my remarks. The Chief Whip and his deputy, with whom I had surprisingly good relations, gave me a verbal warning about leaving parliament without their permission.

My main worry was about how it would affect my relations with John Smith. I have been a Labour activist under Harold Wilson, James Callaghan, Michael Foot, Neil Kinnock, John Smith and Tony Blair. Although I had personal relations with all of them except Blair, I counted myself a personal friend of Smith. It upset me that he might be angry with me. Two nights after the 'apology' I was sitting alone reading the *Evening Standard* in what was then the Members' cafeteria of the Commons. It was crowded with mainly Labour MPs – the Tories preferred the grander Members' Dining Room, as does New Labour – when in walked John Smith, alone. (It is inconceivable that you would ever see Tony Blair in such circumstances.) All the other Labour MPs looked up imploringly, hoping Smith would bring his tray of food and sit down at their table. I put my head down and into the newspaper, embarrassed and at the same time not wishing to embarrass him by seeing me watch him pass me by. To general amazement (especially mine) he came and sat down at my table. We talked as if nothing had happened. Smith didn't even mention the affair. He simply moved into his familiar and hilarious routine of stories of his time on the Scottish court circuit where he still 'tried to get in a couple of good murders a year'. Nevertheless, in the aftermath of the row I felt my usefulness on the Iraq issue had come to an end. Continued campaigning on the subject would not only be bad for me but useless for the Iraqis. I was damaged goods, at least as far as this issue was concerned, and perhaps in general too. I quietly informed the then

Iraqi chargé d'affaires Zuhair Ibrahim and my Iraqi friends in Britain that I was retiring, hurt, from this particular battlefield.

People often asked me, then and later, what Saddam had been like. In a way, how could I know? I had less than two minutes of 'face time' with him and had merely participated in a rather staged 'dialogue' with dozens of others. In any case I came to understand that people did not really want to hear what, in that limited exposure, he had actually been like. They merely wanted their prejudices confirmed.

But for what it is now worth, I'll describe my impressions of him. He was not what I expected. He was not loud, bombastic, aggressive or intimidating. His handshake was soft, not the vice-like grip I expected. I formed the view – buttressed on my second and last meeting with him eight years later – that he was actually rather shy, avoiding people's gaze, looking down at his chest, speaking softly. He appeared touched by the enormous volume of good wishes I had been asked to convey to him from the young people of the Intefadeh raging in Palestine. Virtually alone of all the Arab dictators Saddam's endless protestations of fidelity to the Palestinian cause were sincere and, as the families of the martyred and wounded in the Intefadeh know, he put Iraq's money where his mouth was.

He spoke in a monotonous yet charismatic way. But although some might have been lost in the translation, what he said struck me as messianic rubbish, as he droned on about good caliphs and bad ones. At any rate, almost none of it made any sense to a group of Europeans who had no real grasp of the ancient Arab and Islamic history he was drawing on. The surprise of this was compounded when he interrupted the meeting to go off and pray. Iraq, formerly a bastion of secular 'socialism', had belatedly turned to God. A Koranic inscription *Allah o Akhbar* ('God is Great') had been inscribed on their flag, and Saddam had begun this habit of going off ostentatiously to pray. Alcohol had been banned in public places (though the important Christian population was allowed to continue to buy and sell it – to other non-Muslims), which must have been a wrench to Saddam himself; he famously liked a glass of Mateus Rosé wine with his dinner. All of this was a politically inspired turn to win the hearts of the broader Muslim world and further to marginalize the neighbouring Saudi regime, who sought to portray themselves as worthy custodians of the Two Mosques at Mecca and Medina.

I next set foot in Iraq in 1998. Having been triumphantly re-elected (despite the ruthlessly used 'Saddam Quotes' deployed by my electoral opponents) the year before, and painfully conscious of the continuing though still scarcely known suffering of the Iraqi people, I felt it was time to return to the battle.

The first person I met on this visit was the then foreign minister Tariq Aziz. I had flown in a helicopter with him to the Takrit meeting with Saddam four years earlier. But it was on that trip in 1998 that I formed a lasting bond with him. Though it might profit me to do so, I am not the sort of person to turn my back on my friends, especially when they are in the sort of trouble he is now in. I grew to admire and like Tariq Aziz, as many, like Douglas Hurd, the Pope, even Donald Rumsfeld, had done before me. He is a truly impressive man, with a good, devoutly Catholic family. He had started life as a journalist and ended as the deputy prime minister of Iraq. There was no prime minister. Only Saddam was *primus inter pares*. Aziz was for many years Iraq's voice in the outside world. His owlish intellectualism and his impeccable manners made him the ideal counterpoint to the unworldly, little travelled and uncouth Saddam.

My wife's uncle, the writer Said Abu-Rish, is the biographer of Saddam Hussein. In his book Abu-Rish identifies the many ways – other than the moustache – in which Saddam resembles Joseph Stalin. Both came from, literally, dirt-poor backgrounds. I mean houses with earth floors. Neither knew his father. Both had mothers who drove them ever onwards and upwards by sheer will and sacrifice. Both were determined to industrialize their countries, whatever the cost. Both had chips on their shoulders. Both built police states believing the end justified the means. Both ruthlessly suppressed all tendencies towards the break-up of their country, believing in a strong central authority (themselves). Both were outsiders in their system: Stalin the Russified Georgian who never quite lost his rough edges, Saddam the barefoot boy from the backward backwater of Takrit selling cigarettes from a tray. Both rose to the top ahead of more gifted, more sophisticated, better-loved figures in their party. And, of course, both could be murderous in pursuit of their goals. An important difference, however, was that

Stalin was as cautious in his foreign policy as Saddam was reckless.

This brings us to another set of uncomfortable truths. Neither Stalin nor Saddam Hussein was a psychopath, driven by some inner compulsion to be cruel for no reason. Saddam's crimes, like Stalin's, were first committed against his own comrades. His purges of the party began when, after several years as deputy president – usually described, neutrally, in the Western media as 'strongman' of Iraq – he finally moved aside the president and took the top job that in practice he was already occupying. He knew that there was a faction in the leadership of the Iraqi section of the Ba'ath party, close to neighbouring Syria, which stood as a barrier to his absolute control of the party. In authoritarian societies such a stand-off only ends one way – with the deaths of one or other faction. Stalin gave his factional opponents a show trial and then killed them. Saddam just killed them.

Just months after Saddam's assumption of total power he decided upon the first of his reckless un-Stalin-like gambles – the attempt to over-throw Ayatollah Khomeini and defeat the Islamic revolution in Iran. In this venture he had the wholehearted backing of Britain, America and the Gulf Arab satrapies that trembled before Khomeini's rage.

I opposed this war, and when it started, followed Syria in supporting Iran. I abhorred the carnage created by that First World War style attrition. But the very allies who backed Saddam in his attempt to bring down Khomeini now wish to add it to Saddam's charge sheet.

Let's just take as an example Halabja, where, it must be presumed, Iraqi forces fired chemical weapons into the Kurdish village killing a large number of civilians, including many children. Saddam had chemical weapons because the West – the US and its then close ally West Germany in particular – supplied them to him. US Defense Secretary Donald Rumsfeld twice went to Baghdad to help Saddam use his weapons more effectively. For many months after Halabja, the US State Department in publicly available documents continued to insist that this crime was committed by Khomeini not Saddam. Long after Halabja, both Britain and America continued to arm and support Saddam against Iran. Now, having changed the identity of the per-petrator and inflated the number of victims from 400 to 8,000, they wish to hang Saddam for a war crime in which they were deeply complicit. This was implicitly recognized by the treatment of the affair in the stooge media who would later endlessly throw up their hands in horror about Halabja.

In their wonderful short book *Weapons of Mass Deception: the uses of propaganda in Bush's war on Iraq*,[1] the American authors Sheldon Rampton and John Stauber did an Internet search of the mentions of Halabja in the Western media. It makes grimly comic reading. In 1988, the year of the incident, and when the memory of American support for Saddam was as fresh as the graves of those gassed Kurds, the incident was mentioned 188 times in US articles. This plummeted to only 20 times in 1989 and 29 in 1990, the year of the Kuwait invasion. During the whole of the period from 2 August 1990 till the end of the first war on Iraq on 27 February 1991, Halabja was mentioned only 39 times, and in the subsequent decade it averaged only 16 mentions a year in all US media. During the US presidential election year 2000 it got only ten mentions. After George Bush decided upon his attack on Iraq, however, mentions of Halabja increased sharply. In February 2003 alone it was mentioned 57 times, in March 145 times. Fifteen years after the attack and with memories of which side the US had been on at the time it was suddenly in vogue to care about the Kurds at Halabja. Yet virtually none of the reports that showed how much they cared even mentioned that at the time of the gassing of Halabja's children George Bush's father had, when vice-president, been showering their killers with financial aid.

Saddam's gassing of the Kurds in 1988 in any case was prefigured more than sixty years before when another government sought to crush a rebellion in Iraq by 'rebel northern tribesmen'. The tribesmen were the Kurds, the government that gassed them was the British. Speaking in parliament the minister responsible, one Winston Churchill, said, 'I do not understand this squeamishness about the use of gas against uncivilized tribes.'*

---

* On 19 February 1920, before the start of the Arab uprising, Churchill (then Secretary for War and Air) wrote to Sir Hugh Trenchard, pioneer of air warfare. Might Trenchard take control of Iraq? This would involve 'the provision of some kind of asphyxiating bombs calculated to cause disablement of some kind but not death . . . for use in preliminary operations against turbulent tribes.' Churchill was in no doubt that gas could be profitably employed against the Kurds and Iraqis (as well as against other peoples in the Empire).

Churchill, it emerged after the Second World War, had stockpiled a huge arsenal of chemical and biological weapons along the Channel coast to unleash in the event of a German invasion. I still await an answer to a question that has bothered me for years: why are some people allowed to have, even use, weapons of mass destruction while others are not?

Iraqi society remained remarkably solid during the eight long years of war with Iran. The Shiite majority in Iraq proved that they were Arabs and Iraqis first and co-religionists of Khomeini second. But there was a fifth column, Shiite elements who actively undermined the Iraqi war effort in the interests of their country's enemy. As in all authoritarian societies, this fifth column was ruthlessly annihilated wherever it was found. Some of the graves of these victims are now being uncovered with hypocritical glee by the very governments that helped Saddam's insane invasion of Iran in the first place.

Why, I asked the leaders of Iraq, did you weaken both of your countries, lose the lives of a million souls, and beggar both economies? Why didn't you unite with Iran and challenge the slave dictatorships in the Gulf? You could have changed the world. That is my world view; it is not of course that of Bush and Blair.

The Iraqi answer was always the same. Khomeini was not interested in an alliance with an Arab nationalist secularist government. They would have exported their Islamic fundamentalist revolution to us. We acted against them before they got a chance to act against us. And we 'won' the war. Khomeini was stopped in his tracks. This is, of course, just what the West intended.

The next big crime of which Saddam Hussein stands accused is the putting down of the uprisings in both the north and south of the country in the immediate aftermath of the 1991 war. This insurrection, a revolutionary struggle for power and for the overthrow of the government, involved massive violence on both sides – as in any civil war. Large numbers of local Ba'athist officials, and their families, were massacred in the south by the Shiite uprising. Many were thrown from tall buildings to their death and then their corpses danced upon. But Saddam's regime had the greater firepower and, once the uprising had been betrayed by George Bush Senior, who had actually called on the people to rise up and then abandoned them, the result was inevitable. Saddam crushed his enemies without mercy.

In the north the Kurdish forces sought to use the enfeeblement of the Baghdad regime to liberate themselves and to set up the state of Kurdistan they have coveted for so long. The Western powers have never supported the creation of such a Kurdish state – though they have sometimes pretended to do so – as it would instantly destabilize their NATO ally Turkey, which has brutally suppressed Kurdish aspirations for generations. Turkey has regularly massacred Kurds, destroyed their villages, extirpated their language and culture, even forbidden them to call themselves Kurds. The Kurdish separatist PKK, which launched an armed struggle against the Turkish state, has been brutally defeated by torture, kidnapping and mass murder. But these are the 'bad Kurds', in Jeffrey Archer's immortal words, while those fighting an armed struggle against the regime in Baghdad are the 'good Kurds'.

Throughout the 1990s the Incerlik airbase in south-west Turkey was the scene of a situation so farcical that it still seems scarcely credible. British and American planes would take off to 'protect' Iraqi Kurds in the mountains of northern Iraq, in the self-declared and wholly illegal 'no-fly zones', while jets of the Turkish air force, often on the same day, would fly from the same base over the same mountains bombing the Turkish 'bad Kurds', their flight paths frequently crossing.

Armed separatist rebellions are always put down by force. And civil wars are always the most brutal wars. The Union army literally set fire to the Confederate south in their crushing of the separatist forces in the American Civil War. The bigger the threat of the separatist rebels the greater will be the repression unless something happens – like the entry into the Albanian separatist struggle in Yugoslavia by the British and American air forces in the Kosovan civil war. Britain in Northern Ireland, Spain in the Basque country, India in the Punjab, Pakistan in Karachi, Nigeria in Biafra – the list is a long one.

Again, the hypocritical insistence of Blair and Bush that the extreme violence in the civil war in Iraq was somehow unprecedented and warranted the much greater violence subsequently unleashed by them is exposed by the most cursory examination of even recent history.

Of course the initial pretext for the strangling of the children of Iraq by sanctions – infanticide masquerading as politics – was the regime's possession of weapons of mass destruction. The scale of the fantastic mendacity about this is discussed elsewhere. Iraq, it turned out, by the end, had no weapons of mass destruction. Not one such weapon has been found in a country occupied not by a few hundred of Dr Blix's inspectors but by hundreds of thousands of foreign soldiers. The Iraqi scientists, whom we were told were the key to finding weapons – which couldn't be done under the Blix inspections regime because their 'minders' were intimidating them – are now all under the control of the occupiers. They are the minders now. Yet the only thing found is a single vial of Botox, twelve years old, found in a scientist's fridge. One vial of Botox – less than is carried in the ever-rosy cheeks of Miss Joan Collins – is what we, officially, have to show for the war.

Simple logic shows that Bush and Blair must have known this all along – the only remotely plausible defence being that both men are idiots, fools rather than knaves. If Iraq truly had weapons of mass destruction it wouldn't have been invaded in the first place. Iraq was invaded not because it was dangerous to Britain and America but because it was *not* dangerous. North Korea will not be invaded precisely because it *is* dangerous.

If Iraq had weapons of mass destruction the invading army would have been absolutely petrified of looters finding them and spreading them around the region and the world to the highest bidder. As we all know, they were not concerned about looters at all. If they thought that looters were carrying around those tumblers of chemical or biological agents with which George Robertson used to frighten the horses, the ones that could kill every human being in the world if they could be splashed around efficiently enough, Bush and Blair would have been simply unable to sleep at night, lying in terror and stricken with panic at what might happen next. But they were not.

This brings me to my second and last meeting with Saddam Hussein.

During all my visits to Iraq between 1998 and 2002 I never asked to see Saddam and he never asked to see me. I was very content about that. At the time I thought he was being sensitive to my position in Britain by not inviting me for another public relations disaster. Later it emerged, in a book published in France, translated by *The Times* newspaper, and written by Saddam's long-time translator, Saman Abdul Majid, that in fact Saddam hated me. My very public pronouncement – that I was standing by the people of Iraq and not their president – was, said the author, a source of great irritation to him. He preferred the sycophants who endlessly praised and pledged their loyalty to him. Understandably, this simple revelation about the real relationship between Saddam and me has had no great coverage in the British media.

But in August 2002 I asked to see Saddam Hussein. I did so because I wanted personally to appeal to him to allow the United Nations weapons inspectors to return to Iraq. I knew the reasons behind Iraq's previously less than trusting relations with a succession of inspections regimes. The British and American governments had undoubtedly strung out the work of the inspectors, constantly moving the goalposts, to keep the murderous sanctions in place. I knew, indeed I informed parliament, that previous inspectors, though nominally working for the UN, were in fact double agents working also for the American and the Israeli governments. Though I was rubbished for saying so, it is now a given – and admitted by some of those involved. I knew, though they said differently in public, that Iraq was hoping to trade the return of inspectors for the lifting of sanctions, and I supported that. After the savage bombardment in Iraq in the mangy and disreputable 'Desert Fox' attack during Ramadan and the run-up to Christmas 1998 – an assault largely motivated by Bill Clinton's need to divert attention from the stain on Monica Lewinsky's blue dress – Tariq Aziz outlined the choice facing the West: 'They can have sanctions, or they can have inspections. But they can't have both.'

I knew also that even a climb-down by Iraq and the readmittance of the inspectors – whose withdrawal was ordered by Britain and America to facilitate the attack by the Desert Foxes (I wish I had a pound for every time I heard an ignorant journalist say that Iraq had 'kicked out' the weapons inspectors) – might well not be enough to stop the clear and present danger of an American invasion. But I thought it was worth a try.

After what has happened I am sorry that I helped persuade the Iraqi regime to allow the inspectors to return. It is now clear beyond sane argument that Bush and Blair had decided long before to fall like the wolves of Sennacherib upon the people of Iraq, no matter what concessions the Iraqi leadership made. All that was achieved by the readmittance of the inspectors was that Iraq ended up breaking up its conventional missile defences before the approving eyes of the inspectors and most of the world, while British and American forces massed on their borders waiting for the order to invade. This was scheduled to occur once the window dressing of UN resolutions had been arranged, but in the absence of that cover they would go in nakedly in defiance of international law. And of course, under the guise of weapons inspectors, Britain and America could infiltrate still more spies into Iraq making the whole thing a ramp, a Trojan horse, for the coming attack.

So I asked Tariq Aziz for a meeting with Saddam Hussein. At this stage, with war apparently imminent, there was no telephone contact between the Iraqi leadership and Saddam. Indeed, it later transpired that Saddam had made just two telephone calls to the Iraqi leadership since 1991. Just like in the days of Nebuchadnezzar, it was all done with a word in the ear. Literally in a whisper. Aziz called in an official I had never seen before, presumably a 'runner' working for Saddam. He whispered something in his ear and the man went off in a hurry. I think now that they might have thought I had brought some sort of secret message from the British, such was the alacrity with which the meeting was then arranged. This would not have been as strange as it seemed. I had informed the Iraqi leadership eighteen months before that the then British Middle East minister Peter Hain had asked me to set up a secret channel between him and the Iraqis.

Hain and I had met in the queue in the voting lobby of the Commons – the strange archaic practice whereby every Member of Parliament must physically and immensely time-consumingly walk through a lobby to have their head counted to register their aye or no. One of the positive and indirectly democratic side effects of this system is that it sometimes provides the opportunity for backbenchers to buttonhole ministers on matters of concern. On this occasion the minister, Peter Hain, buttonholed me.

He began by asking me how things had been during my latest visit to Baghdad and Basra. Then he asked how the Iraqi leadership saw things developing. I asked him why he didn't ask the Iraqis that himself – of course knowing full well that all the channels of diplomatic communication had been well and truly closed. After all, as the old war leader Churchill himself was fond of saying, 'Jaw-jaw is better than war-war.' I said that I stood ready to be a go-between, and suggested that he and I should open a secret channel between us, separate from our normal running battle conducted on the floor of the House.

'Let's take a walk,' said Hain. We paced the library corridor, which runs parallel to the Commons chamber, speaking in low almost whispered voices. He was nervous, though I could tell he was excited about the possibilities.

'We will have to be *very* careful,' he said. 'Our intelligence services are *very* clever and very active. I can tell *you* that for certain.' This I inferred was a none too thinly veiled warning that I was under security service surveillance. I expected as much. I have always said that while I have done and said many things I wouldn't want to appear on the front page of the *News of the World*, I don't do and say things of which in my heart I am ashamed. The former head of the security service MI6, Robin Cook, might disagree, but I don't think the security services are that interested in divulging secrets of that variety; if they unearth them they are more likely to make their excuses and leave.

Hain and I parted, having paced the corridor twice and having agreed to stay in touch, person to person, with not a word to anyone.

The next day I called upon the head of the Iraqi Interests Section, Dr Mudhafar Amin, a graduate of Durham University, at the old Iraqi embassy building at 21 Queens Gate. I knew of course that phone conversations were impossible to keep secret and I had no confidence that the Iraqis had codes not already cracked by MI6. And I knew his embassy building was bugged, which was why he always kept his TV on, loudly, during many long difficult conversations I had had with him. So I sat with him writing him notes about my conversation with Peter Hain; notes that I carefully shredded later. He said, in a note, that this was so potentially important that he should travel immediately to Baghdad with the news. He asked me to write out longhand an account of the discussion and my recommendations as to how Baghdad should respond. This I did, adding the observation that Hain's comments about the intelligence services almost certainly meant that I was myself under observation, including telephone tapping.

The next day Dr Amin departed for Baghdad via Jordan carrying the sheets of A4 written in my spidery hand.

He returned with the regime's answer: that I should actively encourage the opening of this channel with the minister and that I was hereby empowered to make the opening gambit I myself had suggested. This was a proposal that, without announcing it publicly, the British should cease to fly their 'no-fly zone' sorties on Fridays – the Muslim holy day. In return the Iraqis would ensure perfect calm on those days in the zones, taking care to avoid anything that might be held to be a provocation. This confidence-building measure would indicate that messages were being received, understood and reciprocated. It might lead to other more important gestures, such as easing up on the highly restricted situation of Dr Amin in London, balanced, say, with increased Iraqi measures to protect and rehabilitate the Church of St George, the Anglican church next door to the Iraqi Ministry of Information, and so on.

Mr Hain soon lost interest in this channel, perhaps because this dialogue between the minister and Saddam through me came to be discovered by our '*very* active' security services, or perhaps because Hain had overstepped his brief in a Foreign Office made increasingly redundant, as in Mrs Thatcher's time, by the prime minister's propensity to conduct his own foreign policy on the telephone to Washington, or maybe for another reason. But somewhere in Baghdad, unless it wasn't treated with the same flame-resistant coating of some other documents, there exists in some bunker in some ministry, the evidence of an unlikely, eventually unfruitful *ménage à trois*: Saddam, Peter and me.

But I bore with me no good news for Saddam, only an extremely pessimistic analysis of the likelihood of war and my earnest plea on behalf of Dr Blix's readmittance.

It was an extraordinary meeting nonetheless. At the crack of dawn a smartly uniformed protocol officer banged on the door of my hotel room without prior notice and bade me join him as quickly as possible. I was driven in a large black Mercedes with tinted windows and drawn black curtains. I had no idea where or even in which direction we were travelling. I was nervous in the car, thinking we'd make a pretty good target for an opportunist with a missile who thought he had some regime big-wig in his sights and who may not have known that the Iraqi leadership had abandoned such cars in favour of nondescript family saloons – I knew because I'd been in one with Tariq Aziz. We stopped five times, each time taking a break and another cup of horridly sweet tea in a succession of utterly anonymous buildings. I kept imagining the president was about to walk in and surprise us – but each time it was another car and on with the mystery tour.

Eventually we came to another unremarkable building but this time got into a high-speed lift down to a tastefully lit room. The walls were curtained and banks of flowers artfully arranged. It didn't feel like the dark heart of the axis of evil. There, in a corner of the room, glancing shyly downwards briefly as I walked towards him, was the most demonized man on the planet.

As eight years before, Saddam proffered a gentle handshake, strange from a man with a record of using such an iron fist. With the aid of some classily deployed hair and moustache dye, a strict health regimen and, of course, no alcohol, Hussein looked little older and somewhat fitter than he had the first time I'd met him. He was not 'a double'; indeed, what happened to all that bilge about proliferating Saddam doubles? Perhaps they are ensconced somewhere with the disappeared weapons of mass destruction.

We were so deep underground that my ears had been popping as we went down in the lift. But he seemed to have taken to that phase at least of the underground life without acquiring a pallid hue. The meeting was attended by all manner of flunkies, interpreters and even soldiers. Their nervousness contrasted sharply with Saddam's almost spooky Zen-like calm.

A white-gloved orderly proffered – in the twelfth year of UN sanctions – an array of Quality Street chocolates, the tin decorated with scenes of London. Saddam was clearly on a British-centred charm offensive.

Little cups of thick sweet Turkish coffee appeared. The president was speaking. Protocol dictated that he took the first sip before other lesser mortals. I goofed, finishing mine before he even started. Pretending he hadn't noticed, Saddam invited me to begin sipping from a coffee cup I'd already emptied.

The Iraqi 'strongman' regaled me with the following anecdote, no doubt gleaned from his reading of war time memoirs.

At the summit in Yalta, he said, Stalin, Roosevelt and Churchill were at dinner when a goldfish in a large bowl of water was brought to the table. The three leaders were invited to use their cutlery to catch the fish. For the wily Stalin the fork was the weapon of choice. Stabbing repeatedly but in vain, Stalin finally conceded defeat and passed the job to President Roosevelt.

Roosevelt tried with the knife, using its flat edge in an attempt to flick the fish out on to the plate. Again, exasperated, the American president had to give up.

At which point Churchill, using his spoon, slowly began emptying the bowl until, bereft of oxygen, the fish finally succumbed.

'What became of the Britain of Winston Churchill?' asked Saddam.

In this anecdote the Iraqi leader displayed an exaggerated belief in the sophistication of British statecraft, at least as compared to that of the barbarous Russian and the brute 'Roman' America, to which Saddam and many around the world believe Britain plays the role of 'Greece', the older and wiser brother-empire.

If this belief is commonly found in the Arab world it is particularly prevalent in Iraq, despite Britain's role as former colonial power and co-tormentor in sanctions and war. Saddam Hussein put it in his own words during my August 2002 meeting.

'You were a colonial power when the USA hadn't been invented,' he said. 'You were not hated like some others when you left your conquests, and unlike those you should have been able to hold your heads up in front of your former subject peoples – but you seem determined to throw it all away.

'Take Iraq. Even at the height of our strategic relationship with the Soviet Union, Britain was the Iraqis' first choice. Whether for holidays – one million big-spending Iraqis a year used to travel to Britain – or for "Made in Britain" goods.

'Our measurements, our scientific standards, our punctual double-decker buses, even our three-pin electric plugs were all based on the British,' he continued.

'Our people trusted your banking system and have had their private savings seized and frozen. Iraqis, some of whom served you in the past, have died at the British embassy in Jordan waiting for visas to go to London.

'We will never understand why you have turned against us more than any other European country. If Britain had taken a more independent policy – one which took more account of your own interests and less of the interests of others – your country could have had a pre-eminent position in the Arab and Muslim world,' said Saddam.

The Iraqi dictator, warming to his Churchillian theme, began to talk about the gathering storm. 'If they come we are ready,' he said. 'We will fight them on the streets, from the rooftops, from house to house. We will never surrender our independence no matter what happens in any invasion.' His admiration for the Dunkirk spirit of the British knew no bounds.

'That is what Winston Churchill promised the invaders threatening England in 1940 and that is what we can promise the Crusader armies if they come here. Churchill and the British people meant what they promised Adolf Hitler. So do we. At the end, the Iraqi people do not love their country less than the British people love theirs.

'Iraq has never harmed Britain, nor its interests. In fact we were a very profitable part of Britain's interests in the Arab world,' concluded the man Tony Blair said was within forty-five minutes of being able to land chemical and biological weapons on British heads on Cyprus.

Towards the end of what I felt had been an interesting though less than encouraging encounter I requested a tête-à-tête discussion with Saddam. This is diplomatic speak for indicating you have something to say to the principals which you do not want to say in front of the others. Saddam instantly dismissed everyone from the room except Tariq Aziz, who would henceforth translate the discussion between us. Naji Sabri, the Iraqi foreign minister, got up to leave with the others but Saddam motioned for him to remain. The book written by the presidential interpreter says that this private part of the meeting lasted fifteen minutes. Here, for the first time, is what happened.

Looking him straight in the eye, I implied that he had not been speaking the truth about Iraq's weapons capability during our earlier discussion and that he should stop grandstanding with me. I was not there as a neutral; I was there as someone who had given much of his political lifeblood to try and help Iraq out of the terrible vice in which it was caught. And I said that he should destroy any and all forbidden weapons systems and comply strictly with the demands of Dr Blix. I was merely stating the obvious, though it will no doubt now be used against me. After all, I said, once Iraq is out from under all this, no doubt the time will come when she can begin to build up her strength again.

This time Saddam looked me straight in the eye and this is exactly what he said.

'Mr George. The Iraqi people owe you a lot. We are forever grateful for everything you have done to try to help us. I hear what you say and I know the sincerity with which you say it. I would not lie to you. So please hear me and believe me. *We do not have weapons of mass destruction.*'

At the time I was deeply despondent about this reply. In truth I did not believe him. I too had been deceived by the relentless barrage of propaganda, of so-called 'intelligence' reports. Even I, a sceptic of sceptics of every statement of the British and American governments, had fallen for their lies. He must have *something*, I remember thinking as he spoke.

As it turns out, the tyrant was telling the truth. And George Bush and Tony Blair, the self-appointed leaders of the civilized world, were the men whose pants were on fire.

My interview with Saddam Hussein, published in the *Mail on Sunday* on 11 August 2002, created a sensation all around the world and in Iraq itself. My prediction, that by saying for the first time from his own mouth 'Iraq accepts and will implement all UN resolutions' Saddam had implicitly agreed to allow Dr Blix to bring his arms inspectors in, was widely ridiculed. I was traduced as a mouthpiece for Saddam all over again. But it was true – he did allow them in. And a fat lot of good it did them.

My plea for those inspectors to be given more time would later be rubbished in the same way. But if they had been we would not now be in the mess we're in. CNN demanded further and better particulars of where exactly the meeting had taken place. They didn't like my answer that even if I knew that I wouldn't tell them because the details could only make it easier for Bush to assassinate the Iraqi leader – and I didn't approve of people killing other people's presidents. Experts worked out how deeply we must have been underground for the lift journey to have taken as long as it did; though I think they may have overestimated the efficiency of Iraqi lifts after twelve years of sanctions. Information minister al-Sahaf – later nicknamed 'Comical Ali' – was not quite up to speed when he denounced my statements about allowing arms inspectors to return, saying, 'the era of arms inspections in Iraq is over'. Saddam himself was furious about my description of the cloak and dagger nature of the meeting and the picture it painted of him skulking underground. The Iraqis put out a statement that the meeting had taken place in a presidential palace. If only all presidential palaces had been so modest.

So that is the story of Saddam and me. Not much of a story really, certainly not the relationship the war and sanctions party tried so desperately to portray. Three separate sets of documents placing me in the pay of the Saddam regime emerged from the ashes after the fall of Baghdad. An American newspaper, the Pulitzer Prize-winning *Christian Science Monitor*, bought documents seeming to show me receiving $10 million in cash from a son of Saddam I never met, starting before I had ever set foot in Iraq (and before the son in question had any role in the regime) and finishing after I had visited Iraq for the last time, including a $1 million payment on a given date when I was in fact on-line to readers of the Guardian Unlimited website from my office in the House of Commons. These documents were purchased (though the newspaper says they did not know at the time that the freelance reporter who wrote their story, Philip Smucker, actually paid for them) from a retired Iraqi general who later sold a second set of documents to the *Mail on Sunday* which claimed payments to me of more millions from Saddam's other son. The *Mail on Sunday* subjected their documents to forensic examination. Their expert, Dr Audrey Giles, former head of the questioned-documents section of Scotland Yard's forensic science laboratory, found them to be forgeries.

Following the *Mail on Sunday*'s revelations, the *Christian Science Monitor* began to forensically examine the documents on which they had based their claim that I had received $10 million from Saddam's son. By testing the age of the paper and the ink they quickly established that the documents purporting to have been written in 1992 and the documents allegedly written eleven years later had, in fact, been written at the same time. These, too, were declared forgeries. Having published an apology and having accepted full responsibility, the *Christian Science Monitor* would later pay me substantial damages and costs and make a statement of contrition in the High Court in London.

On 2 December last year in Court Number 13 – unlucky for some – of the High Court in London, Mr Justice Eady had his say about a case concerning another set of documents making allegations against me. Awarding me £150,000 in damages, and costs estimated to be at least £1.2 million, against the *Daily Telegraph*, the judge administered a judicial caning more severe than any of the public schoolboys running the paper can ever have experienced before.

The newspaper had claimed I was 'in the pay' of Saddam Hussein, and clearly implied that I had bought a '£500,000' villa in the Algarve and a 'vast' £800,000 house in South London from the proceeds. There turned out to be several problems with this story. First, the villa was a cottage, which had in fact cost £82,000 on a 100 per cent mortgage and bank loan. Second, the 'vast house' had cost £220,000 on a 90 per cent mortgage. And most importantly of all, I was never in Saddam's pay.

By the time the case came to court the newspaper had given up trying to show that what they printed had been true. Indeed their defence was that they had never suggested such a thing. But a blind man in a hurry surveying the acres of newsprint published day after day by the *Telegraph* could see that this was not true.

All that remains is for me to draw up a political balance sheet about the Iraqi dictator. Saddam Hussein was a Third World dictator of a kind that was common around the world in the Cold War years and which is slowly but surely dying out or being done to death. He was not Hitler. Hitler was the all-powerful dictator of a powerful, technologically advanced country at the heart of Europe who intended to rule the entire world and who in an industrialized genocide massacred more than six million Jews as well as countless communists, Gypsies, homosexuals, disabled people and occupied peoples of all kinds. Saddam, in contrast, had only regional ambitions and all of them had failed utterly, well over a decade before the wholly unnecessary invasion and occupation of his country. Saddam was a ruthless and cruel man who thought little about signing the death warrants of even close comrades and still less about ordering the merciless crushing of potential threats to his regime. In that regard he was little different to the leaders of most regimes; regime survival is the ultimate priority of most systems – we just don't know it in our own countries, yet.

It was not a dishonourable thing for an Arab ruler to aspire to military might. Iraq is surrounded by dangerous neighbours who have designs upon it or wish to see it disappear. Turkey, Iran and Israel are all militarily powerful and all of them have or have been trying to acquire weapons of mass destruction. In any case the mere possession of WMD is not of itself a threat; it can even help keep the peace. Isn't that the rationale behind our own possession of nuclear weapons? When the USSR acquired its nuclear bomb to balance that of the Americans we were always told that this mutually assured destruction equation was the reason for Europe's most prolonged period of peace.

Unless you are a partisan who believes that the Zionist state should have nuclear weapons while the Arabs whose land it has taken should be broken and destroyed if they try to balance Israeli power, it must be accepted – in the absence of international intervention to obtain justice – that an Arab ruler worth his salt will seek to strike that balance. The same is true as regards Turkey, which covets Mosul and oil-rich Kirkuk in Iraq. And of course with the Persian power to the east.

Saddam Hussein made two gigantic miscalculations, either one of which, had there been any democracy at all in Iraq, would have been his downfall long ago. I refer to the invasion of Iran at the behest of the West and the invasion of Kuwait in defiance of it.

At a time when human rights has become an international phenomenon it was easy for the likes of Bush and Blair, hypocrites both, to demonize a regime as careless of such basic human rights as that of Saddam. But that was not the real reason Iraq was crushed. In truth, since the 1916 Sykes–Picot partition of the Ottoman empire it has been an article of faith of imperialism to keep the Arab world divided and weak.

Just as Stalin industrialized the Soviet Union, so on a different scale Saddam piloted Iraq's own Great Leap Forward. In fact his best days were when he was vice-president before he got the top job. He pioneered the nationalization of the oil industry, the revenues of which, unlike in other Arab countries, were reinvested in the country and its people. The West prefers its petro-dollars recycled into the bordellos, casinos, stock exchanges and property markets of the Occident.

Iraq built the best health service in the Middle East, and made huge advances in the education sector – sending vast numbers of students to the West for postgraduate studies and technical training. My earliest exposure to Iraqis was in the early seventies, when their sleek and prosperous-looking students from the air training school in Scone in Perthshire, reeking of the then unfamiliar and not yet naff Brut aftershave, used to take all the prettiest girls at our local dances. They may well have been pleased to be in Dundee, but those were large rolls of dinars in their pockets, courtesy of their country's oil wealth.

The very fact that there could be such a hullabaloo about weapons inspectors interviewing Iraqi scientists depended on Iraq, an Arab Third World country, having a science base in the first place. This dwarfed that of all other Arab countries, and of course in the other oil-rich lands most people with scientific and technical expertise were simply hired as expat labour from abroad.

By the standards of contemporary dictatorships Saddam himself may have been a killer but he was not a thief. He virtually never travelled overseas and owned no properties or wealth abroad. What good would it have done him? He knew that he would either die, still the all-powerful president of a rich country, or be brought down with a violent crash with no hiding place overseas. The same could not be said of his grasping family, and their orgy of violence and pillaging of the country's wealth played a decisive role in fatally weakening the regime from within.

By all accounts Saddam Hussein was a generous friend as well as a deadly enemy, sometimes at one and the same time. He sent one party opponent – with whom he'd been classmates – to the Iraqi mission at the UN. He told him you have to leave the country or our dispute will turn dangerous for you. While in New York the man was constantly on the telephone asking Saddam for ever more generous spending permissions, on one occasion asking for jewellery his wife had fancied during a breakfast at Tiffany's, the Manhattan gem store. Saddam loved this man and gave him everything. Yet when he returned from the UN to Baghdad and Saddam suspected him of plotting against him, he personally killed him.

In short, Saddam had some significant achievements, and Iraq at first benefited more than it suffered from his rule. But he committed those two gigantic mistakes in invading Iran and Kuwait, for which his country paid severely yet he didn't pay as he should have, with his political life. He managed to keep his country together until 1991 when the West facilitated the severance, which is likely to become final in the years to come, of Kurdistan. Indeed, he is likely to have been the leader in history who came closest to creating a truly Iraqi national identity, and he developed Iraq and the living, health, social and educational standards of his people. But the brutality of his regime and the sheer lack of democracy meant that he could in the end be isolated and defeated. Democracy is not a panacea and the benefits of its Westminster model are often oversold in relation to Third World countries. But in a crew of yes-men where no one can tell the captain he's wrong without paying with his head, the ship only needs to set a course that's out by an inch. Before long it is adrift and lost.

It should be noted that the majority of Arabs and Muslims in the world would not agree with my balance sheet – which ultimately declares Saddam bankrupt. As far as they are concerned, the good he did, perhaps more importantly the defiance he represented, was more important than the many debits. They take a look around at their own puppet presidents and corrupt royals and then they look at Saddam Hussein. For them, in the land of the blind the one-eyed man is king.

9

Wolves, Lions, Donkeys

I saw 'New Labour' conceived, watched it gestate, witnessed its birth and growth. Now I fervently hope I will be present at its death.

Indirectly it was born out of the passion of Tony Benn's campaign for Labour's deputy leadership in 1981, in which I was a Benn partisan. At that time I was the chairman of the Scottish Labour Party and a full-time party organizer. If Benn had won – he lost by an eyebrow to Denis Healey – I would have moved to London on his staff.

Under my chairmanship of the Scottish Labour Party sat three important men. Twenty years on, these three have fallen out and are engaged in a zero-sum game that will end in the political annihilation of one side or the other. But in those days they were as thick as thieves, and ready to steal the Labour Party from under the noses of the rest of us.

They were the Godfathers of 'the Project'; cartographers of the 'Third Way'; the men who put the 'New' into New Labour.

Dr John Reid was a quixotic former communist, former nationalist, former Irish republican, guitar-playing, chain-smoking alcoholic, who fancied himself as an intellectual with horny hands.

He was, like me, the grandson of Irish immigrants. After trying to make the big-time in the music business (unlike the air-guitarist Tony Blair, Reid really can play and sing – it's not just an ugly rumour), Reid went as a mature student to Stirling University. The university was no more fashionable then than it is now but it was a hotbed of student radicalism – once famously embarrassing the Queen on campus with a rowdy and drunken demonstration.

Reid's doctorate, not that he now talks about the subject, centred on the history of the Marxist-Leninist African republic of Benin. An interesting topic, but not one that was then much occupying the attention of the Scottish working class.

His route march across the political landscape had taken the 'Irish rebel' a long way. His hero was the Scottish-Irish revolutionary James Connolly ('Scots steel tempered wi' Irish fire'[1]), executed in a chair by the British after the Easter Rising. The man who as a leading theoretician (his claim) of the Communist Party had taught many of us the whole song book of the 'Bould Fenian Men' of the IRA was now research officer of the Scottish Council of the Labour Party and rapidly, cynically, moving right just as the party seemed to be moving left. He hated Benn with a bitterness that I put down to class envy, to the chip Reid has always carried on his shoulder. He had an analytical brain rather than a creative one, but he peddled a nice line in pseudo-Gramscian dialectics with which he'd try to bamboozle less well-read leftists who crossed his path. He was good company in the early stages of inebriation; but things frequently got ugly later. He seemed to be trying to sublimate something with his drinking, which would turn into macho-man violence at the drop of a hat.

Gordon Brown was an ascetic son of the manse, awkward, shy and bookish. As Presbyterian a figure as Reid was not. Brown was a genuine intellectual, a graduate of Edinburgh University, where he swept the boards of both academia and student politics. Unlike Reid he keeps his doctorate in a drawer, rarely using the title. To a working-class boy like me, he seemed a bit of a weirdo. For all the later rumours of Romanian princesses and the like there never seemed to be any women in his life – at least he never once commented about such things to me in all our times together. He seemed oblivious to the fact that large numbers of educated young women found him devilishly attractive – the Young Lochinvar.

Brown always had his head in a book or a magazine or a newspaper. Indeed, the sight of him shambling through Scottish railway stations weighed down with papers under his arms is my main memory of him at this time. He was a self-styled 'journalist', though none of us was ever aware of much output. Like Reid, Brown was not an original thinker. In fact we called him 'the Amender', listening out for the positions of left and right and putting down amendments carefully pitched between the two – the first glimpse of the kind of triangulation or the 'third way' that Clintonist-Blairism made famous.

Unlike Reid, whose political ideas had become jaded, Brown had passions. He was particularly committed to devolution, the cause championed by his hero James Maxton, the 'Red Clydesider' whose biography he'd written.[2] In the seventies and early eighties this was not a cause espoused by many Scottish Labourites, whose 'conversion' to the cause of a Scottish parliament had been shallow and opportunist, made as it was under the threat of Scottish independence. So passionate was Brown that the day after the defeat of John Smith's legislation in the referendum of 1979 he broke down and wept on the stairs of the party's Scottish headquarters, crying, 'What are we going to do now?'[3]

The third member of the 'Troika' was the lesser known but in those days the most important of the three. Douglas Henderson was an official of the GMB trade union as well as a member of our Labour executive. Though both Reid and Brown curried favour with the trade unions, Henderson was the only one of the three with actual power to achieve things. He was a man of organization, full of million-member schemes and an early enthusiast for one-member-one-vote rather than the union block-vote system (they all were until they got into power). He was also the only popular man of the three, with an easy gregarious style, a passion for football and the know-how to get things done.

These three men considered the left-wing revolt led by Tony Benn to be an infestation that had to be exterminated. The revolt had begun in response to the failures of the Wilson–Callaghan government 1974–79 that had ended in the debacle of the winter of discontent. But it had lurched into ultra-leftism and would end with the triumph of Thatcher and the near-death experience of the second electoral defeat at her hands in the 'khaki' post-Falklands general election of 1983.*

It was not that the Troika thought Callaghan's government had not failed, but rather that they attributed this failure to 'Old Labourism'. They believed that society had fundamentally changed, that the old

---

* Although candidates and electorate did not turn out to campaign and vote in service uniforms, as they had in the most celebrated 'khaki' election of 1945, the wave of euphoria created by the victory in the 1982 Falklands War certainly swept Mrs Thatcher to her landslide the following year.

pattern of alliances and electoral allegiances had gone for ever. That the seemingly inexorable 'forward march of labour' (in the words of Eric Hobsbawm) in the unions, on the municipalities and in parliament had been halted and might never go forward again.

In this they were the mirror of a trend in the communist parties, the so-called Euro-communists, best represented in Britain by the intellectual and historian Eric Hobsbawm (who later recanted) and the magazine *Marxism Today*, edited by Martin Jacques (who has also, up to a point, now recanted).

There was a close intellectual cross-fertilization between these two groups that would fructify in an extraordinary fringe meeting in Bournemouth in 1983, involving the new young leader Neil Kinnock and the old sage Eric Hobsbawm. Foolish press coverage at the time concentrated on the utterly superficial story – 'Labour leader shares platform with top communist' – quite missing the real point, that both men were in the same business of liquidating ancient left-wing parties whose time they felt had gone.

Neil Kinnock was the Troika's 'useful idiot'. They made use of his left-wing reputation, his windy, waffling but occasionally brilliant oratory, and his working-class credentials, in order to begin the butchery of Labour's sacred cows. Kinnock was a shallow, insubstantial individual. He had cost Benn the deputy leadership by leading a group of abstainers – all from the *Tribune* left – in the final ballot with Denis Healey. This despite the fact that Healey, or 'Raging Bull' as we styled him at the time, had recently railed at Kinnock and others of the group that they were 'Toy-town Trotskyists' and were 'out of their tiny Chinese minds'. But for Kinnock, Tony Benn would almost certainly have become Labour leader – Tony Banks MP offered to resign his east London seat to make way for Benn, who had been defeated in Bristol in the 1983 election. We might then have gone on to lose the next election. We did anyway. We might even have lost the one after that. We did anyway. But who knows what the effect of a genuinely Labour leader popularizing socialist ideas over the next decade and a half would have been?

The grandees of today's New Labour who formed a phalanx around Kinnock in those early days were all smarter than him. Blairite succession hopeful Charles 'Two Dinners' Clarke, a privileged son of the

English elite, had been the Falstaffian president of the National Union of Students, stepping down from his ivory tower at Oxford University to play at being a Labourite. He became Kinnock's chief of staff. Patricia Hewitt, the daughter of a Qantas Airways millionaire, had been an ultra-Bennite extremist while I was seeking to tack Benn's campaign to the right; she became Kinnock's press secretary. Players like these, together with Reid (who also worked in Kinnock's office), Brown and Henderson, using Kinnock's 'noble savage' act, began the counter-revolution that changed Labour perhaps for ever and Britain, consequentially, hardly at all.

The sharp-eyed reader will have noticed two important names missing from the roll-call of the founding fathers.

Peter Mandelson had been a communist. A sufficiently serious one that it later turned out he had his very own MI5 file.* He likes to obfuscate now, claiming only to have been a member of the Young Communist League, as if that were a boy-scout troop. In fact he was a member of the Communist Party, he sold the party organ the *Morning Star* and he acted as a steward – a trusted position – at events held by the party and the YCL. He was viewed as a fellow-traveller of the communists in his work at both the British Youth Council and later the Trades Union Congress. This was why MI5 had an interest in him. He was not involved in this embryonic stage of the New Labour project, though he would later play a vital role in its success and ultimate failure. Mandelson, the grandson of the Attlee government minister Herbert Morrison, thus had a background in the labour movement more akin to Kinnock's than did many of the opportunists who now began to clamber aboard the waiting train.

People like Tony Blair for example.

Blair had been completely uninvolved in politics at his public school – 'Scotland's Eton', Fettes College in Edinburgh – and at Oxford University. Though his father had been; he tried to become a Tory MP! I am certain that those involved in 'the Project' at its inception had never heard of Tony Blair. He was a barrister from the London

---

* In August 1997 former MI5 officer David Shayler disclosed information about MI5 activities to the *Mail on Sunday*. Among his claims were that the intelligence service was paranoid about 'reds under the bed' and that it had investigated Labour ministers Peter Mandelson, Jack Straw and Harriet Harman.

chambers of Derry Irvine, who would later be made Lord Chancellor by Blair. Irvine introduced him to Cherie Booth, quite a left-winger with whom I sat on the Labour Coordinating Committee in the early eighties.

Irvine was tangentially involved in Labour politics – at least as much as to be in a position to have stolen the wife of the late Donald Dewar (both men would later sit, without speaking to each other, in Tony Blair's Cabinet). Booth, the daughter of left-wing 'Scouse Git' *Till Death Us Do Part* actor Tony Booth, was a wannabe Labour MP herself. Thus Tony Blair, the man who'd fronted a band called Ugly Rumours at Oxford, circulated the unlikely tale that he was a follower of Michael Foot's old Labour Party. Blair claimed to want to pull out of the Common Market and scrap nuclear weapons – he even joined CND, wore their badge and would later join their parliamentary group. He enthusiastically fought a by-election as a Foot soldier as well as his successful election to parliament, on Foot and Benn's so-called 'suicide note' manifesto in 1983.

As soon as decently possible, though, they buried old Foot at the bottom of the political garden after the 1983 defeat and rallied behind their great white (or rather, red-headed) hope, Neil Kinnock.

The Welsh wizard was full of rhetorical tricks with which he sought to disguise his limited intellect – it was common currency among those in 'the Project' that the leader was 'thick'.

He launched an attack upon the Trotskyist Militant Tendency group, famously ranting about the Liverpool council's policy of confronting Thatcher to the point of municipal bankruptcy. He decried the 'grotesque spectacle of a Labour council, a *Labour* council, scuttling around in taxis handing out redundancy notices to their own workers'.[4] As Kinnock roared his condemnation, left-wing Liverpool MP Eric Heffer dramatically exited the conference stage behind him. (Heffer was a great stormer-outer. Once, he stormed out of the National Executive Committee and marched straight into a stationery cupboard; from which a few sheepish moments later he came out again and rejoined the meeting.)

Down on the conference floor, consoling the Trotskyist deputy leader of the Liverpool city council Derek Hatton, was another ultra-left council boss, Sheffield's David Blunkett. This Bournemouth conference speech inspired a round of purges and expulsions that became emblematic of the Kinnock years. But Kinnock would live to see many more grotesque spectacles than a taxi-borne redundancy notice service.

Under the day-to-day fine-tuning of this group, though a South Wales miners' MP and supposed devotee of left-wing legend Nye Bevan, Kinnock managed effectively to sit out the epic year-long miners' strike. Labour under Kinnock comprehensively betrayed the coal-mining communities of Britain and abandoned them to Mrs Thatcher's industrial depredation. This capitulation had a terrible legacy: of oil dependency, the wilful destruction of a thousand years of coal supplies under our own land, the crippling of effective trade unionism for a generation, and the condemning of once-thriving, virtually crime-free, tightly bonded British mining communities to the wasteland of mass unemployment, deindustrialization, social disintegration, drugs, crime and vice. The consequences of the strike and its aftermath were far graver for the working class, far more grotesque a spectacle than anything contrived by Derek Hatton and the Liverpool Trots.

Hatton and Blunkett meanwhile were as alike as two peas in a pod. Both believed in gesture politics. Blunkett was big on the notion of councils declaring themselves 'nuclear-free zones' – as if the sign at the municipal boundary could be read by radioactivity. Both saw themselves as front-line fighters against Thatcher and not averse to kamikaze acts, such as refusing to set a municipal rate, or otherwise breaking the law at the risk of disbarment, sequestration and disqualification from office. It was quite a magnificent sight in its way; rather like watching the Charge of the Light Brigade at the battle of Balaclava.

I was against it myself, arguing for a posture of militant opposition but stopping short of political suicide in order to live to fight another day. Thus people like Blunkett saw me as a right-wing 'sell-out'.

One such council leader who certainly saw me in those terms was the then leading member of Lothian Regional Council, a certain Alistair Darling, then a bearded Trotskyist. He was keen on the tactic of refusing to set a rate and he helped lead Lothian Council into a ruinous stand-off with the state. The confrontation reached a farcical stage when Darling's close parliamentary ally, 'Afghan' Ron Brown – the

Leith MP who was caught having sex in the House of Commons shower and who later became Colonel Gaddafi's parliamentary echo, becoming the only member of the British parliament to quote the Colonel's 'Green Book' on the Common's green benches – interrupted a parliamentary occasion being addressed by Mrs Thatcher by placing a placard saying 'Support Lothian Council' on the despatch box from which she was speaking and was then thrown, screaming and kicking, out of parliament.* Far from finding this spectacle grotesque, Alistair Darling thought it heroic and (insofar as he ever gets fierce) bitterly criticized my mocking of the adventurism of it all.

Still on the far left at this time, as yet unseduced by Kinnock's turn, were two north-eastern activists, Steve Byers, a supporter of the Militant group of Trotskyist entrists working parasitically within the Labour Party, and Alan Millburn, a supporter of the trendier IMG (International Marxist Group). Millburn ran a bookshop officially called 'Days of Hope' but known universally as 'Haze of Dope' for reasons which were obvious to any who studied the starry-eyed, far-out, far-left fantasies of the fanatics, including Millburn, who hung out there.

Another who guarded his radical reputation fiercely then was Robin Cook. Cook came out of the same Edinburgh University left-wing milieu as Gordon Brown, though he always claimed to me that Brown was a 'fake left'. Cook and Brown were political enemies for reasons that were difficult to fathom other than as an expression of mutual jealousy, two big fish in the small pond of Scottish Labour politics. But certainly, if Brown was a 'fake left', Cook was the real thing.

He had been Kinnock's campaign manager for the leadership in 1983, in exchange for which he wanted a top shadow portfolio, preferably defence. Kinnock disappointed him. I was with Kinnock in his Bedwellty constituency the night he did so. I heard him talking to Cook about his disappointment, pouring balm on his wounded ego. When he put the phone down, the leader, who'd been drinking, unleashed an unprintable stream of abuse about the 'conceited little

---

* On 18 April 1988 the Labour MP for Edinburgh Leith was suspended for 20 days after picking up the mace and throwing it to the ground during a Commons debate. He had the Labour whip withdrawn for three months and paid the estimated £1,000 repair bill.

man' he'd just been schmoozing. And so Cook had begun to tread the path of apostasy.

Cook had an ego out of all proportion to his elfin stature. Once, a 'Red Review' sketch performed at a Scottish Labour conference had him pose in an armchair on a darkened stage. After a blast of the *Mastermind* signature tune the lights came up and a disembodied voice questioned the red-haired, red-bearded man in a red tie and corduroy suit.

'Name?'

'Robin Cook,' came the reply, booming portentously.

'Occupation?' demanded the Magnus Magnusson soundalike.

'Genius,' replied Cook.

Everyone laughed, except Robin Cook.

But as politicians go, Robin Cook *was* a genius. He was a masterful public speaker, a brilliant wit, exceptionally well read with a sharp and acid pen. All over the country he'd travel, unleashing a battery of devastating rhetorical missiles. Against the Bomb; against Ronald Reagan, Margaret Thatcher, imperialism, Cruise missiles, Trident submarines, the Contras, and so on and on. He was a brilliant turn and could have commanded a very considerable political base in the country if he had not begun to sell his reputation for the mess of pottage that was office without power.

The 'everything must go' sale for these socialist idealists would come under Blair, when Cook briefly became a theoretician for the 'Third Way', the fatuous substitute for the Clause Four socialism he had long championed. But the decline began when Kinnock gave him that brusque brush-off on the phone twenty years before.

Cook would go on to be humiliated in turn by Blair. He had been a fanatical propagandist for Blair's wars, developing an unhealthy relationship along the way with Clinton's Secretary of State Mrs Albright, or 'Madeleine', as Robin always called her. He would do this even at party meetings, attended by people who would snigger at the pathetic familiarity of it all (I called them the 'gruesome twosome'). Despite betraying everything he'd ever stood for, he was still unceremoniously dropped as Foreign Secretary for the cipher Jack (Man O') Straw. One minute Cook was on tour, in charge of Britain's less than ethical foreign policy, the next he was the Cook who fixed the price of sausages in the House of Commons canteen as Leader of the House, a non-job from which he jumped before he was pushed a few nights before the invasion of Iraq. Though he now forensically lays bare the bogus case for the war, the uncomfortable truth which I imagine sometimes occurs to him is that much of the preparation of public opinion for this disaster he had himself undertaken.

Cook is not yet finished in public life in Britain. It is possible he could yet lead a campaign from the traditions of British Labour to recapture the party from the usurpers. I myself would welcome such a campaign. (Incidentally, when I asked Robin Cook to stand for the party leadership in 1994 he told me he couldn't because he was 'too ugly'.) But I would never trust Robin Cook as far as I could throw him. Not because he's 'too ugly' – I don't think he's ugly at all, as I told him back in 1994 – but because of the ugliness of the things he's done and for the dirty mouthpiece he became for some of the great crimes of the twentieth century.

Now John Prescott *is* ugly. Big, ugly, rough, tough, and from the traditional trade union base of the Labour Party – this has been precisely his usefulness to New Labour. He is a kind of Lon Chaney, a big palooka, a mascot, a nodding dog in the rear window of Blair's New Labour limousine.

It was not ever thus. Having outlived his usefulness, Kinnock was succeeded by what turned out to be a false dawn under the all too brief leadership of John Smith, a man as generous, deep and sincere as his successor is mean, petty and false. On the death of Smith and in the absence of a challenge from Robin Cook (too 'ugly') or even Gordon Brown (too cowardly) I joined the campaign team of John Prescott.

I had no illusions that he was the Brain of Britain – though his verbal infelicities have always disguised a shrewd policy mind – or that he was the best possible leader. It was just that he was the best on offer. One night he was relaxing in my Glasgow flat after a leadership campaign rally nearby. We were later to go on to a jazz festival event in the city (one of his attractive features is a love of real-life events, which contrasts sharply with the fake, air-kissing, *mwa-mwa* cocktail circuit of the genuine Blairites). My wife was feeding him some Arabic food when they got to talking about Tony Blair's eyes – how Blair's essentially fraudulent nature could be seen by a look deep into the windows on his soul.

According to their impertinent banter, Blair's eyes were 'insincere', 'lying', 'Satanic' . . . it began to get out of hand! I tried to call a halt to such metaphysics.

As we headed for the door, Prescott said to my wife that his wife Pauline felt exactly the same way as she did: that Blair was a 'superficial, insincere creep'. Then he broke into the famous Eagles lyric 'You can't hide your lying eyes.' We all laughed loudly and set off for the jazz.

Alas, Prescott's subsequent Faustian pact with the devil of Blairism has utterly destroyed his reputation in just a few short years. By the time they have wrung everything they can from him (a time that is coming soon, I predict) he will be a caricature of what he was – a militant merchant seaman and genuinely working-class leader.

Already he has ended up in the courts trying to hang on to a Clapham Common flat he didn't use, belonging to his union the RMT, earning 'Two Jags' the additional epithet of 'Three Houses' Prescott. And in the Commons, shamefully laying in to the Fire Brigades Union as wreckers and the enemy within, all the while threatening them with the militarization of their work. It is a sad end to the career of one of the few Labour leaders I genuinely admired.

Peter Mandelson may have been late on the scene but he soon made up for lost time. He did a lot of good for the Labour Party before doing it terminal harm.

Labour badly needed modernization. I myself was never a traditionalist; indeed, I told Tony Blair when he was trying to scrap Clause 4 that 'I was wearing padded shoulders and carrying a cordless phone before Peter Mandelson had even been heard of'.[5]

I hated the rank amateurism of the Callaghan–Foot era in which I worked as a full-time organizer. The campaign literature that read like a page of the factory and railway-workshop premises regulations; clauses and subordinate clauses piled on top of each other like a Gothic house of horrors. The stage backdrop of faded union banners, which were guaranteed to fall down in the middle of the keynote speech, the rickety platforms, the fairground-standard PA equipment, the failure to provide water for the speakers, the open-topped buses bearing bowler-hatted barber-shop quartets in the age of glam-rock. I was all for modernizing the means of delivering our message.

And Mandelson was the man for that. His make-over of the Labour Party, his early feel for public opinion when most on the left thought winning it was an optional extra, his attention to the details that together make a political party run – these were all things for which I admired Mandy. Indeed, secretly, I had a friendly personal relationship, once removed, with Mandelson until the day of my expulsion from the Labour Party in 2003. But like many a good music hall act, Mandelson's went on too far for too long. He started not selling our message to the public but selling what he said was the public's message to us, the very antithesis of the role of a radical party.

He concentrated on the medium so much he forgot the message and its purpose – to change the country and the world.

Mandelson loved power and wealth, sucked up to it in a way that ultimately destroyed his reputation. Like Ramsay MacDonald before him, though not quite in the same way, Mandy loved Duchesses and Dowagers. But he frolicked with the nouveaux riches as well. He had no serious money of his own yet increasingly wanted to live like the 'beautiful people' he partied with. This is what drew him, like a moth to a flame, into the financial scandals that twice saw him resign from the Cabinet in disgrace.

Peter Mandelson was more of an authentic Labour man than his patron Tony Blair. But his peculiarly fatal attraction to Blair has been his undoing. It led him to betray Gordon Brown, whom he knew in his heart to be the man the party wanted to lead it after the death of John Smith. In fatally undermining Brown's reputation and thus his self-confidence, just when he needed it most, he forced Brown out of the race, transforming it from an election into a coronation.

He knew that Brown was a political Titan compared to Blair; as deep as Blair was shallow, as serious as Blair was slick. Brown versus Blair was like a contest between Bertrand Russell and Bob Monkhouse (whose motto, incidentally, could easily be Blair's: 'Once you learn how to fake the sincerity the rest is easy').

This betrayal has been the leitmotif of the Blair government. Relations between Blair and Brown have never recovered from this almost Shakespearian act of treachery from within a band of brothers.

It is the flaw at the heart of New Labour; the fault line between two tectonic plates that continue to grate, sometimes noiselessly, sometimes higher on the Richter scale, but always threatening to bring cataclysmic destruction to 'the Project'. This betrayal split the solidarity of that original band of brothers.

John Reid went with Blair – he had always been jealous and resentful of Brown – while Doug Henderson stayed loyal to Brown. He would later pay for this loyalty with the ministerial sack, while Brown would show his traditional pitiful lack of resolve by being unable (or unwilling) to save him. Brown has only himself to blame for the situation he and his friends now find themselves in. He could have stood up to Blair and Mandy, and contested the leadership. He probably would have won. But he lacked the balls.

He didn't have to encourage New Labour down its path to destroying everything the party had stood for. But he did and he's now finding out that you can't be a little bit pregnant.

Brown is the Chancellor who insisted on privatizing air traffic control and the London Underground, and tried to privatize the Post Office (where he was blocked by Peter Mandelson). He sought to call a halt to the retreat when it came to the betrayals involved in Foundation Hospitals and variable university top-up fees. Even that became the scene of another Brown debacle. Having fomented a rebellion that had the potential to bring Blair down – at the head of which was his 'vicar on earth' Nick Brown, Labour's former Chief Whip – Gordon marched his key men back down the hill again, betraying the students and their parents and allowing another round of derision to be fired off by the Blairite mouthpieces in the media.

New Labour has become a Frankenstein's monster. It has broken free and out of the laboratory that was established by Brown before he'd ever heard of Blair.

David Blunkett, the municipal champion of South Yorkshire's self-styled 'People's Republic', the one-time fan of the Sandinista revolution in Nicaragua and municipal debt-counsellor to Derek Hatton, has become a hanging judge. He is a cartoonish figure, consistently ramping up racism and Islamaphobia in the country, even when he does not seem to know he's doing it.

When police arrested a man in Gloucester in 2003 Blunkett went live on television declaring the person, who had not then even been charged, let alone tried or convicted, to be a member of Al-Qaeda. At a stroke he had nullified the accused's chances of a fair trial in the future.*

Taxed by the BBC about our own 'Guantanamo Bay' in London's Belmarsh Prison, where prisoners, all of them Muslim, languish without trial or representation, he answered: 'I am not concerned that these people are Islam [*sic*] . . . I am concerned about their terrorism.'

He then said that the prisoners could leave prison anytime – if they agreed to be deported. So, in the midst of a 'war on terrorism', people whom the Home Secretary declares to be 'terrorists' (though he will not put them on trial) are 'free to leave'. Presumably, if Blunkett's verdict on them is correct, they will take up terrorism again in somebody else's country.

When a BBC documentary proposed to show undercover film of police racism, Blunkett denounced the corporation for irresponsibility and intervened to bully the BBC governors in an effort to get the programme spiked.†

When it was aired the film showed police cadets openly discussing their hatred of African-Caribbean and Asian people. One cadet, dressed in a Ku Klux Klan hood, demonstrated on camera how he'd like to stab 'Pakis'. Another said the murdered black teenager Stephen Lawrence 'deserved to die'. He accused Stephen's parents of 'milking' their child's death, saying they didn't deserve their OBEs, which should have gone instead to Stephen's racist killers. Still another police cadet, laughing into the secret camera, boasted how he'd fined a 'Paki' driver £200 then forced the man and his wife and children to walk two and a half miles back to their holiday camp.

---

* On 27 November 2003 police arrested a man in Gloucester under the Terrorism Act. Commenting on the arrest David Blunkett said: 'we will know shortly from the forensic scientists the exact nature of the materials that have been obtained in the raid and of course the nature of the connections that this individual has with the wider Al-Qaeda network.'

† The BBC programme *The Secret Policeman* was broadcast on 21 October 2003. Undercover reporter Mark Daly joined Greater Manchester police as a trainee and spent five and a half months posing as a probationary constable: while he was at the Bruche training centre in Warrington, Cheshire, he filmed the footage used to expose racist officers.

Confronted with such blood-chilling evidence of racism within the police, Blunkett chose to attack not the copper in the Ku Klux Klan hood but the BBC journalist who brought him to our attention. The journalist was charged with damaging his police vest by secreting a microphone under it and ordered to pay back the six months' salary he'd received while acting as a police cadet. The Home Secretary was later forced into a humiliating apology – after it was shown he'd mounted a bullying attempt to make the BBC drop the programme – but few believed it was sincere. Blunkett now wants to force us to carry ID cards, which will make life even easier for Klansmen cops like these. Now the police will be able to stop 'Pakis' with even greater impunity. And teenagers who look like Stephen Lawrence will be asked to produce their IDs rather more often than the young white thugs who prey upon them.

The Blairite Home Secretary – built up by Mandelson as a possible challenger to Brown in any future leadership challenge – has decided to take child hostages from refugee families to force their parents to comply with expulsion orders. Once an applicant has exhausted their (greatly truncated) appeal procedure, the asylum seeker will be forced into destitution by the withdrawal of all means of support. Their children will quickly be destitute and must be taken into care. Presumably, if they resisted, this must involve wresting babies from their mother's arms and taking them away in police vehicles; this is Britain in the year of our Lord 2005. King Herod, thou shouldst be with us at this hour.

In the play *The Jasmine Road*,[6] written by a Palestinian refugee, a refugee receives the latest in the torrential stream of letters from Blunkett in which, in one way or another, he demands that they make greater efforts to show their willingness to be 'British'.

'Refugees,' says the letter, 'should make a greater effort to understand British history.'

'Huh,' says the refugee, throwing the letter in the air. 'Who knows better than the refugee about British history? We are refugees *because* of British history!'

Blunkett is busy introducing the umpteenth asylum/immigration/terrorism measure in New Labour's first seven years, he opposed the return of the British detainees from Guantanamo Bay because he knew that no British court would convict them, and in early 2004, in parliament, he boasted to a taunting Tory that he was 'the least politically correct minister in the British government'.

The hyenas, who are whipped in to sit on the backbenches behind him, all laughed at this point. But they are not laughing in Belmarsh, nor in Guantanamo Bay. They are not laughing in the Muslim ghettos of Oldham or Bradford, where the people are living in fear of a resurgent BNP feeding on every scrap of Blunkett's political incorrectness.

One of Blunkett's ministerial colleagues and a fellow Yorkshireman is the Foreign Office junior minister Dennis MacShane.

Now I know a lot about Dennis MacShane, including the fact that he is not Dennis MacShane. His is a family of Roman Catholic refugees from Poland who changed their name to blend in more successfully.

Like Blunkett, MacShane wants Britain's Muslim community, metaphorically, to do the same. In effect to 'disappear', preferably to metamorphose into 'pukka' English gentlemen like him. Supporting the English cricket team; putting their strange ways and customs in a drawer, perhaps to be taken out at weddings and funerals or folkloric festivals.

After the criminal bombing of British targets in Istanbul in 2003, which was in fact condemned forthrightly by all leading authorities among British Muslims, MacShane sat down at his desk in the British Foreign Office. In the building from which the Raj once governed an empire so vast that on it the sun never set (my Irish grandfather said that's because God wouldn't trust the British in the dark), he composed a press release. On government notepaper, MacShane demanded that Britain's Muslims 'must choose' between the 'British Way' and 'Terrorism'.

The 'British Way' he defined as 'peaceful political dialogue and non-violence'. This, written in the building which had been the heart of the darkness of an empire which soaked the world in blood. By a minister in a government which had just ignored the cries of millions of their own supporters, beseeching them to try peaceful political dialogue with Iraq, instead of earth-shattering violence. And these demands to choose – 'are you with us or against us?' – were being made upon a peaceful section of the British population which, despite decades of electoral loyalty to Labour, was now being offered up by a

Labour minister as whipping boys in a part of England where the racist BNP was already on the march.

MacShane later issued a mealy-mouthed 'apology' to his own outraged constituents, whom he'd hurt and who may hurt him later at the polls. But he was not charged with bringing the Labour Party into disrepute. Unlike me!

The former Militant supporter Stephen Byers has been and gone – from Blairite minister to prophet in the wilderness, pressing for even greater betrayal of the cause he once believed in. The man whose aide Jo Moore famously saw 9/11 as a 'good day to bury bad news' now wants greater 'boldness' in carrying out the final interment of Labour's ideals. Likewise former Health Secretary Allan Milburn, another shooting star who crossed the firmament before burning out in a welter of mystery and speculation about why he, the most cosmopolitan of men, really did want to spend more time with his family – in Darlington? Privatization in the NHS, hallucinates the former Haze of Dope man, has not gone nearly far enough.

Alistair Darling, his face like Byers' and Mandelson's now as smooth as a baby's bum, who used to press Trotskyist tracts on unsuspecting railwaymen going in to union meetings, now finds that as Blair's transport secretary it is his job to denounce striking rail workers as mindless militants. (I would often make the joke about the three – and the former beardy communist David Aaronovich – that they all shaved because their hairy faces were tickling the Prime Minister's bottom.)

The party formed by the trade unions to give working people a voice in parliament now treats those unions like 'an embarrassing elderly relative',[7] whose drooling shows the party up in front of their smart, rich, here-today, gone-tomorrow friends. New Labour has expelled the rail workers' union – whose resolution caused the party to be founded over a hundred years ago – because it insisted on spending its political funds in pursuit of its members' interests. The Fire Brigades Union too is on a spiralling ladder out, and the posties' union, the CWU, may also have made its final delivery of funds to New Labour.

The 'one-member-one-vote' schemes of the original founding fathers have gone the same way as the 'million-member party' idea – down the proverbial river. A Heath Robinson labyrinthine constitution has been imposed upon the party in which the individual member's vote means nothing. It can't change the complexion of the ruling committees, it can't make policy, it can't hold MPs or ministers to account. Tony Blair rules as remote as a Roman emperor and looks down just as disdainfully on 'the mob'. Membership, far from growing under New Labour, is falling like a stone – so far and so fast that even members of its National Executive Committee are not told how bad the situation is. Best estimates put paid-up membership at below 200,000 – a fifth of the founding Troika's target twenty years ago.

The party conference has gone from 'parliament of the labour movement', through American-style conventions with trumpets and balloons (I'm not talking about the politicians), to all-out Nuremberg style 'leader-worship' rallies that would turn the strongest stomach. 2003's seven-minute tear-stained standing ovation surely took the biscuit, coming as it did after a leader's speech that conceded nothing to party concerns about Iraq, the NHS, higher education finance or privatization and during which he gloried in saying he'd do it all again exactly the same way. Like Mrs Thatcher, who wasn't for turning, Mr Blair declared he hadn't got 'a reverse gear'; which, given the level of his political intoxication, makes him a truly dangerous driver.

Some say this conference audience was not representative of the delegates, that parliamentary and party staffs were bussed in to bulk the ranks of the true believers and get the hysteria going. Maybe so. But it was the delegates who voted earlier in the week not to have a vote on the war in Iraq, even though it was raging still and was the biggest issue in world politics. A conference voted not to notice the elephant wandering around the aisles dropping copious amounts of trouble to which they'd have to return later.

A party that used to be funded by the voluntary and heart-felt contributions of millions – through the trade union political levy and the fundraising efforts of a genuinely mass membership – is now the plaything of corporate interests.[8] Individual plutocrats, however unsavoury, however alien to the Labour way, are carelessly seduced into massive donations which the party knows full well will have to be repaid with interest somehow, someday. The honours system under Blair makes Harold Wilson's 'Lavender List'* look like a pale imitation. The House of Lords is run by Charlie Falconer, Blair's former flatmate, taking over the job from Derry Irvine, his former boss and cupid. It was Falconer who suggested Blair appoint Lord Hutton to do the whitewashing of the Kelly Affair – how's that for being able to choose your own referee?

Blair boasts about abolishing the hereditary peers yet is unembarrassed at the incestuous, corrupt cronyism with which he has replaced them. Frankly, give me a House of Lords stinking of the putrefying corpses of the English aristocracy rather than one stuffed with the sun-dried-tomato-eating toadies of Blair's cool Britannia, the 'Lloyd George knew my Father' purchasers of seats in parliament by insincere donations and easily covered cheques to New Labour 'blind trusts', or the shady middlemen who make the whole cash nexus possible. In other words, better the decaying relics of ancient earldoms with a sliver of independence in their souls than to be governed by suburban shysters whose main claim to fame is that they have, say, discovered the likes of Alvin Stardust, and who only have ears to hear their master's voice.

The party that once boasted of its traditional ties with the Democrats was left openly hoping for George Bush's re-election for a second presidential term. How could Blair keep his 'special relationship' with a new US president swept to power on a wave of revulsion against the lies and the slaughter in Iraq?

The party that once took such pride in the international esteem of the BBC has cut a swathe through that reputation, humiliating its journalists, gloating in the defenestration of its senior management. They don't appear to have noticed that twice as many people in Britain trust the BBC than trust the swaggering spin-doctors and third-rate politicians of New Labour.

The party that embodied the UN Charter into its own constitution now treats the United Nations with contempt, useful if it agrees with US–UK diktat, useless and redundant if it does not, and listens like sordid eavesdroppers to the private telephone calls of Kofi Annan.

---

* In 1976 Harold Wilson's resignation letter was reportedly scribbled on lavender paper by his then secretary Marcia Williams (Lady Falkender).

The party that prosecuted – through its Attorney General Hartley Shawcross – the Nazi criminals at Nuremberg now says soldiers 'must follow orders' even if they may be illegal.[9]

Labour now has a leader who openly stated to Paddy Ashdown, the former leader of the Liberal Democrats, during Labour's centenary year that the pioneers should never have created an independent Labour Party – which he called an 'historic mistake' – but should have stayed with the Liberals.[10] No parent would wish that its own child, however errant, had never been born. Least of all on the child's birthday.

Tony Blair and the clique of hijackers who are flying Labour to destruction may wish the party had been aborted. They are certainly doing everything they possibly can to coax it into euthanasia.

10

Worse than a Crime

It is said that according to the laws of aerodynamics the bumble-bee cannot fly: its wings are too slight to support its body mass. But it flies all right. By the same token, according to the normal laws of politics, in a democracy with checks and balances, Tony Blair should have been gone long before now. Assailed by heart problems, a clear electoral liability for his party, bed-blocking his Chancellor to whom he has twice promised the succession, caught red-handed in a conspiracy to deceive his own country in the service of a foreign power, Tony Blair should have already moved into his £3.6 million house off Hyde Park – and into the big money job on the promise of which he must have secured the finance to buy it.

In a parliament like the one we had in the darkest days of May 1940 when we stood alone against the Nazi hordes and when the Norway debacle – the ill-conceived and disastrously executed British attack on the Nazi-occupied port of Narvik – proved we were led by bumbling incompetents, the House of Commons came into its own. An adjournment debate tabled by Chamberlain's own Chief Whip Captain Margesson was debated for six hours on 7 May and eight hours on 8 May. Most of the munitions fired at the hapless Chamberlain flew across the chamber from the Labour opposition. But the killer blows were landed by his own side. Leo Amery, a Tory grandee drawing on the immortal words of Oliver Cromwell dismissing the Rump Parliament of 1653, ended his thunderous address to the house with these, some of the most eloquent and powerful words ever uttered in parliament: 'You have sat too long here for any good you have been doing. Depart, I say, and let us have done with you. In the name of God, go.'

In the subsequent vote more than sixty Conservatives abstained. But though he had won the vote, Chamberlain was finished, holed below the water-line by the courage of his own MPs putting country before party. By that amorphous, difficult to define but easy to recognize standard which in the absence of a constitution meant everything in British politics, the prime minister had lost the House even though he was still in possession of a parliamentary majority.

By the end of the day the arch-appeaser Chamberlain had gone and the British bulldog Winston Churchill was in No. 10. By speaking for Britain the House of Commons had saved the day, saved the country, and changed the course of history.

Today parliament is not what it was, not even what it was when I entered it less than twenty years ago. In a recent poll just one New Labour MP said that she would have voted differently on the war on Iraq if she had known then what she knows now. Michael Howard, the so-called leader of the 'opposition' – who receives a handsome emolument from the public purse for holding the government to account – was part of the iron-clad consensus which gripped the Commons in the run-up to the attack. His opportunistic lawyerly twists and turns on the issue since have deservedly received only ribaldry and contempt. The Tories, led by the sad sack Iain Duncan Smith, egged New Labour on to attack Iraq and were more royal than the king in their obeisance towards Washington.

And yet at the same time as parliament stands roughly where it was on 18 March 2003 when the sheep flocked through the lobbies to vote for the slaughter of thousands, the story outside the confines of the House has been very different.

Until the guns began firing, most British people opposed the prospect of war even before they knew what they know now. Once our troops began fighting, roughly half of the British public supported the war. They did so having been softened up by the most remorseless propaganda barrage in history. The 'sexing up' of the case for war was as lurid as the most atrocious top-shelf or even under-the-counter pornography.

Saddam Hussein was painted as the new Hitler, the broken-backed Republic of Iraq as the new Third Reich. In a matter of minutes, Mr Blair told us, Iraq could unleash ballistic missiles capable of reaching us, missiles moreover seeping chemical and biological horrors the consequences of which were described in ever more fantastic detail. Hussein's regime, the government said, was in breach of UN resolutions, an urgent and growing threat which had to be stopped, now.

The regime, it was said, was teaching Al-Qaeda operatives within the fuselage of a redundant airliner how to slit the throats of stewardesses, had procured nuclear materials from the African state of Niger, had developed new long-range missiles, was storing banned weapons under hospitals, in presidential palaces, under lakes, under mountains. Hans Blix's UN weapons inspectors (whose return had been long demanded) were said to be looking for needles in haystacks in a country 'bigger than France', sometimes 'twice the size of France' (it is in fact the size of Texas).

Pulp fiction in the form of 'dossiers' flowed from the pen of the former pornography writer Alastair Campbell, the thuggish prime-ministerial mouthpiece. General Colin Powell, quoting from the dossiers, described them before the Security Council as 'exquisite' evidence of the threat. In the same presentation he played an X-certificate slide and video presentation showing mobile biological weapons laboratories, he played telephone intercepts of Iraqi personnel carrying out a cat-and-mouse game with the inspectors, and he showed factories where assembly lines were churning out obscene weapons. Iraq was said to be shipping weapons to its ancient enemies Iran and Syria, or hiding them under the lawns of its scientists. One claim had them being loaded into 'ships of death' which would sail concentrically around the world, ready to scuttle if approached, poisoning the seas and the food chain for all time.

It is now admitted, even by the Bush-appointed CIA adjunct the Iraq Survey Group, that every single one of those claims was false. Utterly.

It is now a commonplace outside the laager in Westminster and Washington that each of these claims was a wilful, bright, shining, lie. Blair's claim that while wrong these things were honestly believed by him is belied by the distortions he made of even the wrong intelligence he was given.

Yet if the war had gone to plan they might have got away with it.

US Defense Secretary Donald Rumsfeld believed the war could be won with 'light forces', such was the state of internal opposition to the

Saddam regime. Dick Cheney believed it would be like 'the liberation of Paris'; Paul Wolfowitz thought it would lead to a wave of 'pro-democracy change' in the Arab world. British MPs, like Dr Oona King, said she would vote for the war because Tony Blair had promised her that George Bush had promised him that he would make General Ariel Sharon promise to chart a 'road map' to a just peace for the Palestinians. Others said the attack on Iraq would be a 'six-day war' like the Israeli conquest of the remaining Palestinian territories in 1967.

On an aircraft carrier, drifting at great public expense off the coast of the USA, George Bush, the Vietnam draft dodger, having landed an aircraft, declared the Iraq war to be over. 'Mission accomplished,' he said.

Talking of the then embryonic war of national liberation which followed the fall of Baghdad, Bush said of the insurgents, 'Bring them on.'

But, as Bush himself might put it, they 'misunderestimated' the Iraqis.

I had many conversations in Iraq about what might happen if the US invaded the country. I encouraged them to avoid attempting to fight a war of position against a superpower.

'Don't stand in lines, or hunker down in trenches,' I used to say. 'You will be mown down or buried alive.' The only war that can be fought against a superpower is a war of movement. I brought Tariq Aziz all the writings of Che Guevara and Mao Tse Tung on the arts of revolutionary war and he had them translated into Arabic. Fight a war of movement, take the uniforms off, swim among the Iraqi people and whatever their views on the regime, they will undoubtedly provide deep aquifers of support for a patriotic resistance.

I warned in a *Spectator* article on 15 March 2003, just before the invasion, that the inevitable fall of Baghdad would be, in the words of Mr Churchill, not the beginning of the end but merely the end of the beginning, 'and when the crusader army patrols every street in Iraq, they should know they will be as welcome as a pork chop at a Muslim wedding. Or, to put it another way, as welcome as General Sharon's army in the alleyways of Gaza.' I warned there of a future of suicide attacks, car bombs, drive-by shootings, of merciless and ugly resistance as fierce as any war in history. And I warned in parliament that occupied Iraq would be the banner under which every enemy of the United States would gather. I told them they had opened the gates to hell.

I was able to accurately predict all of this not just because I know the Middle East much better than the shallow, superficial wishful thinkers on the front benches and their laptop bombardier adjutants in the media, but above all because I know the Iraqis better than any man in the country.

No British diplomat had set foot in Iraq for more than a decade and virtually no British journalist had got within the skin of this society, unable, as most of them were, to step outside the bounds of whispered conversations in Baghdad hotel lobbies or the paid-for testimonies of exiles working for the American agenda.

I knew the Iraqis to be the most nationalistic of all the Arabs. I knew the deep well of suspicion among virtually all Iraqis that the foreigners wanted to dismember Iraq, to balkanize it, to steal its wealth. I knew the exaltation of fighting spirit in Iraq, the folk memory of resistance to the British occupiers of the last century, the machismo of the Iraqi patriotic image. The Iraqi accent is the toughest version of Arabic spoken anywhere. It matches their character. The tribal allegiance is the most enduring in the whole Arab world. Many Iraqis are very emotional people given to loud, spirited argument, quick to escalate disputes into violence. They weep a lot, remember everything, forget nothing. Iraqis make good friends and very bad enemies. For the best part of a decade I had absolutely absorbed myself among the Iraqis. Virtually alone of all foreigners I never had a minder, I could go where I wanted and speak to whomsoever I pleased. I couldn't walk down a single street in Iraq without being mobbed, asked for autographs, asked to pose for pictures. I estimate that I may have appeared in five hundred wedding portraits, just through having been in the hotels where, gratis, they held their receptions and honeymooned. And those who say the millions, literally, who greeted our London bus's arrival in Baghdad in 1999 were dragooned to do so are welcome to study the more than one hundred hours of film I have to spot the Iraqis who were merely 'acting' like they were pleased to see us.

As the public record shows, I never had the slightest doubt that the

Iraqis would fight the invaders, the occupiers, every step of the way. And for ever if necessary.

That's why I tried so hard to stop the war. Not because I hate my country but because I love it enough not to want to see its reputation sink into a swamp of hatred and blood in a new colonial adventure. Not because I hate our soldiers – young men economically conscripted by low-paid dead-end jobs and poor prospects in the 'civvy streets' of Scotland, the north, rural England and the canyons of depression in South Wales – but because I care for them more than the politicians who sent them to kill and to be killed for a lie.

At the time of writing, the Iraqi resistance are attacking the invaders an average of 87 times a day. By the time you read this it may be more. In the month of September 2004 more than 2,700 military operations were undertaken by the resistance.

According to a remarkable letter written by the pro-war, pro-Bush *Wall Street Journal* reporter Farnaz Fassihi, the war in Iraq has become 'an absolute disaster'. Her private letter home from 'virtual house arrest' because of the collapsing security situation in Baghdad has circulated the world like chain mail. In it she says, 'Iraqis say thanks to America they got freedom in exchange for insecurity . . . and guess what? They'd take security over freedom any day, even if it means having a dictator ruler.' 'Despite President Bush's rosy assessments,' she says, 'Iraq remains a disaster. If under Saddam it was a potential threat, under the Americans it has been transformed to an imminent and active threat, a foreign policy failure bound to haunt the United States for decades to come.'

According to the *Wall Street Journal* star writer the insurgency has spread 'from isolated pockets in the Sunni triangle to include most of Iraq'. The Iraqi government, she wrote, 'doesn't control most Iraqi cities . . . the situation basically means a raging guerrilla war. In four days [in September 2004] 110 people died and over 300 were wounded in Baghdad alone.'

Fassihi records how 'a friend drove thru (*sic*) the Shiite slum of Sadr City yesterday. He said young men were openly placing improvised explosive devices into the ground. They melt a shallow hole into the asphalt, dig the explosive, cover it with dirt and put an old tire or plastic can over it to signal to the locals this is booby-trapped. He said on the main roads of Sadr City there were a dozen land mines per every ten yards. His car snaked and swirled to avoid driving over them. Behind the walls sits an angry Iraqi ready to detonate them as soon as an American convoy gets near. This is in Shiite land – the population that was supposed to love America for liberating Iraq.'

I have quoted this witness at length not only because she is on the spot but also because she represents a newspaper which may have been the most partisan supporter of the war on Iraq in the entire United States.

And if the picture she paints of the beleaguered foreign forces is bleak enough, what of the puppet 'government' they claim to be 'assisting'?

In the original war plan, the convicted bank fraudster Ahmed Chalabi was intended to assume power in Iraq. He had spent a decade milking US government funds in exchange for the provision of false propaganda and fraudulent schemes based on forgery and disinformation.

The State Department knew this from an early stage and made several efforts to sever the Chalabi tentacles, going so far as to accuse the rogue banker of stealing US government money and falsely accounting for taxpayers' dollars. But he had profound support amongst the neo-cons – those whom General Powell described as 'the crazies' – led by Cheney, Wolfowitz, Perle, Feith, Libby and the CIA and Pentagon warriors.

Most of the 'exquisite' documents highlighted by General Powell at the Security Council proved to have been as conveniently fabricated in the Chalabi lie machine as were several of the forged documents later used against me in newspapers like the *Christian Science Monitor* and sold to newspapers like the *Mail on Sunday*. Whatever his misgivings about the sewer, Powell had no compunction about spewing out the sewage.

Quickly after the invasion Chalabi returned to the country he'd left nearly half a century before when his royalist family was expropriated of its vast wealth and estates by the 1958 Iraqi nationalist revolution. Trailing in his wake were the apostate former liberal journalists of the west who'd fawned over the latter stages of his exile. Foaming-at-the-mouth ex-radicals like the *Observer*'s Nick Cohen, *Vanity Fair*'s David

Rose, ex-communist apparatchik David Aaronovitch and bloated bon-viveur and former Trotskyist Christopher Hitchens all penned pan-egyrics of Chalabi. All praise, it seemed, was due to him.

Now that he has been arrested and charged with a multimillion-pound currency fraud, again based on counterfeiting, and has been driven from the puppet administration, his house raided and wrecked by his former American patrons and his nephew Salem – who was the original prosecutor in Saddam Hussein's trial and who is now holed up in London – wanted for murder, it's all gone quiet over there in the fraudster's Farringdon Road fan club.

With Chalabi out of the running – skewered by his kleptomania and utter lack of local credibility – the American colonial governors, first Lt General Jay Garner then Paul Bremer, searched desperately for local heroes to promote. As top dog they settled on a former Ba'athist Rottweiler Iyad Allawi, who by his own account had been on the payroll of at least a dozen foreign intelligence services, including most notably the CIA and MI6. Allawi showed his class when, according to the respected Australian newspaper *The Age* in a story never con-vincingly contradicted, he personally executed no less than six young Iraqi insurgent prisoners by hand in Abu Ghraib jail shortly before he became interim prime minister in 2004.

Allawi set up the Iraqi National Guard and scrambled desperately to create an Iraqi police service. Poorly armed and trained and even more poorly motivated, the puppet forces were quickly massacred. Almost one thousand have already been slain – dozens are murdered most days. In time-honoured Iraqi tradition the resistance have assidu-ously infiltrated these forces, and the infrastructure of Allawi's govern-ment itself. I can reveal that the Ba'athist component of the insurgency has given carte blanche to its supporters to seek posts everywhere within Allawi's administration. And await orders for the next step. In Fallujah, Basra, Najaf and elsewhere, when the going got tough the puppet Iraqi forces got going – out of the battlefield and back to their homes.

The regular assassination of puppet-government ministers and high officials clearly shows the fingerprints of the infiltrators. The move-ments of these stooges are regularly supplied to the resistance groups, the better to plot their demise. These were the very conspiratorial methods so successfully used by the Ba'athists in the bloody coups of 1963 (in which the Ba'ath were assisted by British and American intelligence) and 1968. Enter the ministries and all the organs of the state and wait for your orders is the instruction which is given.

According again to the *Wall Street Journal*'s Ms Fassihi, 'Cops are being murdered by the dozens every day, over 700 to date [September 2004] and the insurgents are infiltrating their ranks . . . the problem is so serious that the US military has allocated $6 million to buy out 30,000 cops they had just trained to get rid of them quietly.' So, who are the resistance?

In the mouths of the US's more sophisticated spokesmen like Colin Powell it is acknowledged that resistance among Iraqis to the occupation is residual, deep and widespread. Every American air-raid, house demolition, round-up, torture case and piece of 'collateral damage' recruits new members, whole families, whole streets, blocks and tribes.

But in the propaganda of Bush and Blair and their little echoes in the media, the resistance is described as a 'terrorist' problem – straight out of the lexicon of Ariel Sharon. If only the 'terrorist' could be extirpated, they seem to say, everything would be sweetness and light. Not only that, but that old reliable saw, the concept of the 'foreign fighter', is dragged as a red herring across the debate. American generals in an occupying army, in their southern drawl, growl at press conferences about 'foreigners' fighting in Iraq as if they themselves hailed from the suburbs of Baghdad.

There were of course no 'foreign fighters' of any description in Iraq before the Anglo-American invasion. There was no Al-Qaeda in Iraq – except for Abu Mussab Al-Zarqawi, the killer of Kenneth Bigley, and he was in Kurdistan in the area under US and British protection – and there were no Islamist fundamentalists running around with weapons competing for power, until Bush and Blair invaded. There was no terrorism in Iraq – except for terrorist attacks paid for by the US's 'Liberation of Iraq Act' and carried out, by their own account, by the Chalabi group Iraqi National Congress and the Allawi group Iraqi National Accord.

Now we are told Iraq is a magnet for 'international terrorism', a 'crucible' in which a 'new war' against fundamentalist 'nihilism' is being waged and that we must all support it! If Al-Qaeda are now in Iraq they came in the whirlwind unleashed by the invasion. And if Iraq now becomes an obscurantist medieval theocracy its midwives will have been the gallant Christian soldiers George Bush and Tony Blair.

But in truth the importance of 'foreign fighters' is dramatically and deliberately hyped by the war-governments and their media allies, who, it being unsafe for them to step outside of the Baghdad 'congestion charge area', simply regurgitate whatever the occupation authorities tell them. Writing in the *Guardian* the respected British-Iraqi academic and commentator Sami Ramadani observed that in September 2004 there were 2,700 military operations launched by the resistance against the occupiers and the puppet forces. Of these just six were claimed by Al-Zarqawi. The Iraqi resistance, or 'Muqawama', is indigenous, disparate, often incoherent and deadly.

Neither can the resistance be easily defined through pre-invasion prisms. For example, the Ba'ath Party and the nationalists generally have become 'Islamicized' not just by the war but by the long years of suffering which preceded it. Equally the Islamic forces, both Sunni and Shia, have become infused with new patriotic Iraqi nationalism. To Islamicize the Arab nationalists and make nationalists of the Islamists, fusing both in the 'crucible' of Mr Blair's rhetoric, is yet another of the 'unintended consequences' of the aggression.

Militarily the most significant force fighting Bush and Blair is the Ba'ath Party. As a general rule of thumb the more straightforwardly 'military' the resistance operation, the more likely it is to have been mounted by former soldiers, policemen and militia loyal to the previous regime. Suicide operations are, generally, carried out by either Iraqi Sunni fundamentalists or the so-called 'foreign fighters' (neither the nationalists nor the Islamists recognize the concept of other Arabs being 'foreigners' – Iraq was the only Arab country where any Arab had the right to come and live, without visa or other encumbrance, as part of the Ba'ath Party's pan-Arab ideology). The higher the disregard for civilian casualties, the more likely it is to have been carried out by non-Iraqis. The more sophisticated the operation – for example, the blowing up of oil pipelines and installations, the mass storming of isolated police stations, the putting to death of the puppet forces inside and the release of those held there – the more likely it is to have been carried out by, say, former members of the now disbanded Republican and Special Guard.

But all factions are learning from each other. Islamists are now turning to non-suicide operations and growing smarter – especially the Shiite Mehdi Army, the force loyal to the young Shiite cleric Muqtada as-Sadr, whose use of improvised explosive devices detonated from the roadside against convoys and patrols is described so vividly by the *Wall Street Journal*'s scribe. And nationalists are themselves turning to tactics they hadn't considered before, like suicide attacks and the taking and killing of hostages. In short, the military and the political paths of all the resistance forces operating in Iraq are slowly beginning to converge. Their nationalist leaders at least hope that a unified command and a single national liberation front will emerge as a result.

But even these classifications can mislead. For example, many of those fighting are now ready to describe themselves as 'Saddamists', but they are not Ba'athists. Such fighters would say that the Ba'ath Party's re-invention of itself as a party of God was insincere. Saddam Hussein on the other hand they regard as a true Muslim, a 'Mujahid' (holy warrior) who was brought down not because he was bad but because he stood up to Israel and the United States. Equally many Ba'athists would now say they were no longer Saddamists. Although many cling to the 'Good Tsar bad advisers' analysis – which blames the disastrous end of the party's rule not on the top man but on the likes of Taha Yassin Ramadan, the vice-president, or Izzat Ibrahim Durri, the real number two in the regime – many now openly condemn Saddam's mistakes. For such people – indeed for virtually all Iraqis – the most bitter denunciations are reserved for Saddam's sons Uday and Qusay, whose incompetence, corruption and all-round venality is widely condemned. This and the president's swing away from the norms of party life into rule by clique, extended family and clan are the most frequently cited gripes against the fallen leader.

Yet another unintended consequence of the American propaganda machine was the inflation of Saddam Hussein's reputation caused by his being publicly paraded before a kangaroo court while in chains. The occupation authorities thought this televised process would humiliate him, demoralize his supporters and persuade the Iraqi public that the beast was caged and soon to be put to death. Like so much else in this story, precisely the opposite occurred. The joke soon circulated in the Arab world that 'after 25 minutes the judge confessed'.

Prior to his appearance in court, the last picture people had seen of Saddam Hussein was of a man who looked like a bedraggled old tramp, dragged from a hole in the ground with US army medics shining lights into his mouth and ears. For many, it was a pitiable sight. Oh, how the mighty have fallen. In court, however, he had quite recovered his poise. Still bearded and wearing casual clothes, he amazed Iraqis by how well he looked. At first the Americans sought to deny them sound, ordering the broadcasters to air the pictures mute. This did not hold and when the sound was turned up, what Saddam had to say struck many chords. Asked his name, occupation and, absurdly, his address by the somewhat juvenile judge, Saddam replied thus: 'I am Saddam Hussein, president of the Republic of Iraq, and I live in the house of every Iraqi.'

Many cheered from the Atlantic to the Gulf. Not because they loved Saddam or because they were oblivious to his many blunders and crimes but because they had inwardly hated seeing an Arab leader dragged from a hole by American invaders. For them a lion, albeit mangy, had roared again.

Charged with invading Kuwait, Saddam pressed the button marked history and regurgitated Iraq's historic complaint against fake colonial boundaries. He stirred ancient enmities about the Persians to the east, the Zionists to the west, the foreigners who were always desperate to keep Iraq divided and weak.

Such was the bravura performance, it is unlikely that the puppet authorities will produce him in court again. Events unexpectedly have produced an unlikely phoenix among the ashes in Iraq – the symbolic reputation of the dictator Bush thought he had laid low. To some extent, though more slowly, a similar process has begun in the west. A letter to the *Guardian* newspaper written with a dash of irony in the autumn of 2003 and in the wake of the collapsing reputations of the coalition leaders said, 'Nowadays you can't believe a word any politician says. Except Saddam Hussein on the issue of Weapons of Mass Destruction.'

So, amazingly, it is now possible to say, as the leader of the Sunni Islamist resistance (who has a dozen profound reasons to hate Saddam Hussein) said to me, 'Most Ba'athists are no longer Saddamists and most Saddamists are not Ba'athists – and if there was a genuinely free election in Iraq right now, the Saddamists would be the largest party. Except they would not be a party but a collection of very different Islamic and nationalist tendencies.' There are others fighting. Cells of very young men form and reform on the basis of family (to avenge the mistreatment or martyrdom of a family member), street, town, city, confession, religion, patriotism. Others fight because the remnants of the old regime have money – and in the most crass blunder made by the occupiers the entire Iraqi Army was dismissed, all dressed up and nowhere to go and no wages to go with. These old soldiers, like the itinerant soldiers from the Kaiser's Army in Weimar Germany, are bitter, angry and broke. The resistance has work for their idle hands and salaries to put food on their families' tables. But the overwhelming majority of the Iraqi people support the resistance, which was estimated over a year ago by the CIA as being 50,000 strong. Polls taken – under military occupation – show as few as 7 per cent now want the British, American, Polish, Italian and other 'foreign fighters' to remain. It is a self-deluding fantasy to describe this as a 'terrorist' or bandit problem. More deluded still is the idea that if the Yanks get lucky and get such ringleaders as Zarqawi this will make any difference to the level of fighting. These tens of thousands are seen and see themselves as a patriotic resistance. As former war-cabinet member Clare Short put it in her controversial 2003 interview in Dubai, they are the heirs of the American revolutionists against British colonial rule, or more contemporarily the French resistance to Nazi occupation and the Palestinian resistance to Sharon.

And they have been stunningly successful. They have the occupiers on the run. They have killed well over a thousand western soldiers – from democratic countries where each of these deaths is a political depth-charge to the ship of state. They have maimed well over ten thousand westerners, many of them – one in ten – to the extent of the amputation of their limbs. Mental illness among soldiers, refusal to serve, desertion, going AWOL, suicide, wife beating, poor morale and unrest within servicemen's families are all among the ancillary damages being sustained by the occupiers. The resistance has changed everything. What began as an exercise in demonstrating the extent of American power has ended up demonstrating the opposite. As Chairman Mao once said, 'Sometimes the enemy struggles mightily to lift a huge stone – only to drop it on its own feet.'

The resistance has brought the neo-con Bush juggernaut to a shuddering halt. They can control the skies (as long as they stay out of RPG range) but they cannot control a single street in non-Kurdish Iraq. Even the so-called 'Green Zone' in Baghdad is insecure. The resistance can and does strike at will; in the 'hero city of Fallujah', in Samarra, Ramadi, Mosul, Baquba, Hilla, Najaf, Basra and all over Baghdad the occupiers treat each day as if it might be their last. They are no longer confident of reaching the end of each patrol alive or undamaged. The resistance have thus stopped in its tracks any early possibility of a US invasion of Syria or Iran – or for that matter Sudan. Bush and Blair know they have bitten off more than they can chew, and that their electorates will simply not swallow any new wars. The political systems in the countries which launched the war continue to reverberate with rage against the dying of the light of clean honest government, civil liberties and their country's reputation abroad. In Spain Aznar's conservatives fell after being caught out in one lie too many when they sought to deceive their own people about the provenance of the Madrid train bombings. In America a new radicalism is on the march. It forced first Howard Dean to the front of the Democratic queue, then, when he imploded, it succeeded in flip-flopping John Kerry from pro-war 'bring 'em on' hawk over Iraq into making opposition to the war the number one weapon in his armoury. More than half of the US thinks that Bush misled them over the war and are unlikely to back him in another. The President it is true was re-elected, but only just. Bush's victory was the narrowest win for a sitting president since the First World War. John Kerry, dubbed 'the number one liberal in the Senate', who ran an increasingly explicitly anti-war campaign, won more votes than had either Reagan, Bush the First, Clinton or Gore. Opinion polls showed that 56 per cent of Americans think their country is headed in the wrong direction, and 51 per cent think the Iraq war wasn't worth fighting. This is unprecedented in a country like America where 'my country right or wrong' runs through the veins of the society and which has attacked more than fifty countries since the Second World War and always with its public's consent.

In Australia, the Labor Party – in all other respects a carbon copy of Blairism – was forced to fight the recent election on a ticket of outright opposition to the participation by Australia in the occupation. In Italy, along with his many other problems, Tony Blair's face-lifted, hair-transplanted dancing partner Silvio Berlusconi will face the wrath of a 90 per cent anti-war population in the forthcoming Italian elections. Politically, Berlusconi is now one of the walking dead, killed by his government's decision to attack and occupy Iraq.

In Poland Prime Minister Leszek Miller was forced to stand down, caught in a pincer movement of Catholic and left-wing opposition to Poland's role in the occupation. Reports of Polish withdrawal of troops are growing more frequent. If they do they will follow Spain, El Salvador and the Philippines in having been forced out of the Coalition of the Killing between the hammer of the Iraqi resistance and the anvil of their own public opinion. But it is perhaps in Britain that the reverberations have most undermined trust in the prime minister, the government, parliament, the political class and the mainstream media. The Hutton Report, whitewash though it was, began the job of smoking out the almost militarized mendacity in which the Blair clique is now ensnared. By exposing e-mails, which would never otherwise have seen the light of day, between No. 10, the intelligence services and the Ministry of Defence it began to be plain that there had been a conspiracy at the very top of the modern British state. The Butler Inquiry established this conspiracy beyond a shadow of a doubt. The so-called Pentagon Papers – revealed in the London *Evening Standard* last September by the same Andrew Gilligan who had been one of the first casualties of the Blair–Campbell counter-offensive – established the international dimension of the conspiracy. These showed that at the time Mr Blair was telling parliament – June 2002 – that there were 'no preparations for war' being made by his government, he had in fact sent our very top military brass to Tampa, Florida, for exactly those preparations. The Foreign Secretary Jack Straw may have thrown away his glasses (part of his leadership-bid makeover) and been unable to spot a looming and controversial handshake with Robert Mugabe at the United Nations as a result, but he was able to read the writing on the wall for Blair. His leak – to the *Daily Telegraph* – of the whole file of correspondence between himself, his officials and Downing Street in the run-up to the war not only revealed his own deep misgivings about Blair's policy but demonstrated without doubt that Blair and Bush made the decision jointly to go to war almost a whole year before Blair told parliament and people that the time had come. Meaning that everything Blair said and did in between had been a calculated deception. The deepening crisis over Iraq and Britain's role has already utterly dwarfed the rest of Tony Blair's period as prime minister. It will be the only thing on which history judges him. It is written all over his face that he knows already what that judgement will be. Like Lady Macbeth, he is trying everything to expunge that 'damned spot', but all the perfumes of Arabia, all the Africa Commissions, relaunches and the bringing back from the political dead of new great white hopes like Alan Milburn will never succeed in washing away what he has done. The media is making up for lost time, pursuing him now relentlessly. The opposition, which once backed him, now openly opines that he is a liar. Robin Cook and Clare Short continue their relentless bombardment of his position, from the commanding heights of having once sat at his right hand. The Stop the War Coalition continues to raid and harry him at every turn. But all of these can only do so, and the audience for them was wholly created, because of the fighters of the Iraqi resistance.

If the occupation of Iraq had not been assailed relentlessly then Iraq would long have faded from the domestic political agenda. The skullduggery of our leaders would have been forgiven by all but the most pure of political opponents of the war. Treason, it is said, never prospers, for if it prospers, none dare call it treason. We can openly say that Tony Blair betrayed us mainly for the reason that his treachery never prospered, indeed has failed disastrously. For that, we must thank the Iraqi resistance. There have been and will be again many times when the actions of the Iraqi resistance have horrified, even repelled their most enthusiastic admirers. But as Tariq Ali, the writer and veteran anti-war leader, wrote, 'If occupation is ugly, how can resistance to it be pretty?'

To western eyes, the ugliest of the acts of resistance groups has been the taking and killing of foreign hostages – especially of course Western hostages (the killing, for example, of Nepalese cooks goes as un-remarked as the killing of most Iraqi civilians).

The day poor Ken Bigley was ruthlessly beheaded, bringing to an end a cruel ordeal which amounted to torturing a prisoner, the US Air Force killed at least ten guests at a wedding party in Fallujah. Of course, this slaughter was barely mentioned on that evening's news or in the next day's papers. That evening Tony Blair emoted before the cameras. 'I feel utter revulsion at the people who did this, not just at the barbaric nature of the killing, but they way they played with the situation over the past few weeks.' Blair was talking about the wicked way in which Ken Bigley's last weeks of life were toyed with. He expressed no revulsion whatsoever at the massacre of the wedding party for which he was co-responsible, as the joint occupier of Iraq.

Like the dozens of British soldiers who, like Bigley, have paid the 'blood price' for the special relationship with George Bush, Bigley's blood was on Blair's hands. True, Blair bore less responsibility for Ken Bigley's death than for the deaths of British servicemen or Iraqis – because Bigley volunteered to work in Iraq, for at least £1,000 a day. By contrast, once British servicemen have joined up, they go where they are ordered and they get paid much less. And when they are killed, their families don't get called up by the Prime Minister or visited by the Foreign Secretary.

What was the work Mr Bigley was doing at the time he was taken hostage? After his death, both Blair and Straw gave the impression that he was engaged in making life better for the Iraqis by doing some sort of reconstruction work. Straw said on 8 October 2004 on the Foreign Office's website, 'He was in Iraq for no other purpose than to earn his living by working for the benefit of the Iraqi people.'

Sadly, there is no other way to describe this than as a lie. Mr Bigley was in fact working for the US military. The Press Association on 24 September described him thus: 'He was working at an American military base at Taji 15 miles north of the Iraqi capital for Gulf Supplies and Construction Services, his employers since 1997. The UAE-based firm protects equipment and camps for the US military and Mr Bigley was part of a team fulfilling a £5 million US Army contract to provide "base-camp life support".'

Ken Bigley didn't carry a gun, but painful though it is to recount, for the resistance he was a part of the military occupation. Blair and Straw successfully kept this from most of us on the day of his death. The purpose of their deceit was to portray his killers as merely evil, barbarians who even beheaded humanitarian workers. The conclusion we were meant to draw from this is that it is Britain's duty to stay in Iraq to save the Iraqi people from this evil and prevent it spreading around the world.

Our government also lied about the hostage-takers' demands, which were for the release of two Iraqi women prisoners. Straw said that this demand could not be met because 'there are no women prisoners in our custody in Iraq'. But there were. Iraqi scientists Huda Salih Mahdi and Rihab Rashid Taha – trained by my parliamentary colleague and Chairman of the House Committee on Science, Dr Ian Gibson MP. These two women had been interned without trial for eighteen months because many years ago they had worked on Iraq's biological weapons programmes, at a time when Western governments were providing the wherewithal for the programmes. Physically, they were held by the US military. However, they were supposed to have been transferred into the legal custody of the so-called Iraqi Interim Government at the end of June, thus, according to the fiction of the handover of sovereignty, their fate was now a matter for the Iraqis rather than the US military. On 22 September 2004, the BBC reported that Dr Gibson's former student, Miss Taha, was going to be released the next day, quoting a spokesman for the 'Iraqi Justice Ministry'.

Within hours and in a statement that constituted a death warrant for Mr Bigley, the US military authorities stated bluntly that Miss Taha was in their hands and would not be released.

Straw was playing word games when he said that there were no women prisoners 'in our custody': as if we and the Americans were separate legal entities in the occupation of Iraq. We are alas nothing of the sort.

Blair, Straw and the other hypocrites all claimed to be shocked and outraged at the fact of the cold-bloodedness of Bigley's killing and its method.

But in what sense, sickening though it is, is beheading with a knife more or less barbaric than murdering from the sky by bomb, rocket or missile or heavy artillery, tank, mortar or rifle fire? The F16, the helicopter gunship, or artillery piece deployed from a kilometre away is a vastly more indiscriminate method of killing. The key difference is that it is a much more impersonal business for the killer, who can go on, perhaps indefinitely, without his conscience being troubled, as if playing a video game, never feeling his victim's warm blood on his hands. For Blair and Straw, obviously that's not barbaric.

Why then did I try to intervene to save the life of the aid worker Margaret Hassan?

There were many reasons. Margaret Hassan was not a foreigner who had arrived in the train of the US–UK invasion of Iraq. She was an Iraqi citizen who had spent thirty years in Baghdad, staying there during the dark days of sanctions and war and opposing both to everyone she was able to reach. Mrs Hassan did not come to Iraq to make money – in fact, she and her husband could have left for the West during a sanctions era in which families were living on less than half a dollar a day. The story of how I attempted to intervene can now be told for the first time.

In the early hours of 30 October 2004, I received a call from Baghdad, from a person whom I knew to be in touch with the nationalist currents in Iraq. He indicated that if I were to make a public intervention on behalf of Margaret Hassan there was a good chance that my voice would be heard. Unlike other voices – Blair, Straw and Bertie Aherne, the Prime Minister of an Irish Republic that claimed to be neutral yet was allowing one thousand American soldiers per day to use Shannon airport to transit occupation forces to and from Iraq.

As it happened, that very morning I was due to make an address to the first annual conference of Respect – the anti-war party. I decided to alert the Arab and other media that, for the first time, I would make an intervention calling for the release of a hostage. By mid-morning I had secured the agreement of the Arabic TV station Al Jazeera to clear six minutes of their main news bulletin for me to make a straight-to-camera appeal for Margaret Hassan's release.

Just before lunchtime, I said the following to the hundreds of Respect Conference delegates and the cameras of Al Jazeera, Abu Dhabi TV and Arab Network News and their viewers in the Middle East beyond:

I want to make an appeal to whichever of the groups within the Iraqi resistance is holding Margaret Hassan. I hope that you know me and that you know of the long years and great efforts I made to try to avert the destruction of your country and the suffering of your people. I hope that you know that my struggle has continued: the struggle for the release of Iraqi prisoners and to highlight the torture to which many of them have been subjected. And the struggle against Britain's role in the occupation in which we have advanced the slogan: 'Not one more British soldier, not one more inch of British occupied territory in Iraq, Troops out now!'

I have called from the beginning of the occupation for all foreigners – with the exception of legitimate, genuine journalists – to leave Iraq. I have said that Iraq has no need of foreigners in the country at this time. Often, when prisoners are taken, we hear that the person was only there to help the Iraqis rebuild their country. Iraq, which contained the world's greatest library almost a thousand years ago, when my ancestors were still painting their faces blue and living in the forests, has no need of such foreign help. Many have come to Iraq to feast upon its suffering, making money from the parcelling out of its wealth. Many others are indirectly making the illegal occupation of the country possible, providing logistical support.

But the person I want to talk to you about is not a foreigner . . .'

I then described the life of Margaret Hassan before looking straight into the eye of the camera and saying this:

I am asking you in my own name to treat her as if she were my sister and not to harm her. Nobody asked me to make this appeal and certainly not the war criminal Tony Blair.

This was to be the basis for my direct and live six-minute Al Jazeera appeal that evening. Just seconds of it in brief news summaries was ever broadcast. Why?

At around 7 p.m. – two hours before I was due at Al Jazeera – I picked up a telephone message from one of my mentors, Tony Benn. In it he said that he was passing on a message from Margaret Hassan's sister. I did not know she had a sister in England and I don't know how that sister knew Tony Benn's telephone number. Suffice to say, he conveyed to me in the strongest terms that Mrs Hassan's family (at least in

England) did not want me to say or do anything on her case. Seeing the yawning chasm of a public relations disaster opening up in front of me, I immediately decided to return a phone call I had deliberately not responded to from earlier in the day. One of the backroom staff of Respect, the redoubtable Rob Hoveman, had taken a call from the British Foreign Office, who, having presumably caught a glimpse on Arabic TV of my earlier speech, were desperately keen to talk to me. I did no respond because I wanted to be able to say – if I did get into a negotiating situation with Mrs Hassan's captors – that I had had no contact whatsoever with Britain's occupying government. Now, I felt, I had no choice. I will not name the Foreign Office official with whom I dealt over the next two hours. Although the official claimed to be acting on their own initiative, I did not believe them. If I had, I would now be naming that official. But so important and ultimately tragic were subsequent events to become, I cannot imagine other than that the official was acting under ministerial orders. I called and was immediately assailed with the argument that what I had said so far was potentially disastrous and that I must say or do no more. I was told that the government had a plan and that the family were furious with me for my intervention. Exactly what had I said? the official demanded. And what did I intend to say and do next?

Scotland Yard had people on the ground, the official said. We don't want to internationalize the situation – we want to keep it a purely local, Iraqi affair. I could be jeopardizing the government's plan.

I hope it's a better plan than the one that killed poor Ken Bigley, I said.

Why can't we work along parallel lines? I said. After all, I had been spurred to make the intervention from sources in Baghdad. Who knows, I said, maybe I'll have more chance of getting her out than your plan.

They are not parallel plans, the official tartly replied. Your line crosses our line, the official said with emphasis.

Clearly, I could not now proceed with my initiative, in defiance – I had to assume the official was telling the truth – of Mrs Hassan's family. But what was I now to do about my six-minute slot on Al Jazeera's flagship news broadcast.

Cancel it, the official said.

At least five phone calls then flew back and forward between us.

It's gone down like a lead balloon with Al Jazeera, I said. They're insisting I use the time in some way, I said.

On your own head be it, the official replied – a little too impertinently for my liking. MPs don't work for civil servants – it's normally thought to be the other way around.

I then negotiated with Doha, Al Jazeera's HQ, who were furious with me. In the end, failing to get an assurance from them that they would not mention Margaret Hassan's name or cause me to, I was forced to pull out of the programme altogether.

I never heard from that official again. Even when a few days later, I received the following e-mail from Baghdad:

A letter from Al Jihad brigades in Iraq ... To Mr George Galloway with respect

To the English and Catholic ... Mr George Galloway ... Kind regards and respect ...

We were extremely happy to know about your newly established British party. We were also filled with joy as we heard your kind appeal to the Iraqi resistance to release Margaret Hassan. We respect your kind appeal as well as your stance and your general support for all Arab and Muslim causes, especially in Iraq and Palestine.

For all these reasons, we wish to address the following to you and every person who has been supporting us:

Firstly, we congratulate you for your newly born British party which you have established, and hope that you will remain the supreme leader of that party, and that you will continue to fight for justice and human rights, especially in regard to the Arab and Muslim causes.

Secondly, we in the Arab and Muslim world regard you and people who share your similar stance as an oasis in the middle of our desert!

While European leaders were exercising the most vicious acts on us and humiliating our Umma, you and many others – such as Roger Garudi and Ramsey Clark – stood honourably and firmly defending and supporting us. We are proud of that, and appreciate your stance, especially that many people who call themselves Arabs and Muslims did not give to our Umma what you have given.

Thirdly, we in the name of the Iraqi people and in the name of the Iraqi resistance would like to give you and your party our support . . . in fact all the support . . . as we would like to prove to those who are in the west, that whoever gives us his hand to support us, we will give him our arm to support him, whoever comes walking to us in support . . . we will run to him and give him ours . . . proving by this that our image is not as the western Zionists portray it . . . We are not a bunch of killers, or terrorists who are thriving for western blood.

We are the ones who taught others in meaning of civilization and respect for human rights, but we also love our country and we want to defend it, and we are willing to give our souls, our money and our children to defend our lands.

What did the west expect us to do, when such idiots like Tony Blair, George Bush and Berlusconi and many others, invade our country, slaughter our children, destroy our civilization, take over our wealth, take away our dignity, and destroy the image of our religion. Were they really expecting us to greet them with flowers? Or to defend our country, as all laws – whether human laws or Godly laws – give us the right to. It is our right to defend our country, and we shall keep defending our country against the occupation just as you – the west – have when under occupation.

Mr George Galloway, we have been witnessing for the past decade a vicious Anglo-American attack on everything that is Muslim; an attack on its culture, its land, its laws and its history. All this has caused us great misery and despair.

[The letter then goes into describing the effects of the Anglo-American policies/wars on both the Arab and Muslim world, including Iraq and Afghanistan of course.]

And these George Galloway are the reasons why we hate the west, hoping that you will forgive us.

However, because of your endless support to our causes, and your famous bus to Baghdad – which we will never forget – we would like to return your favour by supporting your appeal and sharing our voice with yours, we are calling our sincere brothers in the resistance to immediately release Margaret Hassan, as a gesture of respect and honour for Mr George Galloway, he who deserves all the respect and appreciation from us . . .

The e-mail then appended the text of a message they said they had addressed to the group holding Mrs Hassan:

Our hero brothers, who are holding Margaret Hassan, we ask you in the name of Allah, and in the name of our brotherhood, and in the name of the holy jihad, to release Margaret Hassan as a gesture of respect to the kind man . . . George Galloway . . . We are waiting for your kind reply.

It was dated Sunday 31 October 2004.

The next day, I called the Foreign Office and read this to them. I expected it might cause a flutter in the dovecot. It sounded like a useful lead to me. I was ready – despite the many difficulties I would undoubtedly have faced – to travel to Baghdad to follow it up. Alas, 'Carruthers of the FO' was completely uninterested. It was a seed which had fallen upon stony ground. That very day, the strategy of de-internationalizing the Hassan case – the treating of it was a 'local Iraqi affair' – saw Irish Prime Minister Bertie Aherne with the three sisters of Margaret Hassan making a heartfelt appeal for Mrs Hassan's release. Some weeks later, her body turned up. A video tape showing her execution had been sent: to Al Jazeera, the very station to which I had been on my way to try and save her life before Jack Straw's Foreign Office, for whatever reason, let down my tyres.

Of course, it may well have been that no one could have saved her. Her murder was a grotesque, unspeakable, incomprehensible crime. Whoever committed it – and there are very many strange and inexplicable elements to her tragic story – not only broke the hearts of her surviving relatives but disfigured the face of the Iraqi resistance. If, and it is a very big 'if', it was a resistance group which killed her.

For Iraqis, it is the intercommunal outrages – most notably the series of bomb attacks on Shi'ite worshippers in Najaf and Baghdad during the mourning of Ashura – which are most unreservedly condemned. If they were carried out by Sunni fanatics seeking to divide the country on confessional lines then almost certainly they will have been carried out by those with no interest in a united Iraq surviving and are likely to have come from outside Iraq's borders. Many Iraqis, however, believe that such outrages are carried out by the occupation itself, or by those collaborators who need it to continue. This will sound far-fetched, except to those who have read Graham Greene's *The Quiet American*, set in the early stages of the war in Vietnam, or seen the Michael Caine movie based upon it. It has been in fact a tried and tested tactic of both America and Israel to stage horrific outrages for political effect.

More controversially there is the vexed subject of the taking and killing of hostages. From the beginning of the occupation I and others warned all foreigners – with the exception of genuine journalists – to leave Iraq. It was, I said, going to be a war zone and there would be no 'third way'. To borrow a phrase from George Bush, foreigners there would be either with the occupiers or against them. The Iraqi resistance many times issued their own warnings to the same effect. Yet still, drawn like moths to a flame, foreign workers came, lured by the big bucks which were there to be had. The US has so far spent $200 billion of American taxpayers' money (the resistance has made sure that no profit has yet been possible from Iraq) on the Iraq war and occupation. Much of it has been handed to mainly US contractors and some of that has provided rich pickings for foreign workers. When they are captured by the resistance they are always there, their families say, to 'help the Iraqi people' or to 'help rebuild Iraq'. With all respect to obviously hopelessly distressed relatives, this is balderdash which certainly doesn't fool those who have captured the hostages. To come to Iraq to build military bases for the invaders is a crime which the resistance fighters will inevitably punish by death. This is an ABC of liberation warfare. To serve the occupation authorities in any way, even if it is only scooping out mashed potatoes in the US Marines canteen, is equally to make oneself an enemy of those struggling to liberate their country. Part of the privatization mania of the neo-cons running the war is to subcontract out as much of the war effort as they can. Consequently all manner of 'contractors', 'consultants', 'security staff' and technicians of all kinds are in fact thinly disguised essential personnel of the occupation. They are legitimate targets for acts of resistance – and have been throughout history. Don't forget that if, as Kofi Annan said, the war on Iraq was illegal then the only people fighting lawfully in Iraq are the Iraqi resistance. Inevitably a heart-rending human tragedy unfolds whenever one of these hostages is taken, held in orange jumpsuits in a cage, maltreated, even killed. Forgotten is the fact that the jumpsuit and cage are US designs, made in Guantanamo Bay. Ignored is the fact that we have thousands of our own hostages – in 'Gitmo', at Bagram airbase in Afghanistan and scattered around in countries like Egypt, to whom we have sub-contracted the torture of allied prisoners. We are left oblivious to the fact that we ourselves are holding thousands of Iraqi hostages – held without charge or trial (indeed there is nobody with the lawful authority to try them) – at Baghdad airport and in the torture chambers of the likes of Abu Ghraib. Hostages of the resistance are no doubt treated horrifically. But they are not filmed being buggered, stripped, humiliated, dirty underwear placed over their faces, forced to perform sex acts on each other or being bitten by savage dogs in their naked private parts. That kind of pornography is a US army speciality. The whole world, it seems, stops in its tracks at the prospects of a westerner being killed by his captors. Yet in the same week Britain was fixated by the tragic fate of Kenneth Bigley more than three hundred Iraqis were killed by American bombing. Many of them were decapitated in their homes in cold blood by high-explosive rockets. Bush condemns the executioners, while he himself executed more Texan prisoners in the time he was governor of Texas than any governor in the history of the state. He condemns the method of execution while retaining obscenely close and profitable relations with the House of Saud – the most remorseless head-choppers in the world. The taking of hostages, the bartering of their freedom for money for the struggle or political concessions, and often their brutal slaying, is an historic and inevitable part of the asymmetrical war being fought out in the new colonial conflicts. We shall, I am sorry to say, have to get used to it, or get out.

In summary, Bush and Blair turned the world upside down, defaced international law, gutted the United Nations, destabilized the Middle East, and profoundly undermined their own political positions for reasons which turned out to be either deliberate lies or just downright wrong.

In the name of the war on terror they opened a new front, in which they are sunk as deep as the British Expeditionary Force in the mud of Flanders. They have recruited a whole army of new enemies and galvanized the legions of foes they already had. They are now locked into a battle they cannot win. Every attempt they make to try and win it engenders still greater levels of hatred against them and weakens internal cohesion in their own societies, forcing them in turn to abandon more and more of the very liberties and values which they claim as the jewels in the crown of their civilizations.

Two hundred years ago the legendary French statesman Talleyrand was told breathlessly, by an aide, of the murder of a political opponent. 'It's a terrible crime,' said the aide to the wise old fox Talleyrand, who replied, 'It's worse than a crime, it's a blunder.'

Such an epitaph seems perfect for the Bush and Blair war upon Iraq.

11

R.E.S.P.E.C.T.

'Respect: the Unity Coalition' was launched, out of the anti-war movement, to challenge Tony Blair's New Labour at the polls. One of the best things about its name is that we get to use one of the greatest hits in popular music on our bandwagon. Respect: it's a young word. It's a black word. It sums up perfectly the different world we seek to build. Respect others – their cultures, religions, interests; respect yourself; and respect the earth we are busily incinerating.

It's the first 'post-modern' name for an electoral political movement; most are one or other arrangement of the words The, Something, and Party.

With respect, we're different.

And best of all, the name was invented by an eight-year-old girl called Hope.

Little Hope Nolan was asked by her mother, the Liverpool journalist and activist Carmel Brown, what name she thought would be suitable for a movement like ours; a peace movement, a justice movement, an equality movement, a green movement. Hope, who with her mother, sister Seren and father Stuart had been on the anti-war marches, came up with two names. One was the 'Give all your sweeties to Hope Party'. The other was Respect.

The Unity Coalition was born out of the great anti-war movement, the peace and justice movement that sprang out of the post-9/11 conflicts. The Stop the War Coalition, although led from the left, followed a strategy of uniting the widest possible cross-section of the British public against the lurch to endless war and the whittling away of the hard-won civil liberties that allow us to live in a relatively free and democratic society.

Using war as an answer, said the coalition, would make all the world's problems worse. The Iraqis would resist foreign occupation and the country would become a blood-filled swamp. And not all the blood would be Iraqi. America was doing this for oil, for profit, for Sharon's Israel, for the recolonization of the Middle East. Terrorism would get worse, not better; the war would give a massive impulse to extremism, fundamentalism, scarring the face of the world for a generation. The British people want more, deserve more, than to see their government reduced to the status of tail to a stupid and vicious dog.

Unity can only be built on the basis of respect for the points of view and the sensibilities of others. The leadership of the Stop the War Coalition itself contained strands of opinion never before united – Muslims, peace activists, feminists, Jews, orthodox communists, Sikhs, Trotskyists, Greens, trades unionists, Christians, town and country people, young and old, black and white – from all political backgrounds, including traditional Labour people disgusted at the role of their government. All these strands were woven into the greatest mass movement the country has ever seen.

Look at some snapshots. A group of ultra-Orthodox Jewish rabbis walked all the way from North London (it was their Sabbath) to march at the head of an anti-war demonstration. Muslims who were fasting during Ramadan arranged Iftar (the breaking of the fast) when they reached Trafalgar Square. Thousands of school students – a phenomenon which hadn't been seen since the early seventies – marched out of classes 'on strike' against the war. Ladies from the Cotswolds carried sweetly handwritten placards saying things like 'War will be a very bad thing . . .', or the very English 'Make tea not war'. Although the British anti-war movement was not the biggest in the world – that honour belonged to Spain, closely followed by Italy – it was arguably the most important, certainly the most surprising and definitely the most inspirational. 'It's like Hyde Park!' became a benchmark for anti-war events from Cairo to Vancouver.

And it almost did stop the war. The movement created the most serious crisis for Blair, both in the House of Commons, where he faced the biggest parliamentary revolt against a government since the days of the Duke of Wellington 170 years before, and in the country, where opinion polls showed the people to be deeply split, roughly fifty–fifty (and this before his case for war was unmasked as a tissue of lies). Blair told us himself, in his interview with his muse Trevor Kavanagh of the *Sun*,[1] that he had gathered his family in the Downing Street salon – a rather touching scene if a shade melodramatic – to tell them: 'Look, I might lose my job over this.' We know that the British military top brass – never that keen on the war from the start – were ordered to prepare a contingency plan that would involve withdrawal of British troops from the region just before the war. That was the trigger for Donald Rumsfeld's apparently clumsy declaration just before the start of the war that 'we can do it alone'[2] if Britain had to withdraw through a vote in parliament.

In any case the sheer scale of the opposition (and the outcome thus far of the war and occupation) has made it impossible for Tony Blair to join any new American military adventures, and thus in all likelihood has stopped such wars as were being planned. It exacted a heavy political toll on him, wiping billions off his prime ministerial 'share price'.

And it's not over yet. The war and subsequent occupation of Iraq has been a political earthquake that reverberates still. Nearly two years after the war the issue continues to dominate the news. Practically every day the discrediting of the mendacious case for the conflict takes another twist. The Hollywood-style presentation to the United Nations made on the eve of the war by General Colin Powell, Bush's Secretary of State – where he quoted Tony Blair's 'exquisite' and soon to be ridiculed 'dodgy dossier' – now stands contradicted even by the Iraq Survey Group picked by Bush to find, or plant, the incriminating evidence. The head of the ISG, David Kay, a hawkish Republican, resigned saying there are no stockpiles of banned weapons in Iraq and may never have been since the early 1990s – just as the Iraqi regime had claimed all along. Later General Powell would say that it was now 'an open question'[3] whether or not Iraq had the weapons he himself had so confidently described as his case for war before the Security Council. At this rate, the anti-war movement may yet hold Tony Blair finally to account for the great blunder, the great crime he has committed. Either Britain has an incompetent fool for a prime minister, who has made the gravest possible mistake. Or we have a brazen liar. But whether fool or knave we surely have in him someone who is not fit to be at the helm of a great country.

Housed in the basement of the lecturers' union NATFHE and staffed largely by volunteers, the Stop the War Coalition spawned 500 local groups, thousands of local activities and national demonstrations of people numbering in the millions. It hit the ground running and never stopped.

When the Egyptian president Hosni Mubarak visited the little studio complex in tiny Qatar of the Al-Jazeera television network, he famously remarked: 'All this noise coming from this little shoebox?' Any visitor to the ramshackle King's Cross headquarters of the Stop the War Coalition might have said the same.

But the failure to stop the war demonstrated the limits of the politics of protest.

- We could march in unprecedented numbers but hundreds of sheep in the House of Commons could still flock into the lobbies for the slaughter of war.
- We could speak for at least half the country yet still hardly get a look in on the media, including the corporation we paid for through our BBC licence fee.
- We could represent the majority of trade unionists yet still be let down by the apparatchiks of the TUC.
- We could find an echo among most Labour people but we could still be denied a vote or even a debate in the Labour Party conference.

In the midst of a great movement of tens of millions in Europe, the British representatives in the European parliament could vote to back the war, confident that scarcely anyone knew who they were, or cared. Scarcely an elector in the land could name two of them, a body of men and women not even legends in their own households.

The marchers walked straight into the brick wall of the power-lessness, the disenfranchisement, of the mass of the British people locked out of the mainstream political system.

And so we have decided to try to knock down that wall.

I had been thinking, and later talking – *sotto voce* – about the need for such a demolition squad throughout the emergency.

I first raised it with the *Guardian*'s Seumas Milne and Stop the War Coalition chairman Andrew Murray, both longstanding and close comrades of mine, in a Greek restaurant in Camden nearly a year before the Iraq war, when it became obvious to me that Blair and Bush had secretly embarked upon the path to slaughter – whatever the people thought. The next day I discussed it with John Rees and Lindsey German, influential in organizing the coalition and the most important 'power-couple' on the British left since Nye Bevan and Jennie Lee.

I was then still a member of the Labour Party, but, as I told a horrified meeting of the Labour Left Briefing (a left-wing but 'Labour to the end' group) around this time, I could not guarantee that I would remain so. My show-trial was held at the headquarters of the Iron and Steel Trades Confederation in London's King's Cross on 22 and 23 October 2003.[4] I had been promised it would be dealt with before the Labour conference, which took place three weeks before, but in the end the hearing was delayed deliberately so that the matter could not be raised on the conference floor. It was the first straw in the wind. The Blairites were out for my blood.

The tight-lipped Mrs Malaprop – Rose di Georgiou Burley – chairing the panel could not have made her intentions plainer had she dangled a noose throughout the proceedings. Or if like the Tricoteuses – the women who attended the bloodfest of the Terror in the French Revolution – she had knitted her way through the testimony of the Rt. Hon. Michael Foot, the former leader of the party, the Rt. Hon. Tony Benn, the former Cabinet minister and at fifty years in the House the party's longest-serving MP, Tony Woodley, the newly elected leader of Labour's largest affiliate, my own union, the TGWU, and not least Mark Seddon, the talented young editor of *Tribune* and member of the party's National Executive Committee.

Burley and I had history, if indirectly. She was married to the legendary Wally Burley, a right-wing apparatchik of the Wilson–Callaghan years. When I was a full-time Labour organizer Burley was the head of the sweetheart association the National Union of Labour Organizers (NULO). He hated me and everything I represented then. I was young, he was old. I was left, he was right. I saw my job as being the organizer of Labour victories, he saw his as keeping the left at bay. Later he would play a key role in the extirpation of the Militant group of Trotskyists – witch-hunted out of the party following Neil Kinnock's famous speech at the Bournemouth Labour conference in 1985.

As soon as I saw that Burley's wife Rose was to chair the Tribunal I felt I was doomed for the chop, because I knew her political outlook was similar to his. She was flanked on one side by a Darlington woman councillor, a dead-spit for Les Dawson – all folded arms, chins and bosoms. I have already forgotten her name. I never heard her voice. On the other sat a fat, red-faced Manchester union official whom I had felt was sympathetic. I had reasons for this. First, he winked at me several times at key moments of the trial. Second, important interlocutors, friends of mine with real influence in his union the GMB, told me he would be. Third, my union leader Tony Woodley had 'squared' his important ally, the new GMB leader Kevin Curran. I guess the ruddy representative just had a nervous twitch – or being named Jenkins he'd never forgiven me for the defenestration of his namesake Roy on my election to parliament in 1987. By the way, I never heard his voice either.

One voice I got to know well during the two-day hearing was that of the Labour Party's deputy general-secretary, the formerly far-left Unison union official Chris Lennie. Lennie was New Labour's sole witness, and the slovenliness of his preparation and presentation of the case has made him a laughing-stock in the Labour movement.

Lennie's stuttering, stammering, shambling incompetence and shameless distortion – even of words themselves – gained him star billing in Mathew Norman's popular diary in the *Guardian*. One line from Mathew summed up Lennie's performance.

Question: 'Are you not concerned, Mr Lennie, at the damage you are doing to the English language during these proceedings?' Answer: 'Is that relevant?'

I even had a history, again indirect, with the expensive QC hired by New Labour to prosecute me. James Goudie QC is a character right out of Dickens. Bumptious, pompous, sounding like a member of the royal family, Goudie, poor fellow, is married to Baroness Goudie, one of 'Tony's cronies' in the House of Lords. During most of the thirty

years I spent in Scottish Labour po
bag-carrier for my worst enemies. She v
'Solidarity' group, the right-wing backla
an adviser to, and seemingly inseparable
now a life peer and the former secretary-ge
used to call him before he became an arms s
sector and of no further interest to me, 'Robl
equally close to the late Donald Dewar, against who   y
took up arms in the 1970s in a battle which laste   death
(ironically, he once told the House he looked forwar   seeing me
carried out of the Commons in a box). Poor Mr Goudie, there had
been so many others labouring away in his marriage – Robertson,
Dewar, Hattersley, Blair . . . No wonder he seemed out of sorts during
our tribunal – going through the motions, knowing full well what the
outcome was going to be, knowing too that his wife wore the family's
ermine and that it was unlikely that he'd be able to snuggle up to her
on the red benches now filled with Robertson, Hattersley et al.

An indication of the pre-cooked nature of the outcome comes not
just from the most cursory glance at the transcript but from a couple
of bizarre postscripts. As I waited in an ante-room for the verdict, on
political death row, I switched on my mobile phone to pick up my
messages. One of them, which I've saved, was from Mohammad
Sarwar, Britain's first Muslim MP, calling me from Pakistan. In the
message, with remarkable clairvoyance, Sarwar – whom New Labour
intends to field in my seat in the next general election in Glasgow –
said he'd just heard the news of my expulsion from the party (this is
two hours before the tribunal brought in its 'considered verdict') and
how sorry he was, etc. Well, news obviously travels fast these days.

My expulsion was announced around 5 p.m. on Thursday
23 October. At 9 a.m. on Saturday 25th every member of my constituency Labour Party received in the post a considered letter – written
in good English, so clearly drafted by someone else – from Ian
McCartney, the Labour Party's 'chairman' (in fact this is a misnomer
as he is appointed by Tony Blair and better described as the prime
ministerial pouffe), explaining the reasons, many weeks before they
were officially issued, for my expulsion. If this letter really was produced after 5 p.m. on Thursday and delivered in Glasgow a little over

...ter, it is easily the most efficient direct mail operation ...'s history.

...thirty-six-year membership of the party was ended in a thirty-second statement by the fragrant Rose. 'You are expelled from the party forthwith.' I loved the forthwith bit. It was exactly the kind of Labour-speak she and I had grown up with. Right out of Lord Citrine's *ABC of Chairmanship*, which is filled with words like 'forthwith', 'outwith', 'homologate', 'move the previous question', and of course, as had been said to the likes of Aneurin Bevan, Stafford Cripps, S. O. Davis and other greater men than me: 'You are expelled from the party forthwith.'

I swear that it was just at that moment I realized where I'd smelt this Rose before. She works in the House of Commons, for the chairman of the Defence Select Committee, the lifelong 'Atlanticist' sometimes known as the Member for Pentagon Central, the Rt. Hon. Bruce George MP – one of my most inveterate Commons opponents and Chairman of the All-party Weight Watchers' Group.

There was no time to mope. As I walked out of that door another one opened. It is a door behind which lies a potential audience of millions of people. People who waited a long time for a Labour government only to find Tony Blair presiding over a grotesque carica-ture of what the Labour party stands for. People like the millions of trade union members whose financial and other contributions sus-tained the party over most of a century, yet were treated, in the words of John Monks, like an 'embarrassing elderly relative' locked away for the most part in the attic, out of sight. People like that have been systematically betrayed by New Labour, although you wouldn't know it if you depended on listening to the supine squeaks of complaint from some of the union leaders. In the immortal words of the great Ernest Bevin – founder of the TGWU and Attlee's Foreign Secretary – the party had been born 'from the bowels of the trades unions', yet in recent years it has treated the unions with contempt.

One of many groups of workers betrayed by New Labour was Britain's forty thousand firefighters. In 2002 the Fire Brigades Union, a loyal affiliate of the Labour Party for eighty-five years, who hadn't had an industrial dispute for a quarter of a century, launched a cam-paign for a professional salary for a professional service – £30,000 a year, or pay of £8.50 per hour. I spoke at the launch, the only politician to do so, atop a fire engine in Trafalgar Square, because of my twenty-five years of close involvement with the union. The FBU balloted its members – under the Thatcher anti-union laws which have not only not been repealed by Mr Blair but are acclaimed by him as a reason for capitalists to invest here – who voted by 9 to 1 for industrial action in pursuit of the claim. Given the immense popularity of firefighters within the general public – as men and women who at the behest of a 999 call will plunge, without question, into however severe a blaze to save our lives and property – Blair seemed to be risking a bonfire of his vanities.

When on 11 September 2001 the blood-streaked sky of New York began to fall, the world watched in awe as the firefighters, in the words of Bruce Springsteen, disappeared into the dust, up the stairs, into the fire, many to the darkness of a smoky grave.

But the union had underestimated the venality of the leagues of journalists who turned upon them when they struck – many of them earning three times as much as fire-crews for reporting cats stuck up trees or inflaming popular prejudices as columnists. But not as much as they underestimated the venality of New Labour.

Formerly militant Cabinet ministers who had recently voted themselves a 40 per cent pay increase and were at that moment planning to set fire to Iraq – their fifth conflagration abroad in five years – attacked them for endangering 'people's lives and properties'. For twenty years most white-collar workers had seen their living standards inexorably rise as pay, tax and public expenditure policies had been skewed towards them. Blue-collar workers, virtually unrepresented in parliament since the miners' strike nearly twenty years before, had been increasingly left behind. If their demands had been won, the firefighters might have blazed a trail down which postal workers, car workers and others might have followed.

Refusing to pay the firefighters their due was akin to injuring a loyal friend. But New Labour had to add insult as well. Led by that blustering donkey John Prescott they laid into the firefighters as the 'enemy within'. They were accused of being wreckers, agents of Saddam Hussein, saboteurs, lead-swingers, misogynists, racists, even fascists!

And then there were Britain's 11 million old age pensioners[5] – the generation that fought for the country, to defend the country – for a time (the only time we actually were under attack and under threat of invasion) entirely alone while the Americans watched the war on newsreel and might have gone on doing so had not the Japanese attacked them at Pearl Harbor and Hitler declared war on them (the US did not, as is frequently and falsely alleged, declare war on Nazi Germany). This generation, which built the wealth of the country, which paid for the National Health Service, and the other comforts of the Welfare State under which all the New Labour ministers grew up. The demands of pensioners' champions like Barbara Castle and Jack Jones for the restoration of the link between pensions and average earnings – which would boost pensioner income by the 26 per cent that has been stolen from them – was treated, like the demands of the firefighters for a professional wage, with unalloyed contempt. Our country, incomparably richer than it was in the 1970s, simply 'couldn't afford' justice for our old people, said New Labour. Our economy, the fourth largest in the world, would simply be 'wrecked' if we increased the living standards of our older people at the same rate as the rest of us.

Mrs Thatcher the 'milk-snatcher' (as Edward Heath's Education Secretary in the 1970s she ended the free provision of school milk, which had given 'old Labour' the calcium for a little more backbone) became the pension-snatcher, when in one of the first acts of her brutal premiership she axed the link between pensions and average earnings. Thus began a process that has robbed millions of pensioners of billions of pounds. The result has been the birth of 'grey power' – an army of dissatisfied militant pensioners, living longer and more vibrant lives than their fathers and mothers did, and able to deploy techniques like e-mail and the Internet. They are led by well-known figures from the British left – like Jones, more than ninety years young, Gordon McLennan, the former leader of the Communist Party, and Rodney Bickerstaffe, the outstanding retired trade union leader who built Unison, the country's largest union. But if these are the general staff, their army, like that of the anti-war movement, is deep and broad.

In the Home Counties and rural England pensioners' revolts against council tax rises well in excess of the rise in pensions threatened can't-pay-won't-pay rebellions. Some 'refuseniks' threatened to go on hunger strike. The crisis in Britain's pensions system is growing. Robber barons are increasingly found to have plundered or at least mismanaged company pension schemes. Increasingly they are scrapping such schemes altogether. The mis-selling of private pensions has led to the potential beggaring of huge numbers of pensioners coming on stream. This is an army whose numbers and alienation can only grow in the years to come. Respect aims to provide them with a potent weapon with which to fight for justice for Britain's 'Grey Warriors'.

Anyway, by expelling me New Labour took the decision about what was to be done out of my hands. I became free to proceed as I believed in my heart to be correct – with a political and electoral challenge to Blair.

This did not imply that I thought Labour was a closed book. I was born into the Labour Party and spent my life in it. I had left thousands of good people behind in it and was – and am still – committed to them. These people felt, as I had, that this was our party, stolen from us by 'here today, gone tomorrow' hijackers bent on flying the party to its destruction as a vehicle for social democracy.

The question was whether there were enough brave passengers left on board New Labour to take back control; and whether even if there were, the democratic space still existed in which they could do so.

New Labour's membership is sinking fast, and those still in the party are bound by draconian chains of bogus democracy and are being gagged, or in some cases are queuing up to gag themselves.

But the Labour Party has been over a hundred years in the making. It is a household brand in every sitting room in the land. It has hundreds of MPs, thousands of councillors and millions of voters. Even with its shrinking membership it still dwarfs every other organization on the centre-left of British politics.

The task of trying to re-create a party of labour, for the working people, outside its ranks, would be like climbing Everest. But so would any attempt to climb back into control of New Labour. Whether the north face or the south face turns out to be the harder remains to be seen.

Many of my friends have placed their faith in a campaign to 'Reclaim the Party'. I wish them luck. They will need it. I believe they will not succeed, but I sincerely hope that they do.

Any success achieved by Respect should not be seen as a threat to them but an opportunity. Surely, if it can be demonstrated that there is life outside New Labour and that the Blairites cannot take for granted the allegiance of swathes of voters – whom they are engaged in betraying on the assumption that such people have nowhere else to go – a counter-revolution will be more likely to take place in the Labour Party.

Respect's foundation conference took place on 25 January 2004. Attended by nearly 1,500 activists, it set itself an ambitious target: the bringing down of the Blair clique and the severing of the special relationship with George W. Bush. Respect: the Unity Coalition is the fastest-growing political organization in Britain. It is not the Stop the War Coalition in a different guise; many of STWC's members and supporters are Greens, Liberal Democrats, Nationalists, Labourites, even Conservatives. But it is an attempt to grow out of the anti-war movement a new political force against war and the causes of war. In most places the activists of Respect are the same people who made the anti-war movement such a huge force. Many of the leaders of the one are also the leaders of the other: John Rees, Lindsey German, Anas Al-Tikriti and Dr Azzam Tamimi of the Muslim Assocation of Britain, Mark Serwotka of the civil service union, the award-winning film director Ken Loach, Salma Yaqoob, one of the young women who have emerged to give the lie to the canards about the supposed 'subservience' of Muslim women.

Sometimes it's difficult to know, looking at a platform, whether it is a Respect meeting or a gathering of the anti-war movement.

Sometimes I'm on the platform and have to ask the others, 'Which of the two are we speaking for tonight?'

Put shortly, it is our case that it is not enough to be *FOR* peace. Without justice in the world there will be no peace. We believe that these kinds of wars do not come out of thin air, nor even occur because we have the misfortune to have lived through the era of the unholy alliance between Bush and Blair. Rather we believe that wars flow ineluctably from the prevailing social and economic system that now rules the world.

Imperialism needs wars. It needs wars to pump-prime the economy.

The military-industrial complex, the great war industries like Boeing, McDonnell Douglas, BAe are welfare junkies. That is to say their immense profitability depends upon the subventions of the taxpayer who must endlessly be frightened or dragooned into spending more and more on war or, to put it in Orwellian Newspeak, defence.

The governments give the tax-funded contracts to the military industries, which make a fortune and give some of it back to fund the re-election of the governments, who give them another round of contracts. It's nothing personal, purely business, capitalist-style; there is no McDonald's without McDonnell Douglas.

Of course, the war industries need their products to be used regularly so that new generations of weaponry can be demonstrated in these deadly 'live-firing' exercises, to show their paymasters what they can do and to terrify potential as well as actual victims. And then the stockpiling begins again.

The weapons are also exported to the pet dictatorships of their own governments who pay for them with their country's wealth, if it has any, or with their indebtedness if they don't. The utterly corrupt Al-Yamamah multi-billion-pound deal between BAe and the Saudi regime is a case study in this. The House of Commons Public Accounts Committee conducted a thorough investigation into the alleged widespread corruption involved in the contract to sell (and maintain) weapons systems to the Saudi regime, and then promptly decided never to release their findings. In a truly *Catch-22* scenario the British taxpayers pay for the weapons sold by British arms companies at the behest of the British government to foreign dictatorships who for one reason or another can't or won't stump up.

One such incident occurred in the early nineties, when Britain's export credit guarantee scheme paid up for the arms sold to a tin-pot dictator whom we had favoured but with whom we subsequently fell out. His name was Saddam Hussein; I wonder what happened to him?

Imperialism needs wars because it must dominate markets – and you can't get more dominating than physically invading and occupying another's country. Iraq is now being carved up and parcelled out like a succulent shawarma, and guess which companies are getting the choicest pieces? And it needs to be sure of the raw materials on which it depends for the fool's paradise; the orgy of over-consumption that is the lifestyle in the West, not just for the small elite but for a significant proportion of its population. And not just the availability of the raw material; after all, no government is going to leave under the ground any resources from which it could be earning big money. Imperialism's demand is to *control* the resources – the price, the rate of extraction or production, the pace of exploration. If Americans are going to drive their eight-miles-a-gallon 'Hummers', the General Motors civilian version of the military Humvee beloved of Governor Schwarzenegger and the 'only motor out of Detroit which sells without incentives', then not only must the oil keep flowing but the price must be right.

The US now physically occupies four Arab Gulf countries: Saudi Arabia, Iraq, Kuwait and Qatar. Between them these four have five hundred and fifty years of oil and gas under their soil and waters. By comparison the US has only twenty-five years' worth of reserves and Britain less than fifteen. You don't have to be Einstein to work it out!

But of course there are many other countries where there is a profusion of those things that the rich and powerful countries want to have without paying the proper price and without sharing them fairly with others. In the past they were simply taken, colonized, incorporated into what was openly celebrated as 'The Empire' (indeed, OBEs, MBEs, etc., today still commemorate the Empire, and shame on all who partake of it). Now the process has to be dressed up a little more elaborately, in the fine clothes of 'human rights', for example, 'humanitarianism' or, laughably from leaders who cavort on the floor with Rupert Murdoch, 'women's rights'.

One of the salient characteristics of Britain's anti-war movement today, as opposed to say the anti-Cruise missile demonstrations in the early eighties in which I was involved, is the crystal-clear understanding of all these arguments on the level of the activists and, judging by the responses of the crowds on the demonstrations, by a significant percentage of the supporters too.

This is the source of the optimism we share about the short- and medium-term prospects of Respect.

Our basic platform is simple but effective and in stark contrast to that of New Labour.

- No more participation in US wars.
- An end to the slavish obeisance to George W. Bush.
- An end to illegal foreign occupations, in Palestine, Afghanistan and Iraq – bring the British armed forces home.
- No more arms trading with General Ariel Sharon.
- Restoration of the link between our state retirement pension and average British earnings.
- An end to privatization of Britain's public services and the return of essential national utilities like the railways and air traffic control to democratic public ownership.
- A return to a truly National Health Service free at the point of need and funded from a progressive system of taxation; no more bogus Trojan Horse 'partnerships' with the private sector, no elitist 'Foundation' hospitals and no 'market-led' solutions in the service – the health of the nation is a public concern and not a business for profit.
- Scrap tuition fees and top-up fees for students; education spending is not a cost but a benefit, an investment in the country's future from which all of us benefit.
- Save Our Civil Liberties – put an end to the witch-hunting of minorities, immigrants, asylum seekers; the incitement of hatred against 'the other' is tearing apart the social fabric of our country. Restoration of the right to trial by jury and to legal aid, and the scrapping of plans for anti-libertarian so-called 'Identity Cards'. Close the immigration 'detention centres' – detention is for criminals who have been tried and convicted, not for those who fled here thinking they were coming to a free country.
- Restoration of trade union freedoms enshrined in the charter of the International Labour Organization; ILO standards are the UN-approved minimum conditions for the existence of free trade unionism; scrap the Thatcher anti-union laws.
- No to the Bankers' Euro, the anti-democratic European Constitution and the sublimation of our national sovereignty to unelected, unremovable European institutions. Yes to a People's Europe, No to the Europe of the Commission, the Eurocracy and the faceless remote mandarins who increasingly control our destiny.
- For internationalism but against so-called 'Globalization', a cover for the theft of the resources of the world by corporate brigands, the

homogenization of the cultures of the peoples of the world; let a thousand flowers bloom.

Foreign occupations are not the answer to the problems of Palestine, Afghanistan and Iraq; they are the main problem and no solution can be based on foreign troops endlessly fighting growing insurrections among the occupied people. These insurrections can only be described as 'terrorist' by those willing to sacrifice the English language as well as everything else to George Bush's 'War on Terror'. In any war of national liberation, truly horrific, sometimes indefensible, even inexplicable, things will happen. If military occupation is ugly, how can resistance to it be pretty? But the primary responsibility for those acts lies with those who have embarked upon illegal violent occupation of other people's countries. The Iraqi resistance are no more 'terrorists' than were the Maquis – the French Resistance – who tore the heart out of the German occupation of France by any means necessary, or the Greek, Italian, Yugoslav or Albanian Partisans. When the heroes of Telemark, the brave Norwegian Resistance fighters, in one of the most daring acts of the Second World War, blew up the German factory trying to produce heavy water for atomic-energy research on occupied soil, they were of course denounced as 'terrorists' by the Quisling collaborator government and their Nazi masters. But they were not; they were resistance fighters and moreover went on to star as such in their own movie.

This is why we say, bring the British army home from these occupations. We don't want our young men to kill or be killed in such an ignoble enterprise. We want them home with their families, not standing in the deserts of southern Iraq, a fatwa away from disaster in the inevitable uprising. Just a hundred yards away across the Clyde from my Glasgow constituency used to live a teenager called Gordon Gentle. He should be playing football today or preparing for a night out finding a girlfriend, thinking of marriage, a family, a life. Instead, he is dead in a box under the ground. Thanks to Bush and Blair. Gordon Gentle was a young Scottish soldier sent to die not for his country, but for the political vanities of dangerous fantasists. In that, he was like well over a thousand others from the coalition countries which invaded Iraq. Now, his brave mother with the beatific name Rose Gentle is touring the country as part of an embryonic 'families for justice' campaign of Forces families who have seen through the lies of our leaders. If the government does not bring our soldiers home safe and sound, undertakers will be doing so in increasing numbers in the years to come. This is not a wish on my part; it is the opposite of a wish. But it is the considered judgement of one who, alas, has been proved right already about all the major particulars of our long war against Iraq. Let the Iraqis work out their future for themselves, just as the 'regime-changed' countries of the former Soviet bloc have done and just as happened in the European countries Greece, Portugal and Spain after the 1970s overthrow of their military dictatorships. None of them needed British and American armies on their soil in order to create their new systems and neither do the Iraqis. If (and it is a big if) any outside assistance is needed in Iraq, then it will have to be drawn from the Arab world. Iraq is an overwhelmingly Arab country and it is to the Arab League that it should look for any help. But it shouldn't need much outside assistance to hold a free and fair general election, which is the overwhelming necessity now. By the rivers of Babylon they can organize the placing of a mark on a ballot paper and count up the results; it is after all the land where the alphabet was first written down in a place where mathematics was invented.

Although we are not directly participating in Israel's occupation of the Palestinian territories we are indissolubly linked to it by our history and by our association with the great power, the United States, which financially, militarily and diplomatically makes it possible. Blair's government has sold more weapons to Ariel Sharon than any previous British government to any Israeli government. These weapons – tank parts and avionics for the helicopter gunships and fighter jets that frequently dive-bomb the refugee camps of Gaza and the West Bank – the use of which was smoked out by me in parliamentary questions, are being used in and against the occupied territories by Sharon in defiance of international law and of assurances given by Sharon to Blair; assurances that he passed on to parliament and which proved to be worthless. The arms trading nonetheless continues.

It is not because we hate America that we refuse to be the tail to the American dog. It's because we love Britain and would refuse to be the tail of anyone. We acknowledge the special relationship that inevitably exists between Britain and the USA, on grounds of culture, language and history. We want a special relationship with the people of America. We just don't want the Lewinsky-type special relationship: one-sided, unequal, illicit, easily dispensed with by the more powerful partner and requiring the weaker partner to be endlessly on her knees.

We neither want nor need American bases on our soil. We don't want to be a forward base for the George Bush 'Star Wars' missile defence system that has its early-warning front line at Fylingdales in Yorkshire. We are an independent European country, not the fifty-first state of the United States of America.

Like the pigs on George Orwell's *Animal Farm*, who, having come to power decrying the two-legged elite that ruled Farmer Jones's roost, ended up themselves walking on two legs braying the slogan 'Four legs good, two legs *better*', New Labour's greatest betrayal of social democracy lies in the field of the public–private dichotomy. For them 'private good, public bad' is the fundamental apostasy, a mantra learned by rote from the previous Thatcher rulers and adopted by them, even though it represents the diametric opposite of Labour values.

An essential tenet of social democracy is that there are some things too important to the country, the nation, the society, to be left to the free market.

Roy Hattersley, the former deputy leader of the Labour Party, who used to be regarded as a right-wing Labour man, put this very well in an article in the *Guardian*.[6] He described how he had spent four long hot hours crawling along a motorway in England on a Sunday. None of the drivers in the traffic jam knew why they were being delayed but, as the slow miles unfolded, steam was almost literally coming out of the ears of the drivers as well as the radiators of their cars. Only towards the end of the journey did Hattersley realize the reason for the delay, which as he said had caused personal, environmental and no doubt economic havoc among the tens of thousands of drivers delayed. A very wide, very heavy boat was being transported on a low loader with police escort down the motorway. As Hattersley explained, the owner of this boat had made a private economic decision that suited his own private interests. Having calculated the cost of transporting this boat by sea or by rail he had decided his interests lay in taking it by road. In an untrammelled free-market system he was free to do so. But the real interests and well-being of everyone else on the road that day dictated a different decision. The public interest would have been served by regulating the activity of the boat owner, and forcing him to behave less selfishly. It would, no doubt, have been inconvenient and more expensive for the owner. But it would have been better, cleaner and cheaper for the rest of us.

The public good and the interests of private wealthy people are not always synonymous, indeed they very often clash and lie in opposite directions. Social democracy's historic mission is to fight the corner of those left trailing in the queue for the good things in life, those whom, if the local and national state will not stand up for them, will always be handed the short straw in life. It is this mission that New Labour has abandoned, and appears to glory in having done so. In Andy De La Tour's brilliant drama of New Labour's degeneration, the play *Question Time*, he puts the following gem in the mouth of an Old Labour retired trade union official, speaking to his daughter, a 'Blair babe' and wannabe cabinet minister. 'I've never shirked compromise; but tell me this? When does a Labour government, that carries out Tory policies, in the name of compromise, actually turn into a Tory government? When they no longer see them as compromises; that's when; when they start to believe Tory policies are better.'

This used to be the philosophical (or at least ideological) dividing line between the two big parties, and was summed up brilliantly by, ironically, the 'useful idiot' of the New Labour 'project', Neil Kinnock. It was intended as a counterpoint to an extraordinary speech given by Mrs Thatcher to the General Assembly of the Church of Scotland, at their headquarters on The Mound in Edinburgh. Naturally it became known as her 'Sermon on the Mound'. During the course of rewriting the Bible – she said that the Good Samaritan was clearly a Tory capitalist, not as we had long suspected an early socialist – Mrs Thatcher said that 'there is no such thing as society', only individuals. Kinnock's answer was magnificent and still gives me goose pimples. I know it by heart nearly twenty years on.

'No such thing as society?' he asked. 'No such thing as honouring other people's mother or father? No such thing as cherishing other people's children? No such thing as us, and always? Just me – and now. Me and now.'[7]

Free-market capitalism holds that society is merely a collection of atomized individuals making the best private decisions for themselves. Somehow, by alchemy perhaps, this we are told will produce a common good – with everyone behaving selfishly, pursuing their own interests first and foremost. On the philosophical level it is an absurd concept. Yet that concept has been implicitly accepted by the New Labour privateers. New Labour's first act was to privatize the national bank. The Bank of England had been nationalized by the post-war Labour government on the fairly standard notion that a state needs a central bank, answerable to the government for the purposes of monetary oversight. After all, none but the government can be allowed to set the tax rate for a country, so why would any state allow private individuals to set its interest rates, for example, when such a decision can be much more important in setting the national economic course? This privatization belonged with the many of which it could be said, 'Mrs Thatcher would never have had the gall to do that.' But New Labour did.

Having embarked on the privatization trail New Labour soon showed that was how they meant to go on.

'Our air is not for sale,' said the Brownite then shadow chief secretary to the Treasury Andrew Smith MP at the Labour Party's pre-election conference in 1996. He was referring to the Tories' outlandish proposal to privatize the air traffic control service – which would have made Britain the only country in the world so to do. It would have been a 'Railtrack in the skies', said New Labour spinners, an accident waiting to happen. Imagine putting the safety of millions of people – air passengers and those down below – in the hands of people whose first priority, by definition, would be to make a profit from the service. Shortly afterwards New Labour sold off our crowded skies. The accident has not yet happened; but if it does it will be still more blood on the hands of the Blair cabinet.

On the London Underground the same cavalier carelessness for passenger safety has been displayed. The Bechtel Corporation, whose day job is receiving contracts in Iraq worth billions of dollars from American politicians with whom they have an obscenely close corporate relationship, are moonlighting as the privateer of choice on the Tube – thanks to New Labour. Despite opposition from across the board, including that of the right-wing London *Evening Standard*, Gordon Brown insisted on railroading through yet another rip-off on the public good for the sole benefit of private interests.

In a moment beyond satire, the chocolate firm Cadbury offered to sponsor school sports, and the government welcomed the prospect of schoolchildren doing the hop, skip and jump into the arms of the purveyors of sweet, fat-filled calories. Why not? McDonald's, the pushers of greasy fat-filled junk food, are already in charge of 'Eating Zones' – what used to be called the school dinner hall – in schools throughout the land. Junk food may thicken the child but it is the thin end of the wedge of privatization of education.

Public Private Partnerships (PPP) or Private Finance Initiatives (PFI) are painted by the Blairites as a panacea for the crumbling school buildings and cramped overcrowded conditions left to them by the Thatcher era. Look, they say, new schools and brand new wings are rising everywhere thanks to the input of private finance. It is certainly true that if your family borrowed money from a local loan shark or money lender you could build that new conservatory you've been thinking about. But how would you pay it back? The cost of borrowing money at commercial rates is obviously much higher than if the state financed the school building itself, either from its resources or from money it has borrowed at the preferential rates only a state can obtain. And in many of these PFI–PPP scams the money is not a loan at all. The lender does not want his money back. He wants to remain a cuckoo in the nest, forever being endlessly fed resources as charges for his 'services' – what we used to call the school caretaker and the like – which would otherwise be available for the books and the computers and the sports fields for the children.

So, tell your kids to gaze at the wonders of the PPP phoenix rising from the ashes and tremble. For they will be paying the private financiers for that school throughout their lifetime, and so will their children yet unborn. And the public will never own these buildings – not until the end of time.

The devotees of the 'private good, public bad' cult know the price of everything and the value of nothing. That explains their constant search for ways of introducing 'market principles' into the most sensitive sector of all – the National Health Service. This was the jewel in the crown of the 1945 Attlee Labour government, the towering achievement of the legendary socialist Nye Bevan. Free health care provided equally for all from the cradle to the grave and paid for by collective contribution in a progressive tax system. This was once the single most defining characteristic of Britain in the capitalist world, a strong contrast to America, where in excess of seventy million people have no health insurance of any kind, tens of millions of people have only the most basic, and if you fall down in the street the ambulance man must feel for your wallet before he feels for your pulse.

Thatcher's introduction of the internal market into the NHS sparked an uprising of opposition. Royal Colleges made known their concerns, as did the unions, including the moderate RCN representing a section of nurses – the very 'angels' who enjoyed perhaps the highest public affection of any group of workers. Patients began to complain about the scant junk food snack-type catering being offered by private contractors who'd won competitive tendering contracts to feed vulnerable sick people in hospitals. And about how dirty the toilets were now that they were being cleaned not by hospital staff, but by even more lowly paid, more insecure, unmotivated workers from private cleaning companies. Rates of infections in British hospitals began to rise. New Labour, when in opposition, was regularly highlighting horrific stories about patients being bundled around the country from one hospital 'trust' to another, looking for a bed or a health board with any space left on its budget in order to treat their complaint. Patients were dying in transit, dying on trolleys in hospital corridors, dying on interminable waiting lists. The NHS – the best loved institution in the country – was being slowly murdered by the Tory government. Of all the many reasons why the British people fell out of love with the Tories, their butchery of the health service (which few members of the Thatcher government would have dreamt of using for themselves or their families) was probably the main one.

Upon their election Tony Blair's government had a mandate to transform the NHS. But they were hamstrung by their promise not to increase taxes, their tilt towards a tango with the private sector to provide private 'solutions' to public problems, and their leader's determination to show how 'modern' he was. As with education, the result has been a return to the mentality of the thirties. Private medicine is proliferating. So-called centres of excellence – magnets for the best staff, the most resources and the most articulate and mobile patients – are what the Blairites call such retrogressive solutions as Foundation Hospitals. Instead of spending big money to bring us up to the level of public health spending in neighbouring countries like, er, right-wing conservative France, Blair has tried to move the problem 'off the books' by a plethora of semi-privatizing and 'pathway' to privatization policies. Waiting lists are falling but not as fast as promised and sometimes only because of the fixing of figures rather than sick people. Hospitals are not cleaner – in fact reinfection rates in our hospitals are higher than they were under Thatcher – and public morale about the NHS has begun to fall again into dangerous territory.

Time is running out for the idea of the NHS. If the government continues to fail, more and more people will opt out and into the private sector. This in turn will make raising taxes for health spending even more difficult, and so a vicious circle will have turned again. Before we know it we will have a two-tier health service – we're almost there by postcodes already – with plush, hotel-like private treatment for those who can afford it and increasingly second-rate, Victorian, or at least US-style 'poor-house' provision for the rest. The health service is in double jeopardy and Respect's aim is no less than to save its life.

Virtually every one of the New Labour High Command was educated, entirely free of charge, at some of Britain's best universities – and received a state-funded student grant with which to do so. Having climbed up this ladder into the elite of British society they have begun to pull up that ladder out of the reach of today's students, and place new and ever higher obstacles in front of tomorrow's. Mrs Thatcher abolished student grants. Some of today's Labour MPs were among the leaders of the National Union of Students that railed against her. But New Labour has attacked student opportunities with a verve Mrs Thatcher can only have dreamed about. Under them few students finish their courses with an albatross of debt around their shoulders of less than £10,000, sometimes far higher. This of course does not include the thousands of pounds they have 'borrowed' from their parents and which they will never pay back. Student loans, bank loans, credit cards, hire-purchase debts, loan-shark charges, are driving more and more students to despair, overwork in the black economy, and some even into prostitution and the lap-dance culture growing like topsy in the country. Many more potential students will decide not to become students at all in the years to come. The new environment of tuition fees and variable top-up fees will force young people into a decision to abandon the idea of education just when the country needs a more educated workforce. It will force many young bright people and their parents into choosing shorter courses, cheaper courses and the poorest universities, leaving the long, expensive and best courses in the elite universities for the children of the rich and powerful.

'Back to the Future!' seems to be New Labour's slogan. We are seeing a return to the prevailing culture of the 1930s – before the Welfare State, before the Robbins principles, which created a cross-party 1960s consensus that higher education must be available to all who would benefit from it, irrespective of their social background or parental means. This was the consensus that made the country the fourth largest economy in the world and made Great Britain a cultural, medical and scientific force to be reckoned with.

It seemed at first that this would be the last straw for the largely quiescent ranks of Labour MPs. All sorts of revolts were threatened, early day motions were tabled in the Commons attracting hundreds of signatures. Michael Howard wrong-footed the government by moving to their left and joining the 'revolt', opening up the possibility of a humiliating defeat for Tony Blair on an issue on which he publicly staked his premiership. But once again, as with the war, Blair correctly calculated that most of the New Labour 'rebels' were all wind and water. And at the first sign of a few cosmetic concessions the ranks of the rebellion would thin to the 'usual suspects'. Britain's students, like her pensioners, have been betrayed not just by the New Labour cabinet but by the vast majority of New Labour MPs. Gordon Brown's sabotaging of the Labour rebellion – which he had encouraged for entirely cynical inner-party reasons to do with his long-running feud with Blair – when he pulled out the former Chief Whip Nick Brown at the eleventh hour, showed the worthlessness of any illusory belief in him. Blair and Brown are two sides of the same coin; to argue that the replacement of one by the other would represent change is to draw a false dichotomy. It would be no more than the Thatcher–Major 'regime change', and would end for the party in the same tears.

If David Blunkett is not removed soon from the Home Office it will become the most repressive 'Interior Ministry' in the whole of the European Union. In my lifetime we have gone from disparaging such 'continental' practices as armed police, imprisonment without trial and denial of access to justice for those without the means to hire counsel, to the situation now where we are becoming a byword for police state methods more appropriate to a dictatorship.

An exaggeration? Not at Belmarsh, where prisoners are entombed without trial or even charge or proper legal representation. Or at Dungavel, the Home Office detention centre where whole families are incarcerated for the crime of asking for political asylum. You won't think it's an exaggeration when British policemen are asked by their government to seize the children of asylum seekers, as hostages, to be released only if their parents decide to leave the country. The lunatics have taken control of Britain's asylum policy and the fruits of Blunkett's 'tough guy' approach (which leaves Michael Howard and Ann Widdecombe trailing in his wake looking suddenly soft) are already tumbling, bruised, on to the streets of Britain's cities.

One night when I was speaking at a public meeting in a sleepy little fishing town on the Kent coast, my eyes were constantly drawn to a group of around twenty young black men sitting together wearing shabby tracksuits. The image I could not expel from my mind was that they looked like a chain gang from the deep south of the USA. It turned out they were on hunger strike because, having been refused asylum, all support and benefits had been removed, and either begging or stealing was the only way to stay alive. The men chose the dignified path of going on hunger strike. In Britain. In 2003.

It turned out that they were refugees from the Congo. The Congo has been a war zone for many years and what could have been one of the richest countries in Africa is now a pitiful basket case. How did it get that way; why didn't it live up to its 1960s potential?

Because British and American imperialist interests murdered Patrice Lumumba, perhaps the greatest of all African leaders, and dumped his body in the trunk of a motor car. They put President Mobuto Sese

Seko in charge, perhaps the greatest international thief of all time, who proceeded to steal more than thirty billion dollars from his country, investing it in chateaux, huge landed estates, stocks and shares, concubines and front companies operating out of the very countries – our own included – which had elevated him to power as they dumped the corpse of Lumumba. Of the many blood-soaked crimes of British imperialism, this, for me, is one damned spot that will not out, and all the perfumes of Arabia could not disguise the guilt I felt watching those poor African men in Kent that evening.

Blunkett talks of fear of the country being 'swamped' – a deliberate revisiting of Thatcher's famous scarecrow – but it is his whole approach to issues of crime, punishment, asylum, immigration, race relations and civil liberties that belongs in the swamp. The swamp of the 'semi-house-trained polecat' Norman Tebbit, the swamp of the British National Party, the swamp of his ultra-right US counterpart John Ashcroft and the rest of the Nixon–Reagan–Bush crew he now runs around with.

The European elections on 10 June 2004 and the elections to the Greater London Assembly were the first of Respect's firefights with New Labour. At just twenty weeks old amidst a virtual media blackout, Respect polled more than a quarter of a million votes. In some places, we emerged as the second biggest party. In one place, Tower Hamlets, we came first. There we won eight out of eighteen wards, coming second in five others. In the neighbouring London borough of Newham, Respect came second, but it was first choice for 40 per cent of the Newham electorate. Within a couple of months of the Euro elections, Respect claimed its first scalp, winning a council by-election in the Stepney ward in Tower Hamlets, pushing New Labour into third place, and later coming second in Millwall, again driving the Blairites into third.

Leaked documents from the council leadership in Newham make clear the New Labour leadership's terror about the Respect insurgency. They predict that in the council elections next year we could well control the authority.

A hundred years before, Keir Hardie and the pioneers began the task of building an independent Labour Party for Britain in the East End of London. They rallied to their resplendent red banner the poor masses of east London in unity with the teeming immigrant populations – mainly Jews. Less than a quarter of a century later, that independent Labour Party formed a government. History is having to repeat itself now that Keir Hardie's party is dead and buried, at least as originally envisaged.

New Labour has the gall still to sing 'The Red Flag' at the conclusion of their annual conference. Yet the 'cowards that flinch' and the 'traitors that sneer' are all up there on their platform. The 'dungeons dark' and the 'gallows grim' have been built around the world by them. That New Labour is no longer the champion of working people and internationalism is as clear as the dawning realization that Respect is the voice of the labour cause, which remains the hope of the world.

In parliamentary by-elections, while still less than six months old, Respect scored the biggest fourth-party election vote in more than a century of British political history, gaining more than 12 per cent in the tightly fought Leicester South constituency and nearly 7 per cent in Birmingham Hodge Hill. In Hartlepool, a 98 per cent white constituency, Respect came in fifth – after the Conservatives – polling more than double the thirty-year-old Green Party in a constituency in the shade of a nuclear power plant with ships full of radioactive waste tied up in the quay.

Proportional representation elections – where every vote counts – are of course our battlefield of choice. But we are ready to fight New Labour wherever and whenever we choose. It will be a war of movement rather than position. We will not stand in orderly ranks to be mown down by the Gatling guns of the hyper-parties; ours is a guerrilla army that will hit and move and prepare to hit again.

It is of course certain that there will be more Westminster by-elections. Without wishing any unusual harm to my parliamentary colleagues (hmmm . . .), as Nye Bevan once said, 'where there's death there's hope'. If a by-election occurs in a suitable place we will move heaven and earth and a huge chunk of the movement to wherever it is. We believe there are millions of pensioners, students, Muslims, trade unionists, peace campaigners, civil rights activists and others who would dearly love the opportunity to give Blair and his sycophants a bloody good hiding. We will be their best instrument to do so.

Respect will fight for traditional British values of tolerance, freedom, democracy, equality; for respect for other people's colour, religion, language, way of life, rights and responsibilities. We will defend Muslims against the kind of rabid attack mounted by Mr Blair's friend Richard Desmond, the owner of the *Sunday Express* (as well as, though now at arm's length, the magazines *Asian Babes* and *Spunk Loving Sluts*) and a big donor to Blair election funds, in the twice-published column by Blair's admirer Robert Kilroy Silk. We will defend the rights of religious people to wear whatever clothes and headgear they wish in pursuit of their religious practice. We will defend Jews against anti-Semitism whether from the far right or from fundamentalist Christians or Muslims. We will fight for the rights of all minorities. We want our country to be a rainbow society. We like the fact that so many colours, cultures, traditions, religions and languages are mixing in our green and pleasant land. We love to see our children making friends who are different from themselves and yet, fundamentally, the same. We want our society to be a rich and wonderful weave of many colours and hues, like the threads in the tartan that together produce something much more beautiful than the sum of their parts. This can only be done by proceeding on the basis of respect.

In my country in the late summer the hills and mountains are carpeted with lovely purple heather. It is a joy to behold. But sometimes, if rarely, it is possible to come upon the precious white heather, so treasured that people wear it in their lapels as a good luck charm, hoping it will bring them better days. That is how I see Respect: the Unity Coalition – 'a sprig of white heather, in the future's lapel'.

12

Bursting the Bubble

General elections are a wonderful time for generating political action. This year, with no chance of a Michael Howard victory – who wants to leap from the clutches of Dracula into the arms of someone else with a touch of the night about them? – the temptation to say 'this is not all there is' has been an obvious one. That's why Respect has gone from strength to strength. Just a year old, members have joined us as fast as they have deserted New Labour, which is now down to lower membership levels than the early 1930s. Being a genuinely democratic party, where the members call all the shots and the leaders don't want to go around the world volleying them at people, surely helped too. We remain the fastest growing political organization in Britain – from nought to 5,000 plus in twelve months. How to choose Respect? See the end of this chapter, and turn a new page for a new politics in Britain. There are many other things a self-respecting civilized person could and should be doing to make a difference. Britain's trade unions remain the biggest and most important non-government organizations in the country. I myself joined the Transport and General Workers' Union on Christmas Eve 1973 and have been a paid-up member ever since. All those who work for a living should be trade unionists. If there is no union where you work, start one.

The TUC will help you with information about the most appropriate one for you. Remember unions are no more than the sum of their members – and their members can change them by uniting with others who want to make them more effective. Respect has a network of Respectable progressive trade union activists; we can put you in touch with someone like you!

In the Middle East and on the mainland of Europe they are perfecting the art of consumer boycott, and it's an idea heading our way too. Anything produced by McDonald's, Marlboro, Coca-Cola, Esso, Johnson & Johnson and Estée Lauder should be struck off every Respectable person's shopping list, as should all Israeli products. No right-thinking person would have been seen dead buying the fruits of apartheid South Africa in the days of white supremacy, because by doing so they were killing the children of Soweto. Ditto, every dollar earned by the apartheid state of Israel, whether from 'Dead Sea' cosmetics (the Dead Sea and the whole of the Jericho Valley is illegally occupied territory), or from oranges and avocados allowed special access to the European Union despite being either the fruit of illegal settlement land-grabs or blooming by dint of the grand larceny of Palestinian water. Jaffa, the once beautiful seaside town that was the apple of the Palestinian cultural eye, the home of poets, painters and writers, is now the name of an orange providing the hard currency juice which oils the wheels of the Israeli apartheid system. At the same time the oppression of the Palestinians could not begin to be effective without the billions given in US aid – public and private – every single year to Sharon's Israel. Every dollar spent on American or Israeli goods is another bullet in the back of a Gaza refugee child, another brick in Israel's 'Apartheid Wall', another nail in the coffin of a just settlement of the conflict.

Respect is working closely with the Palestine Solidarity Campaign and the Friends of Al-Aqsa.

We encourage twinning – of the kind pioneered in Dundee a quarter of a century ago. Towns can twin, but so can colleges, universities, schools, workplaces, community groups, churches, mosques, trade union organizations. Either Respect, the PSC or Friends of Al-Aqsa can show you how it's done. Moves are afoot in Preston, Tower Hamlets, Newham and elsewhere – why not join in? It is not enough, however, to fight racism abroad; justice begins at home. Respect supports the Campaign against Political Terror, which fights the use of the so-called 'war on terror' to bring terror to bear in Britain's minority communities and slash and burn our ancient liberties. We fight the particular terror of the resurgence of the BNP, NF and other openly fascist organizations now winning seats in local councils and garnering almost a million votes last year. These Nazis have now substituted the Muslim population of Britain as the subjects of their hate campaigns. But they are the same Holocaust deniers who in earlier times exulted in the genocide against the Jews. Any minority – racial, religious, sexual – which might prove a useful whipping boy from which to exact a blood-price will do for them.

The TUC campaign against this fascist filth can count on Respect to be there and be counted. The civil rights group Liberty, now led by Shami Chakrabarti, one of the brightest new stars on the scene, is another organization campaigning against the drift in Blunkett's Britain to shred the very freedoms we used to cherish as the British way of life. Greenpeace, defending mother earth with verve, imagination and style, and Amnesty International are also of course people travelling in the same direction as us on the environment and against repression and torture around the world – torture now being sub-contracted out by the United States to third countries like Egypt to extract information from prisoners without dirtying its own hands.

War on Want remains the lead organization, fighting in the progressive way the only war worth fighting: against poverty, ignorance and disease. Our support for the on-going work of the Stop the War Coalition is of course guaranteed. Respect was born out of this, the most successful ever British political campaign. We regard her as our 'mother ship' from which we will never stray too far – unless the day comes when there are no more wars to stop. The aftermath of the European Social Forum, when tens of thousands of mainly young Europeans gravitated to the heart of the 'new empire' in London, was enormously heartening. A beginning of the end of the isolation of these islands from our continent could be glimpsed there, a kind of People's Europe which had the style and passion to melt at least some of the Europhobic hearts. Let our ruling classes tremble at the gathering storm of which they are the eye and the heart. They and we stand for a really new world order in which war is abolished and justice is the only marching order. Justice, for the poor and the marginalized. Justice, for the immigrant, the refugee, the worker, who makes everything – every product, every service – all around us, yet generally is rewarded with only enough to find the strength to work again the next day.

The Campaign Against the Arms Trade takes aim at another of the dragons we intend to slay. Britain, with full government involvement and even, through the export credit guarantee scheme, with taxpayers' subsidy, is one of the world's leading players in the merchandise of death and destruction. We sell every conceivable part of the paraphernalia of torture and slaying – and we don't much care to whom. Under New Labour (remember the 'ethical' foreign policy?) the Metropolitan Police even used Blunkett's anti-terrorism laws in London's dockland two years ago during the international arms fair. Not against the representatives of some of the world's grisly generalissimos gathered by the Thames to calibrate the killing potential of some of the world's ghastliest weapons (Made in Britain); but against the perfectly peaceful souls gathered outside to demonstrate against this most sinful of commerce.

Activism, too, is merely the sum of all the activities of individuals just like you. There wasn't a picket outside Oxford Street's Marks and Spencer urging shoppers to boycott the Israeli good inside until somebody started one. And then it grew and grew. You too can be a picketer, a leafleter, a door-knocker, a meeting organizer, a steward on the demonstrations, an office-bearer, a leader.

But there are limits to the power of protest and activism. In the end we will have to storm the political fortresses; they are unguarded by many of any worth. That's what Respect will be up to in the months ahead. We hope you'll join us because, in the words of the Russian writer Nikolai Ostrovsky:

> Our dearest possession in life
> And since it is given to us to live but once
> We must so live as not to be seared by the shame of a cowardly or trivial
>   past
> So live that dying we may say
> All my life and all my strength I have given
> To the finest cause in the world;
> The liberation of humankind.

So come and join us in bursting the bubble, the one the boys have been living in and from which notice of eviction is hereby given.

13

Mr Galloway goes to Washington
TESTIMONY BEFORE THE U.S. SENATE

Committee on Homeland Security and
Governmental Affairs

SUBCOMMITTEE ON
INVESTIGATIONS (MAY 17, 2005)

SEN. COLEMAN: Mr Galloway, I'm pleased to have you before the committee today.

What I'm going to do is briefly summarize the evidence before we give you a chance to give your sworn testimony.

The Oil-for-Food program was used to support those who were favorable to Iraq. Former Iraqi Deputy Prime Minister Tariq Aziz and Iraqi Vice President Taha Yassin Ramadan confirmed this.

I would think that you would admit that your efforts to oppose the sanction were well received by the regime. I know it's been quoted to you many, many times – but your, I would say, infamous statement to Saddam Hussein on January 21, 1994, where you said to Saddam, 'Your Excellency, Mr President, I greet you in the name of many thousands of people in Britain who stood against the tide and opposed the war of aggression against Iraq and continue to oppose the war by economic means, which is aimed to strangle the life out of the great people of Iraq.'

You then went on to say you greet the Palestinian people, you went on to note that you thought 'the president would appreciate knowing that even today three years after the war I still meet with families who are calling their newborn "son of Saddam."'

You went on ultimately at the very end to say, 'Sir, I salute your strength, your courage, your indefatigability, and I want you to know that we are with you.' And I believe it was in Arabic 'thowra hat'l nas'r, thowra hat'l nasr, thowra hat'l quds', which means 'Until victory, until victory, until victory in Jerusalem.' And I also would note that you would say that you deeply regret those comments and that the comments were not aimed directly at Saddam but were aimed at the Iraqi people.

In the fall of 1999 you headed a two-month London-to-Baghdad bus trip to gain support for lifting the sanctions on Iraq.

We have your name on Iraqi documents, some prepared before the fall of Saddam, some after that, which identify you as one of the allocation holders, that your allocations were then used by Fawaz Zureikat, operating under the name of Aredio Petroleum and Middle East Advanced Semiconductor to actually lift the oil.

We note too, based on the statements of former Iraqi officials as well as some documents and in the cases of Vladimir Zhirinovsky and Alexander Voloshin correspondence in documents, that allocation holders knew that surcharges or oil allocations were paid to Saddam Hussein, and that allocation holders were aware of this and were responsible for the payments.

We have also heard testimony regarding several documents retrieved from the Iraqi Ministry of Oil that demonstrate how Iraq allocated oil to its friends and allies.

That chart also lists Contract N1104 with Middle East Advanced Semiconductor.

Footnote 93. Your testimony regarding a SOMO commercial invoice dated June 27, 2002, that shows Middle East Semiconductor loaded 2,360,860 barrels of Iraqi crude oil pursuant to SOMO crude oil sales contract N1104.

Exhibit 12. We heard testimony regarding correspondence between the executive director of SOMO to the Iraqi Oil Minister providing details of contract N1104 and listing your name in parentheses, next to Middle East Advanced Semiconductor and Fawaz Zureikat, who we know lifted the oil. Again statements of detainees, including former Vice President Ramadan, confirm that the name in parentheses – your name – is the allocation holder.

Your testimony regarding Contract N1104, which was signed on December 12, 2001, between SOMO and Fawaz Zureikat, president of Middle East Advanced Semiconductor.

Your testimony regarding SOMO commercial invoice B13201 that shows Aredio Petroleum lifted 1,014,403 barrels of Iraqi oil pursuant to SOMO crude oil sales contract N923.

Exhibit 45. We heard testimony regarding SOMO chart entitled 'Crude Oil Allocation during Phase 9 Memorandum of Understanding' that indicates that contract N923 was executed between SOMO and Mr Fawaz Zureikat (slash) George Galloway (slash) Aredio Petroleum.

Exhibit 9. We also heard testimony regarding the memo from the executive director of SOMO to the Oil Minister requesting approval of contract N923. The document includes an official Ministry of Oil stamp dated 1/15/2001 and provides details of a contract N923 signed with Aredio Petroleum Company, (parens) Fawaz Zureikat (dash) Mariam's Appeal, indicating that the allocation recipient of the contract N923 was Fawaz Zureikat – Mariam's Appeal.

Mr Galloway, as I indicated in my opening statement, this is not a court of law. This committee has simply made available information obtained during the investigation from interviews with former Iraqi officials and Iraqi documents to lay out how the Oil-for-Food program worked – how allocations were given to favored friends, how allocation holders made substantial commissions on those allocations to oil companies, what Ramadan called 'compensation for support.'

But another official in talking about another allocation holder said, 'Of course they made a profit. That's the whole point.' Surcharges and oil contracts were given back to the Saddam regime and were the responsibility of the allocation holder.

The evidence clearly indicates you as an allocation beneficiary, who transferred the allocations to Fawaz Zureikat, who became chairman of your organization Mariam's Appeal.

Senior Iraqi officials have confirmed that you in fact received oil allocations and that the documents that identify you as an allocation recipient are valid.

If you can help provide any evidence that challenges the veracity of these documents or the statements of former Iraqi officials, we'd welcome that input.

Mr Galloway, you're appearing before the subcommittee without asserting any privilege or immunity. Indeed, your appearance before the sub-committee is entirely voluntary and on your own accord. No subpoena was issued to secure your appearance.

You're appearing before the subcommittee concerning matters that do not arise out of the performance of any of your official duties as a member of the British Parliament but instead concern actions taken by you in your capacity as a private citizen.

Before we begin, pursuant to Rule 6, all witnesses who testify before this subcommittee are required to be sworn.

At this time I'd ask you to rise and please raise your right hand.

[Swearing in]

We'll be using a timing system today, Mr Galloway. You have ten minutes for an opening statement. If you need more time, we'll certainly accommodate that, and you may proceed.

GALLOWAY: Senator, I am not now, nor have I ever been, an oil trader. And neither has anyone on my behalf. I have never seen a barrel of oil, owned one, bought one, sold one – and neither has anyone on my behalf.

Now I know that standards have slipped in the last few years in Washington, but for a lawyer you are remarkably cavalier with any idea of justice. I am here today but last week you already found me guilty. You traduced my name around the world without ever having asked me a single question, without ever having contacted me, without ever having written to me or telephoned me, without any attempt to contact me whatsoever. And you call that justice.

Now I want to deal with the pages that relate to me in this dossier and I want to point out areas where there are – let's be charitable and say errors. Then I want to put this in the context where I believe it ought to be. On the very first page of your document about me you assert that I have had 'many meetings' with Saddam Hussein. This is false.

I have had two meetings with Saddam Hussein, once in 1994 and once in August of 2002. By no stretch of the English language can that be described as many meetings with Saddam Hussein.

As a matter of fact, I have met Saddam Hussein exactly the same number of times as Donald Rumsfeld met him. The difference is Donald Rumsfeld met him to sell him guns and to give him maps the better to target those guns. I met him to try and bring about an end to sanctions, suffering and war, and on the second of the two occasions, I met him to try and persuade him to let Dr Hans Blix and the United Nations weapons inspectors back into the country – a rather better use of two meetings with Saddam Hussein than your own Secretary of State for Defense made of his.

I was an opponent of Saddam Hussein when British and Americans governments and businessmen were selling him guns and gas. I used to demonstrate outside the Iraqi embassy when British and American officials were going in and doing commerce.

You will see from the official parliamentary record, Hansard, from the 15th March 1990 onwards, voluminous evidence that I have a rather better record of opposition to Saddam Hussein than you do and than any other member of the British or American governments do.

Now you say in this document, you quote a source, you have the gall to quote a source, without ever having asked me whether the allegation from the source is true, that I am 'the owner of a company which has made substantial profits from trading in Iraqi oil.'

Senator, I do not own any companies, beyond a small company whose entire purpose, whose sole purpose, is to receive the income from my journalistic earnings from my employer, Associated Newspapers, in London. I do not own a company that's been trading in Iraqi oil. And you have no business to carry a quotation, utterly unsubstantiated and false, implying otherwise.

Now you have nothing on me, Senator, except my name on lists of names from Iraq, many of which have been drawn up after the installation of your puppet government in Baghdad. If you had any of the letters against me that you had against Zhirinovsky, and even Pasqua, they would have been up there in your slideshow for the members of your committee today.

You have my name on lists provided to you by the Duelfer inquiry, provided to him by the convicted bank robber, and fraudster, and conman Ahmed Chalabi, who many people in your country to their credit now realize played a decisive role in leading your country into the disaster in Iraq.

There were 270 names on that list originally. That's somehow been filleted down to the names you chose to deal with in this committee. Some of the names on that committee included the former secretary to his Holiness Pope John Paul II, the former head of the African National Congress Presidential office and many others who had one defining characteristic in common: they all stood against the policy of sanctions and war which you vociferously prosecuted and which has led us to this disaster.

You quote Mr Dahar Yassein Ramadan. Well, you have something on me, I've never met Mr Dahar Yassein Ramadan. Your sub-committee apparently has. But I do know that he's your prisoner, I believe he's in Abu Ghraib prison. I believe he is facing war crimes charges, punishable by death. In these circumstances, knowing what the world knows about how you treat prisoners in Abu Ghraib prison, in Bagram Airbase, in Guantánamo Bay, including I may say, British citizens being held in those places, I'm not sure how much credibility anyone would put on anything you manage to get from a prisoner in those circumstances. But you quote 13 words from Dahar Yassein Ramadan, whom I have never met. If he said what he said, then he is wrong.

And if you had any evidence that I had ever engaged in any actual oil transaction, if you had any evidence that anybody ever gave me any money, it would be before the public and before this committee today because I agreed with your Mr Greenblatt [Mark Greenblatt, legal counsel on the committee].

Your Mr Greenblatt was absolutely correct. What counts is not the names on the paper, what counts is where's the money. Senator? Who paid me hundreds of thousands of dollars of money? The answer to that is nobody. And if you had anybody who ever paid me a penny, you would have produced them today.

Now you refer at length to a company named in these documents as Aredio Petroleum. I say to you under oath here today: I have never heard of this company, I have never met anyone from this company. This company has never paid a penny to me and I'll tell you some-thing else: I can assure you that Aredio Petroleum has never paid a single penny to the Mariam Appeal Campaign. Not a thin dime. I don't know who Aredio Petroleum are, but I daresay if you were to ask them they would confirm that they have never met me or ever paid me a penny.

Whilst I'm on that subject, who is this senior former regime official that you spoke to yesterday? Don't you think I have a right to know? Don't you think the Committee and the public have a right to know who this senior former regime official you were quoting against me interviewed yesterday actually is?

Now, one of the most serious of the mistakes you have made in this set of documents is, to be frank, such a schoolboy howler as to make a fool of the efforts that you have made. You assert on page 19, not once but twice, that the documents that you are referring to cover a different period in time from the documents covered by the *Daily Telegraph* which were a subject of a libel action won by me in the High Court in England late last year.

You state that The *Daily Telegraph* article cited documents from 1992 and 1993 whilst you are dealing with documents dating from 2001. Senator, the *Daily Telegraph*'s documents date identically to the documents that you were dealing with in your report here. None of the *Daily Telegraph*'s documents dealt with a period of 1992, 1993. I had never set foot in Iraq until late in 1993 – never in my life. There could possibly be no documents relating to Oil-for-Food matters in 1992, 1993, for the Oil-for-Food scheme did not exist at that time.

And yet you've allocated a full section of this document to claiming that your documents are from a different era to the *Daily Telegraph* documents when the opposite is true. Your documents and the *Daily Telegraph* documents deal with exactly the same period.

But perhaps you were confusing the *Daily Telegraph* action with the *Christian Science Monitor*. The *Christian Science Monitor* did indeed publish on its front pages a set of allegations against me very similar to the ones that your committee have made. They did indeed rely on documents which started in 1992, 1993. These documents were unmasked by the *Christian Science Monitor* themselves as forgeries.

Now, the neo-con websites and newspapers in which you're such a hero, senator, were all absolutely cock-a-hoop at the publication of the *Christian Science Monitor* documents, they were all absolutely convinced of their authenticity. They were all absolutely convinced that these documents showed me receiving $10 million from the Saddam regime. And they were all lies.

In the same week as the *Daily Telegraph* published their documents against me, the *Christian Science Monitor* published theirs which turned out to be forgeries and the British newspaper, *Mail on Sunday*, purchased a third set of documents which also upon forensic examination turned out to be forgeries. So there's nothing fanciful about this. Nothing at all fanciful about it.

The existence of forged documents implicating me in commercial activities with the Iraqi regime is a proven fact. It's a proven fact that these forged documents existed and were being circulated amongst right-wing newspapers in Baghdad and around the world in the immediate aftermath of the fall of the Iraqi regime.

Now, Senator, I gave my heart and soul to oppose the policy that you promoted. I gave my political life's blood to try to stop the mass killing of Iraqis by the sanctions on Iraq which killed one million Iraqis, most of them children, most of them died before they even knew that they were Iraqis, but they died for no other reason other than that they were Iraqis with the misfortune to born at that time. I gave my heart and soul to stop you committing the disaster that you did commit in invading Iraq. And I told the world that your case for the war was a pack of lies.

I told the world that Iraq, contrary to your claims, did not have weapons of mass destruction. I told the world, contrary to your claims, that Iraq had no connection to al-Qaeda. I told the world, contrary to your claims, that Iraq had no connection to the atrocity on 9/11, 2001. I told the world, contrary to your claims, that the Iraqi people would resist a British and American invasion of their country and that the fall of Baghdad would not be the beginning of the end, but merely the end of the beginning.

Senator, in everything I said about Iraq, I turned out to be right and you turned out to be wrong and 100,000 people paid with their lives; 1600 of them American soldiers sent to their deaths on a pack of lies; 15,000 of them wounded, many of them disabled forever on a pack of lies.

If the world had listened to Kofi Annan, whose dismissal you demanded, if the world had listened to President Chirac who you want to paint as some kind of corrupt traitor, if the world had listened to me and the anti-war movement in Britain, we would not be in the disaster that we are in today. Senator, this is the mother of all smoke-screens. You are trying to divert attention from the crimes that you supported, from the theft of billions of dollars of Iraq's wealth.

Have a look at the real Oil-for-Food scandal. Have a look at the 14 months you were in charge of Baghdad, the first 14 months when $8.8 billion of Iraq's wealth went missing on your watch. Have a look at Halliburton and other American corporations that stole not only Iraq's money, but the money of the American taxpayer.

Have a look at the oil that you didn't even meter, that you were shipping out of the country and selling, the proceeds of which went who knows where? Have a look at the $800 million you gave to American military commanders to hand out around the country without even counting it or weighing it.

Have a look at the real scandal breaking in the newspapers today, revealed in the earlier testimony in this committee. That the biggest sanctions busters were not me or Russian politicians or French politicians. The real sanctions busters were your own companies with the connivance of your own government.

SEN. COLEMAN: Thank you, Mr Galloway.

Mr Galloway, can we start by talking about Fawaz Zureikat. Do you know the individual?

GALLOWAY: I know him very well.

SEN. COLEMAN: In fact you were best man at his wedding?

GALLOWAY: I was.

SEN. COLEMAN: And at some point in time he became chair of Mariam's Appeals. Is that correct?

GALLOWAY: He did. Yeah.

SEN. COLEMAN: And can you tell me when that occurred?

GALLOWAY: I think in late 2000 or early 2001.

SEN. COLEMAN: Before Mr Zureikat was chair of Mariam's Appeal, who had that position?

GALLOWAY: I was the founding chairman.

SEN. COLEMAN: Was there someone between you and–

GALLOWAY: Mr Halford.

SEN. COLEMAN: And do you recall when he had that position?

GALLOWAY: I don't.

SEN. COLEMAN: Mr Zureikat was a significant contributor to Mariam's Appeals. Is that correct?

GALLOWAY: He was the second biggest contributor. The main contributor was Sheik Zayed, the ruler of the United Arab Emirates, which you've glossed over in your report because it's slightly embarrassing to you. And the third major contributor was the Crown Prince of Saudi Arabia, which you've equally glossed over because it's embarrassing to you.

And both of those individuals are your friends.

SEN. COLEMAN: How much did Mr Zureikat contribute to Mariam's Appeals?

GALLOWAY: Roughly 375,000 English pounds.

SEN. COLEMAN: About $600,000?

GALLOWAY: I don't know the conversion. But it's 375,000 Sterling.

SEN. COLEMAN: If you can, uh . . . By the way, Mr Zureikat was your representative – uh, designated representative – for the activities of Mariam's Appeals. Is that correct?

GALLOWAY: For the activities of Mariam's Appeals. Yes.

SEN. COLEMAN: And when did he get that position?

GALLOWAY: I think late 2000.

SEN. COLEMAN: Late 2000. Looking at Exhibit 9 – and I think you have the books in front of you – that appears to be a document from the Ministry of Oil that testimony has indicated that the signature is an accurate signature.

Do you have any reason to believe that that document is false?

GALLOWAY: Well, I have told you that I have never heard of Aredio Petroleum, and I've told you that the Mariam Appeal never received a single penny from Aredio Petroleum. So the information at the top of the page, if you've translated it accurately, is false.

SEN. COLEMAN: Have you heard of Middle East ASI company?

GALLOWAY: Yes. That's Mr Zureikat's company.

SEN. COLEMAN: I turn to Exhibit 12.

And that purports again to be a stamp of the Ministry of Oil of Iraq and this purports to be showing the details of a contract signed with Middle East ASI company, Mr George Galloway and Fuwaz Zureikat. So Middle East ASI is Mr Zureikat's company?

GALLOWAY: Middle East ASI is Mr Zureikat's company. He may well have signed an oil contract. It had nothing to do with me.

SEN. COLEMAN: He was chair of Mariam's Appeals in 2000. I take it you knew him well. Did he ever talk with you about his dealings with oil in Iraq?

GALLOWAY: He did better than that. He talked to everybody. He talked to every English journalist that came through Baghdad – who he helped at our request to get the interviews and to get to the places that they wanted and needed to go. He was introduced to everyone as a major benefactor of the Mariam Appeal and as a businessman doing extensive business in Iraq and elsewhere in the Middle East.

SEN. COLEMAN: I'm asking you specifically, in 2001 were you aware he was doing oil deals with Iraq?

GALLOWAY: I was aware that he was doing extensive business with Iraq. I did not know the details of it. It was not my business.

SEN. COLEMAN: So this is somebody who was the chairman of committee that you know well and you're not able to say that he was . . .

GALLOWAY: Well, there's a lot of contributors – I've just been checking – to your political campaigns.

SEN. COLEMAN: There's not many at that level, Mr Galloway –

GALLOWAY: I've checked your website. There are lots of contributors to your political campaign funds. I don't suppose you ask any of them how they made the money they give you.

SEN. COLEMAN: Certainly not at $600,000 American.

But let me ask you again, just so that the record is clear – that it's clear on the record – that you're not contesting then the validity of Document 12, Exhibit 12. You're indicating that Mr Zureikat could have had dealings with Iraq. You're saying that at that point in time you're not aware that he had oil dealings with Iraq?

GALLOWAY: First of all, I've only seen this document today. And I'm telling you that insofar as my name is in a parenthesis the information in it is false.

I've no reason to believe that Mr Zureikat's company didn't do that particular oil deal.

But this is your problem in this whole affair. There is nobody arguing that Mr Zureikat's company did not do oil transactions and many other – much bigger, frankly – business contracts with Iraq. There is nobody contesting that Mr Zureikat made substantial donations to our campaign against sanctions and war.

My point is – you have accused me, personally, of enriching myself, of taking money from Iraq. And that is false and unjust.

SEN. COLEMAN: Mr Galloway, do you recall an interview you had with a Jeremy Paxman in April 23 of 2003,

[Addressing aide] Can we have a copy of the transcript of that?

I'd like to refresh your memory.

[To aide] Can you get a copy of that.

As we get you a copy, you were asked a question, talking about business dealings with Mr Zureikat in Iraq. And at the least the transcript that I have – and I'd ask you to let me know if it's incorrect – your quote is, something about business in Iraq

'Well, I'm trying to reach him' – this is in 2003 – 'I'm trying to reach him to ask him if he's ever been involved in oil deals because I don't know the answer to that.' So in 2003 you're saying you don't know the answer to whether he was involved in oil deals?

GALLOWAY: Well, I told you in my previous two answers – I knew that Mr Zureikat was heavily involved in business in Iraq and elsewhere, but that it was none of my business what particular transactions or business he was involved in – any more than you ask the American and Israel Public Affairs Committee [AIPAC] when they donate money to you or pay for your trips to Israel, where they got the money from.

SEN. COLEMAN: So Mr Galloway, you would have this committee believe that your designated representative from the Mariam's Appeal becomes the chair of the Mariam's Appeal, was listed in Iraqi documents as obviously doing business, oil deals with Iraq, that you never had a conversation with him in 2001 on whether he was doing oil business with Iraq.

GALLOWAY: No, I'm doing better than that. I'm telling you that I knew that he was doing a vast amount of business with Iraq. Much bigger, as I said a couple of answers ago, than any oil business he did. In the airports he was the representative of some of the world's biggest companies in Iraq. He was an extremely wealthy businessman doing very extensive business in Iraq.

Not only did I know that, but I told everyone about it. I emblazoned it in our literature, on our website, precisely so that people like you could not later credibly question my bonafides in that regard. So I did better than that.

I never asked him if he was trading in oil. I knew he was a big trader with Iraq, and I told everybody about it.

SEN. COLEMAN: So in 2003, when you said you didn't know whether he was doing oil deals, were you telling the truth at that time?

GALLOWAY: Yes, I was. I've never known until the *Telegraph* story appeared that he was alleged to be doing oil deals. But his oil deals are about one-tenth of the business that he did in Iraq. So I did better than telling people about his oil deals. I told them he was doing much, much more than that.

SEN. COLEMAN: So Exhibit 14, which purports to be a contract with Middle East Semiconductor, Contract M1214. Middle East Semiconductor, again, is Mr Zureikat's company, is that correct?

GALLOWAY: Yes, it is.

SEN. COLEMAN: So do you have any reason to believe that this document is false?

GALLOWAY: Well, the parenthesis, if the parenthesis implies – as you've been arguing all morning that it implies – that this was being signed for by Middle East Advanced Semiconductors in order to pass the money on to me, is false.

Mr Zureikat and Middle East Semiconductors or any other company have never given me any money. And if they had, you would have it up here on a board, and in front of the committee here.

SEN. COLEMAN: I take it, Mr Galloway, that in regard to any surcharges paid to Saddam – I think it's Footnote 89, which refers to the surcharge for the contract, focused on Mariam's Appeal – you're saying that that document, first of all, any contract between Iraq and Mariam's Appeals is false?

GALLOWAY: Well, Senator, I had gotten used to the allegation that I was taking money from Saddam Hussein. It's actually surreal to hear in this room this morning that I'm being accused of giving money *to* Saddam Hussein.

This is utterly preposterous, utterly preposterous, that I gave $300,000 to Saddam Hussein. This is beyond the realms of the ridiculous.

Now. The Mariam Appeals finances have been investigated by the Charity Commission on the order of Lord Goldsmith.

(You'll recall him, Senator. He's the attorney general. Practically the only lawman in the world that thought your war with Iraq was legal, thought Britain joining your war with Iraq was legal.)

He ordered the Charity Commission to investigate the Mariam Appeal. Using their statutory powers, they recovered all money in and all money out ever received or spent by the Mariam Appeal. They found no impropriety. And I can assure you, they found no money from an oil contract from Aredio Petroleum – none whatsoever.

SEN. COLEMAN: And the commission did not look at these documents relating to this contract with Iraq. Is that correct? –

GALLOWAY: – No, but they looked better than that, Senator.–

SEN. COLEMAN: – I'm not asking you better. I'm asking the question whether they looked at these documents. –

GALLOWAY: – Senator, you're not listening to what I am saying. They did better than that.

They looked at every penny in and every penny out. And they did not find, I can assure you, any trace of a donation from a company called Aredio Petroleum, or, frankly, a donation from any company other than Mr Zureikat's company. That's a fact.

SEN. COLEMAN: If I can get back to Mr Zureikat one more time. Do you recall a time when he specifically – when you had a conversation with him about oil dealings in Iraq?

GALLOWAY: I have already answered that question. I can assure you, Mr Zureikat never gave me a penny from an oil deal, from a cake deal, from a bread deal, or from any deal. He donated money to our campaign, which we publicly brandished on all of our literature, along with the other donors to the campaign.

SEN. COLEMAN: Again, Mr Galloway, a simple question. I'm looking for either a yes or no. Did you ever have a conversation with Mr Zureikat where he informed you that he had oil dealings with Iraq, yes or no?

GALLOWAY: Not before this *Daily Telegraph* report, no.

SEN. COLEMAN: Senator Levin.

SEN. CARL LEVIN (D): Thank you, Mr Galloway.

Mr Galloway, could you take a look at the Exhibit Number 12 . . .

GALLOWAY: Yes.

SEN. LEVIN: . . . where your name is in parenthesis after Mr Zureikat's? –

GALLOWAY: Before Mr Zureikat's, if I'm looking at the right exhibit –

SEN. LEVIN: I'm sorry. I was going to finish my sentence – my question, though. My question was, where your name is in parenthesis after Mr Zureikat's company.

GALLOWAY: I apologize, Senator.

SEN. LEVIN: That's all right. Now, that document – assuming it's an accurate translation of the document underneath it – would you . . . you're not alleging here today that the document is a forgery, I gather?

GALLOWAY: Well, I have no idea, Senator, if it's a forgery or not.

SEN. LEVIN: But you're not alleging.

GALLOWAY: I'm saying that the information insofar as it relates to me is fake.

SEN. LEVIN: I – is wrong?

GALLOWAY: It's wrong.

SEN. LEVIN: But you're not alleging that the document –

GALLOWAY: Well, I have no way of knowing, Senator.

SEN. LEVIN: That's fine. So you're not alleging?

GALLOWAY: No, I have no way – I have no way of knowing. This is the first time –

SEN. LEVIN: Is it fair to say since you don't know, you're not alleging?

GALLOWAY: Well, it would have been nice to have seen it before today.

SEN. LEVIN: Is it fair to say, though, that either because you've not seen it before or because – otherwise, you don't know. You're not alleging the document's a fake. Is that fair to say?

GALLOWAY: I haven't had it in my possession long enough to form a view about that.

SEN. LEVIN: All right. Would you let the subcommittee know after you've had it in your possession long enough whether you consider the document a fake.

GALLOWAY: Yes, although there is a – there is an academic quality about it, Senator Levin, because you have already found me guilty before you – before you actually allowed me to come here and speak for myself.

SEN. LEVIN: Well, in order to attempt to clear your name, would you . . .

GALLOWAY: Well, let's be clear about something.

SEN. LEVIN: Well, let me finish my question. Let me be clear about that, first of all.

Would you submit to the subcommittee after you've had a chance to review this document whether or not, in your judgment, it is a forgery? Will you do that?

GALLOWAY: Well, if you will give me the original. I mean, this is not – presumably, you wrote this English translation.

SEN. LEVIN: Yes, and there's a copy underneath it of the –

GALLOWAY: Well, yes, there is a copy of a gray blur. If you'll give me – if you'll give me the original –

SEN. LEVIN: The copy of the original.
  [Crosstalk]

GALLOWAY: Give me the original in a decipherable way, then of course I'll –

SEN. LEVIN: That would be fine. We appreciate that.

GALLOWAY: Yes.

SEN. LEVIN: Now, at the bottom of this document, assuming – assuming it's not a forgery for a moment, it says 'surcharge.' Are we together?

GALLOWAY: Yes.

SEN. LEVIN: 'As per the instructions of Your Excellency over the phone on 12/11/01 of not accepting the company's proposal unless they pay the debt incurred since phase eight.'

If, in fact – if, in fact, Mr Zureikat's company paid a surcharge or a kickback to the Iraqi government in order to obtain an allocation of oil, would that trouble you?

GALLOWAY: Well, as it turns out, from your own testimony, that practically everyone in the world, and especially the United States, was paying kickbacks.

SEN. LEVIN: My question . . . It troubles me a great deal. As you've heard from my statement today, I'm very much troubled that we have an oil company that was involved in this and we're going to go after that oil company.

Now let me ask you. I've expressed my view about Bayoil. So now let me ask you about Mr Zureikat's company.

If in fact Mr Zureikat's company paid a kickback to the Iraqi government in order to obtain this allocation, would you be troubled? That's my question.

GALLOWAY: Yeah. That's a good question. And will you allow me to answer it seriously and not in a yes-or-no fashion? Because I could give you a glib –

SEN. LEVIN: Providing you give us an answer, I'd be delighted to hear it.

GALLOWAY: Here's my answer and I hope it does delight you.

I opposed the Oil-for-Food program with all my heart. Not for the reasons that you are troubled by, but because it was a program which saw the death – I'm talking about the death now; I'm talking about a mass grave – of a million people, most of them children, in Iraq. The Oil-for-Food program gave 30 cents per day per Iraqi for the period of the Oil-for-Food program – 30 cents for all food, all medicine, all clothes, all schools, all hospitals, all public services. I believe that the United Nations had no right to starve Iraq's people because it had fallen out with Iraq's dictator.

David Bonior, your former colleague, Senator, whom I admired very much – a former chief whip here on the Hill – described the sanctions policy as 'infanticide masquerading as politics.' Senator Coleman thinks that's funny, but I think it's the most profound description of that era that I have ever read – infanticide masquerading as politics.

So I opposed this program with all my heart. Not because Saddam was getting kickbacks from it – and I don't know when it's alleged these kickbacks started. Not because some individuals were getting rich doing business with Iraq under it. But because it was a murderous policy of killing huge numbers of Iraqis. That's what troubles *me*. That's what troubles me.

Now, if you're asking me, 'Is Mr Zureikat in some difficulty?' – like all the other companies that it would appear paid kickbacks to the Iraqi regime – no doubt he is. Although it would appear he's quite small beer compared to the American companies that were involved in the same thing.

SEN. LEVIN: Now my question . . .

GALLOWAY: That's what – I told you what troubles me.

SEN. LEVIN: I'm not asking you – [Crosstalk]
My question . . . Now that you've given us your statement about your feeling about the Oil-for-Food program – My question is, Would you be troubled if you knew that Mr Zureikat paid a kickback in order to get an allocation of an oil contract? That's a very simple question.

GALLOWAY: It's Mr Zureikat's problem, not mine.

SEN. LEVIN: It would not trouble you?

GALLOWAY: It's Mr Zureikat's problem, not mine.

SEN. LEVIN: And so that if a kickback, which was illegal under international – now you may not agree with the U.N., but that's the international community that you're attacking, which is fine. You're entitled to do that. You're entitled and I'll defend your right to do it. But you're attacking a U.N. program – which is your right to do – which was aimed at providing humanitarian assistance to try to alleviate the problems that the sanctions provided – which is your right to do. But my question – which you are so far evading – is, Would you be troubled if that U.N. Oil-for-Food program was being circumvented by the kind of kickbacks which were taking place and being given to Saddam Hussein in order to obtain allocations under that program *if* Mr Zureikat participated in that kickback scheme, which violated the U.N.sanc ... You may not have agreed with it, but it violated the program. Would it trouble you if he violated that U.N. program in that way? That's my question.

GALLOWAY: Senator, there are many things –

SEN. LEVIN: I know. Other things trouble you. But can you just give us a straightforward answer? You've given us a long explanation of other things that trouble you, which is your right. Now I'm asking you whether *that* troubles you.

GALLOWAY: It troubles me that it might put him in difficulty. It troubles me that it might now lead to a prosecution of him. It troubles me that this will be further smoke in the smokescreen. But I, root and branch, opposed this [SEN. LEVIN: I understand . . .] Oil-for-Food program.

SEN. LEVIN: There were a lot of things you opposed, but you don't believe should be circumvented in illegal ways. Isn't that –

GALLOWAY: But, please, Senator! You supported the illegal attack on Iraq. Don't talk to me about illegality –

SEN. LEVIN: Sorry about that. I didn't. But that's beside the point. [Crosstalk] That's beside the point. You're wrong in your –

GALLOWAY: Well, I'm collectively talking about the Senate. Not you personally.

SEN. LEVIN: Well, that's okay. Let me go back to my question. I don't want to get involved in –

GALLOWAY: Why not? You want to talk about illegality?

SEN. LEVIN: No.

GALLOWAY: You launched an illegal war, which has killed 100,000 people. You want me to be troubled?

SEN. LEVIN: No, I want you to answer questions which are fairly put and directly in front of you. Now I'll ask you one last – two last questions. *If* – if – Mr Zureikat's contribution to Mariam's Appeal came from the sale of oil – or his share of the sale from oil – which he was able to obtain because he paid a kickback in violation of the U.N. program. Would that contribution trouble you? That's my question.

GALLOWAY: Well, Senator–

SEN. LEVIN: If you can't give a short answer, just–

GALLOWAY: I'll give as short as I can, and I appreciate your fairness in this.

Fundraising for political purposes is seldom pretty, as any American politician could testify. I took the view – I can be criticized for it, have been criticized for it – that I would fundraise from the kings of Arabia whose political systems I have opposed all my life in order to raise funds for what I thought was an emergency, facing a disaster. And I did not ask Mr Zureikat which part of his profits from his entire business empire he was making donations to our–

SEN. LEVIN: That wasn't my question. My question was, would it trouble you if you found that out?

It's okay. You're not going to answer. I want to go to my next question.

You're simply not going to answer. I will say, American politicians who find the source of money after it's given to them is troubling – they find out something they didn't know afterwards – frequently will – and hopefully, I think always – at least frequently will return that money, will say they disagree with the source of the money. Hopefully all of us will do that. But whether or not we all live up to that standard, you clearly do not adopt that as a standard for contributions to Mariam's Appeal. You're not going to look at the source of the money; you're just simply going to accept the money, and you've made that clear.

I wanted just to ask you about Tariq Aziz.

GALLOWAY: Yeah.

SEN. LEVIN: Tariq Aziz. You've indicated you, you – who you didn't talk to and who you did talk to. Did you have conversations with Tariq Aziz about the award of oil allocations? That's my question.

GALLOWAY: Never.

SEN. LEVIN: Thank you. I'm done. Thank you.

SEN. COLEMAN: Just one follow-up on the Tariq Aziz question. How often did you uh . . . Can you describe the relation with Tariq Aziz?

GALLOWAY: Friendly.

SEN. COLEMAN: How often did you meet him?

GALLOWAY: Many times.

SEN. COLEMAN: Can you give an estimate of that?

GALLOWAY: No. Many times.

SEN. COLEMAN: Is it more than five?

GALLOWAY: Yes, sir.

SEN. COLEMAN: More than ten?

GALLOWAY: Yes.

SEN. COLEMAN: Fifteen? Around fifteen?

GALLOWAY: Well, we're getting nearer, but I haven't counted. But many times. I'm saying to you 'Many times,' and I'm saying to you that I was friendly with him.

SEN. COLEMAN: And you describe him as 'a very dear friend'?

GALLOWAY: I think you've quoted me as saying 'a dear, dear friend.' I don't often use the double adjective, but—

SEN. COLEMAN: – I was looking into your heart on that.–

GALLOWAY: – but 'friend' I have no problem with.

Senator, just before you go on – I do hope that you'll avail yourself of this dossier that I have produced. And I am really speaking through you to Senator Levin. This is what I have said about Saddam Hussein.

SEN. COLEMAN: Well, we'll enter that into the record without objection. I have no further questions of the witness. You're excused, Mr Galloway.

GALLOWAY: Thank you very much.

Contacts

Respect: the Unity Coalition
259–269 Old Marylebone
    Road
London NW1 5RA
020 7170 4030/4031
www.respectcoalition.org
office@respectcoalition.org

Trades Union Congress
Congress House
Great Russell Street
London WC1B 3LS
020 7636 4030
www.tuc.org.uk

Palestine Solidarity Campaign
Box BM PSA
London WC1N 3XX
020 7700 6192
www.palestinecampaign.org

Friends of Al-Aqsa
PO Box 5127
Leicester LE2 0WU
(Fax) 0116 253 7575
www.aqsa.org.uk

Unite Against Fascism
c/o NATFHE
27 Britannia Street

London WC1X 9JP
020 7833 4916
www.uaf.org.uk

Liberty
21 Tabard Street
London SE1 4LA
020 7403 5354
*www.liberty-human-
    rights.org.uk*

Greenpeace UK
Canonbury Villas
London N1 2PN
020 7865 8100
www.greenpeace.org

Amnesty International
    (International Secretariat)
1 Easton Street
London WC1X 0DW
020 7413 5500
www.amnesty.org

War on Want
Fenner Brockway House
37–39 Great Guildford Street
London SE1 0ES
020 7620 1111
www.waronwant.org

Stop the War Coalition
PO Box 3739
London E5 8EJ
020 7053 2153
www.stopwar.org.uk

London European Social
  Forum
ukesfcommittee@gn.apc.org

Globalise Resistance
PO Box 29689
London E8 2XR
020 7053 2071
www.resist.org.uk

Campaign Against the Arms Trade
11 Goodwin Street
London N4 3HQ
020 7281 0297
www.caat.org.uk

Notes

Chapter 1: The Boys in the Bubble

1. Alan Clark, testimony to the Matrix Churchill trial, 1992.
2. Tony Blair, interviewed on the BBC programme *On the Record*, 16 November 1997.
3. David Blunkett, speech to the Federation of Small Businesses, 5 September 2002.

Chapter 2: New World Odour

1. 'Jute Mill Song' by the Dundee poet Mary Brooksbank, 1964.
2. *New Musical Express*, 11 April 2000.
3. Study by Energy Action and University of Strathclyde, January 2004.

Chapter 4: My War with Uncle Sam

1. Michael Moore, *Dude, Where's My Country?*, Allen Lane, 2003.
2. Sheldon Rampton and John Stauber, *Weapons of Mass Deception: the uses of propaganda in Bush's war with Iraq*, Constable & Robinson, 2003.
3. Christopher Hitchens, *The Trial of Henry Kissinger*, Verso, 2002.

Chapter 5: Last Refuge of the Scoundrel

1. The *Sun*, 1 April 2003.
2. Dr John Reid, interviewed on the BBC programme *Breakfast with Frost*, 27 April 2003.
3. Tariq Ali, *Bush in Babylon*, Verso, 2003.

Chapter 6: A Line in the Sand

1. Statistical extracts from official reports and quotations from newspapers and other publications cited in this chapter are all taken from Geoff Simons, *The Scourging of Iraq*, Palgrave Macmillan, 1996.
2. Madeleine Albright, interviewed on the CBS programme *Sixty Minutes*, 12 May 1996.

Chapter 7: Ave Mariam

1. Leader, *Daily Telegraph*, 16 April 1998.
2. The *Scotsman*, 15 April 1998.
3. *The Times*, 11 November 2000.

Chapter 8: Saddam and Me

1. Rampton and Stauber, *Weapons of Mass Deception*, op.cit.

Chapter 9: Wolves, Lions, Donkeys

1. As Hugh MacDiarmid said of James Connolly in his poem 'The Weapon'.
2. *Maxton: a Biography* by Gordon Brown, HarperCollins, 1988.
3. Private conversation with the author.
4. Neil Kinnock, speech to the 1985 Labour Party Conference, Bournemouth.
5. Speech by the author to the Scottish Labour Party Conference, March 1995.
6. *The Jasmine Road* by Ghazi Hussein opened at the Theatre Workshop, Edinburgh, on 9 October 2003.
7. John Monks, speech to the Fabian Society Conference, 19 June 1999.
8. See Greg Palast, *The Best Democracy Money Can Buy: an investigative reporter exposes the truth about globalization, corporate cons and high finance fraudsters*, Constable & Robinson, 2003.
9. See *The Trial: how New Labour purged George Galloway*, Bookmarks Publications, 2003. Go to *www.bookmarks.uk.com*.
10. Paddy Ashdown, *The Ashdown Diaries: 1977–1999*, Penguin, 2002.

Chapter 11: R.E.S.P.E.C.T.

1. The *Sun*, 18 April 2003.

2. 12 March 2003.

3. 25 January 2004.

4. A verbatim account of the trial is available at *www.stopwar.org.uk*. Excerpts from the transcript are published in the pamphlet *The Trial* published by Bookmarks Publications and available price £1.00 from the Bookmarks shop, 1 Bloomsbury Street, London WC1B 3QE.

5. Statistic from: *http://www.dwp.gov.uk/asd/asd1/state_pension/SP_summ stats_Mar03.asp*.

6. The *Guardian*, 8 July 1996.

7. Neil Kinnock speech to the 1985 Labour Party Conference, Bournemouth.